*Favorite Brand Name*™

# GRILLING

*and More*

Publications International, Ltd.

Favorite Brand Name Recipes at www.fbnr.com

**Microwave Cooking:** Microwave ovens vary in wattage. Use the cooking times as guidelines and check for doneness before adding more time.

**Preparation/Cooking Times:** Preparation times are based on the approximate amount of time required to assemble the recipe before cooking, baking, chilling or serving. These times include preparation steps such as measuring, chopping and mixing. The fact that some preparations and cooking can be done simultaneously is taken into account. Preparation of optional ingredients and serving suggestions is not included.

# CONTENTS

28

156

348

# BARBECUE
## BASICS

*New and innovative grilling and flavoring techniques have turned standard backyard fare into cookout cuisine. This tantalizing style of cooking with its mouthwatering aromas offers endless opportunities for both the novice and experienced pro. A simple review of the basics will ensure great success with all the delicious recipes in* Great Grilling & More. *Your grill is sure to be fired up all summer—and possibly, all winter long!*

### CHOOSING A GRILL

Before you choose a grill, consider where you grill, what you'll be cooking, the seasons when you'll be grilling and the size of your budget. A small portable grill is fine if you usually barbecue smaller cuts of meat for a few people. For larger cuts of meat, bigger groups of people and year-round grilling, a large covered grill is worth the expense. Basic types of grills include gas, covered cooker and portable.

**Gas Grill:** Fast starts, accurate heat control, even cooking and year-round use make this the most convenient type of grill. Bottled gas heats a bed of lava rock or ceramic coals—no charcoal is required. Fat from the meat drips onto the lava rocks or coals and produces smoke for a grilled flavor. Hickory or fruitwood chips can be used to create the typical smoky flavor of charcoal.

**Covered Cooker:** Square, rectangular or kettle-shaped, this versatile covered grill lets you roast, steam, smoke or cook whole meals in any season of the year. Draft controls on the lid and base help control the temperature.

Closing the dampers reduces the heat; opening them increases it. When the grill is covered, heat is reflected off the inside of the grill, cooking the food evenly and keeping it moist. When grilling without the cover, the coals are hotter since added air circulation promotes their burning.

**Portable Grills:** These include the familiar hibachi and small picnic grills. Portability and easy storage are their main advantage. When choosing a suitable portable grill, consider what would be best for your cooking and transporting needs, and make sure it is sturdy.

### FIRE BUILDING

• The number of coals required for barbecuing depends on the size and type of grill and the amount of food to be prepared. Weather conditions also have an effect; strong winds, very cold temperatures or highly humid conditions increase the number of coals needed for a good fire. As a general rule, it takes about 30 coals to grill one pound of meat under optimum weather conditions.

• To light a charcoal fire arrange the coals in a pyramid shape about 20 to 30 minutes prior to cooking. The pyramid shape provides enough ventilation for the coals to catch. To start with lighter fluid, soak the coals with about ½ cup fluid. Wait one minute to allow the fluid to soak into the coals. Light with a match.

• To start with an electric starter, nestle the starter in the center of coals. Plug the starter into a heavy-duty extension cord, then plug the cord into an outlet. After 8 to 10 minutes, when ash begins to form on the coals, unplug the starter and remove it. The electric starter will be very hot and should cool in a safe, heatproof place.

• To start with a chimney starter, remove the grid from the grill; place the chimney starter in the base of grill. Crumble a few sheets of newspaper; place in the bottom portion of the chimney starter. Fill the top portion with coals. Light the newspaper. Do not disturb the starter; the coals will be ready in 20 to 30 minutes. Be sure to wear fireproof mitts when pouring the hot coals from the chimney starter into the base of the grill. This method is essentially failure-proof since it does not use starter fluid.

When the coals are ready, they will be about 80% ash gray during daylight and will glow at night. Spread the coals into a single layer with barbecue or long-handled tongs. To lower the cooking temperature, spread the coals farther apart or raise the grid. To raise the cooking temperature, either lower the grid or move the coals closer together and tap off the ash.

## COOKING METHODS FOR CHARCOAL GRILLING

**Direct Cooking:** The food is placed on the grid directly over the coals. Make sure there is enough charcoal in a single layer to extend 1 to 2 inches beyond the area of the food on the grill. This method is for quick-cooking foods, such as hamburgers, steaks and fish.

**Indirect Cooking:** The food is placed on the grid over a metal or disposable foil drip pan with the coals banked either to one side or on both sides of the pan. The drip pan keeps the grill clean and minimizes flare-ups. To cook with moist heat, add liquid to the drip pan during cooking if necessary. This method is best used for foods that require longer

cooking time and even, less intense heat, such as roasts and whole chickens.

When barbecuing by indirect cooking for more than 45 minutes, add 4 to 9 coals around the outer edge of the fire just before you begin grilling. When these coals are ready, add them to the center of the fire as needed to maintain a constant temperature.

*Here's how to determine the number of coals needed:*

### Number of Coals Needed for Indirect Cooking on a Covered Grill

| Diameter of Grill (inches) | Number of Coals |
|---|---|
| 26¾ | 30 |
| 22½ | 25 |
| 18½ | 16 |
| 14 | 15 |

### Number of Coals Added for Longer Cooking

Place coals on each side of drip pan every 45 minutes.

| Diameter of Grill (inches) | Number of Coals |
|---|---|
| 26¾ | 9 |
| 22½ | 8 |
| 18½ | 5 |
| 14 | 4 |

## CHECKING CHARCOAL TEMPERATURE

A quick, easy way to estimate the temperature of the coals is to cautiously hold your hand, palm-side down, about 4 inches above the coals. Count the number of seconds you can hold your hand in that position before the heat forces you to pull it away.

| Seconds | Coals | Temperature |
|---------|-------|-------------|
| 2 | hot | 375°F or more |
| 3 | medium-hot | 350° to 370°F |
| 4 | medium | 300° to 350°F |
| 5 | low | 200° to 300°F |

## USING A GAS GRILL

Carefully follow the instructions in your owner's manual for lighting a gas grill. Once the grill is lit, turn on all burners to "high." The grill should be ready to use in about 10 minutes.

**Direct Cooking:** Leave the burners at the "high" setting to sear the food, and then reduced immediately to "medium." Continue to cook at "medium" or "low." Gas grills cook the most evenly and with the fewest flare-ups at "medium" or "low," with temperatures in the 250° to 375°F range. This is equivalent to medium-hot to low for charcoal. If flare-ups are a problem, one or more of the burners can be turned to a lower setting.

**Indirect Cooking:** Preheat the grill as directed above. Turn the center burner to "off" and the two side burners to "medium." Place a metal or disposable foil drip pan directly on the lava rocks in the center of the grill. Place the food on the grid directly over the drip pan. If you wish to sear the food, first place it over a side burner, then move it to the center. For indirect cooking on a dual burner grill, turn one side of the grill to "off."

Place the food on the unheated side of the grill, over the drip pan.

Do not use water to quench flare-ups on a gas grill. Close the hood and turn the heat down until the flaring subsides. Trimming as much fat as possible from the meat before grilling or using a drip pan also helps.

## FLAVORED SMOKE

Although the distinctive smoky flavor of charcoal is missing on a gas grill, wood chips and chunks are great flavor alternatives. Most manufacturers advise against putting these directly on the lava rocks, since ash can clog the gas lines. Simply soak the chips or chunks for 20 minutes, drain and place in a metal or disposable foil drip pan. Poke several holes in the bottom of the pan and place it directly on the lava rocks. Preheat it with the grill.

## BASIC TEMPERATURES

This chart gives the basic internal temperatures of meat to determine cooking doneness.

| Meat | Doneness | Temperature |
|------|----------|-------------|
| Poultry | Whole | 180°F |
| | Breast | 170°F |
| Pork | Medium | 160°F |
| Beef* | Rare | 140°F |
| | Medium-rare | 145°F |
| | Medium | 160°F |
| | Well Done | 170°F |
| Lamb | Medium-rare | 145°F |
| | Whole | 160°F |

*When cooking burgers using ground beef, be sure that the burgers' internal temperature reaches at least 160°F.

# SIZZLING
## STARTERS

## Roasted Eggplant Dip

2 eggplants (about 1 pound
    each)
¼ cup fresh lemon juice
3 tablespoons sesame tahini*
4 cloves garlic, minced
2 teaspoons hot pepper sauce
½ teaspoon salt
    Paprika
1 tablespoon chopped fresh
    parsley
    Pita bread rounds, cut into
      wedges
    Red chili pepper slices
      (optional)

*Available in the ethnic section of the
supermarket or in Middle Eastern grocery
stores.

Prepare grill for direct cooking. Prick eggplants in several places with fork. Place eggplants on grid. Grill, covered, over medium-high heat 30 to 40 minutes or until skin is black and blistered and pulp is soft, turning often. Peel eggplants when cool enough to handle. Let cool to room temperature.

Place eggplant pulp in food processor with lemon juice, tahini, garlic, pepper sauce and salt; process until smooth. Refrigerate at least 1 hour before serving to allow flavors to blend. Sprinkle with paprika and parsley; serve with pita bread wedges. Garnish with red chili pepper slices, if desired. *Makes 8 (¼-cup) servings*

**Roasted Eggplant Dip**

# Spicy Apricot Sesame Wings

½ cup *French's®* Napa Valley
Style Dijon Mustard
⅓ cup *Frank's® RedHot®*
Cayenne Pepper Sauce
2 tablespoons Oriental
sesame oil
1 tablespoon red wine vinegar
½ cup apricot jam
2 pounds chicken wings, split
and tips discarded
2 tablespoons toasted sesame
seeds*

*To toast sesame seeds, place on baking sheet
and bake at 375°F 8 to 10 minutes or until
golden.*

**1.** Stir mustard, *Frank's RedHot* Sauce, sesame oil and vinegar in small measuring cup. Spoon ¼ cup *Frank's RedHot* Sauce mixture and apricot jam into blender or food processor. Cover; process until smooth. Reserve for basting and dipping sauce.

**2.** Place wings in large bowl. Pour remaining *Frank's RedHot* Sauce mixture over wings; toss to coat. Cover; marinate in refrigerator 20 minutes.

**3.** Place wings on oiled grid and discard any remaining marinade. Grill over medium heat 25 to 30 minutes or until crispy and no longer pink, turning often. Brush with ¼ cup reserved sauce during last 10 minutes of cooking. Place wings on serving platter; sprinkle with sesame seeds. Serve with remaining sauce.

*Makes 8 servings*

**Prep Time:** 15 minutes
**Marinate Time:** 20 minutes
**Cook Time:** 25 minutes

## GRILLING TIP

*Cleaning the grill is easier if the grill rack is coated with vegetable oil or nonstick cooking spray before grilling. A clean and oiled grill rack also prevents foods from sticking and makes the cooked food taste better.*

# Grilled Garlic & Herb Pizzas

Homemade Pizza Dough
(page 14)
8 cloves Grilled Garlic
(page 31)
1 medium yellow onion
Olive oil
1 medium red, yellow or
orange bell pepper
1 cup crumbled goat cheese
¼ cup chopped fresh herb
mixture (thyme, basil,
oregano and parsley) *or*
4 teaspoons dried herb
mixture
¼ cup grated Parmesan cheese

Prepare Homemade Pizza Dough. While dough is rising, light KINGSFORD® Briquets in covered grill. Arrange medium-hot briquets on one side of the grill. Prepare Grilled Garlic. Lightly oil grid to prevent sticking. Cut onion into ½-inch-thick slices. Insert wooden picks into onion slices from edges to prevent separating into rings. (Soak wooden picks in hot water 15 minutes to prevent burning.) Brush onion lightly with oil. Place whole bell pepper and onion slices on grid around edge of briquets. Grill on covered grill 20 to 30 minutes until tender, turning once or twice. Remove picks from onion slices and separate into rings. Cut pepper in half and remove seeds when cool enough to handle; slice pepper halves into strips.

Roll or gently stretch each ball of dough into 7-inch round. Brush lightly with oil on both sides. Grill dough on grid directly above medium-hot KINGSFORD® Briquets 1 to 3 minutes or until dough starts to bubble and bottom is lightly browned. Turn; grill 3 to 5 minutes or until second side is lightly browned and dough is cooked through. Remove from grill. Spread 2 cloves Grilled Garlic onto each crust; top with onion rings, pepper strips, goat cheese, herbs and Parmesan cheese, dividing equally. Place pizzas around edge of coals; grill covered 5 minutes until bottom crust is crisp, cheese melts and toppings are heated through.

*Makes 4 individual pizzas*

**Note:** A 1-pound loaf of frozen bread dough, thawed, can be substituted for Homemade Pizza Dough. Or, substitute 4 pre-baked individual Italian bread shells, add toppings and warm on the grill.

*continued on page 14*

Grilled Garlic & Herb Pizzas

### Homemade Pizza Dough

2¾ cups all-purpose flour, divided
  1 package quick-rising yeast
  ¾ teaspoon salt
  1 cup water
1½ tablespoons vegetable oil

Combine 1½ cups flour, yeast and salt in food processor. Heat water and oil in small saucepan until 120° to 130°F. With food processor running, add water and oil to flour mixture; process 30 seconds. Add 1 cup flour; process until dough comes together to form ball. Knead on floured board 3 to 4 minutes or until smooth and satiny, kneading in as much of the remaining ¼ cup flour as needed to prevent dough from sticking. Place dough in oiled bowl, turning once. Cover with towel; let rise in warm place 30 minutes until doubled in bulk. Divide dough into 4 equal balls.

# Western Lamb Riblets

5 pounds lamb riblets, cut
    into serving-size pieces
¾ cup chili sauce
½ cup beer
½ cup honey
¼ cup Worcestershire sauce
¼ cup finely chopped onion
1 clove garlic, minced
½ teaspoon crushed red
    pepper flakes

Trim excess fat from riblets. In saucepan, combine chili sauce, beer, honey, Worcestershire sauce, onion, garlic and pepper flakes. Bring mixture to a boil. Reduce heat; simmer, covered, 10 minutes. Remove from heat; cool.

Place riblets in resealable plastic food storage bag. Pour cooled marinade over riblets in bag. Close bag securely and refrigerate about 2 hours, turning bag occasionally to distribute marinade evenly.

Drain riblets; reserve marinade. Arrange medium-hot KINGSFORD® Briquets around drip pan. Place riblets on grid over drip pan. Cover grill; cook 45 minutes, turning riblets and brushing with marinade twice. Bring remaining marinade to a boil; cook 1 to 2 minutes. Serve with riblets. *Makes 6 servings*

# Gorgonzola Buffalo Wings

**Dressing**
- ¼ cup mayonnaise
- 3 tablespoons sour cream
- 1½ tablespoons white wine vinegar
- ¼ teaspoon sugar
- ⅓ cup (1½ ounces) BELGIOIOSO® Gorgonzola

**Chicken**
- 2 pounds chicken wings
- 3 tablespoons hot pepper sauce
- 1 tablespoon vegetable oil
- 1 clove garlic, minced

**For dressing**
Combine mayonnaise, sour cream, vinegar and sugar in small bowl. Stir in BelGioioso Gorgonzola; cover and refrigerate until serving.

**For chicken**
Place chicken in large resealable plastic food storage bag. Combine pepper sauce, oil and garlic in separate small bowl; pour over chicken. Seal bag tightly; turn to coat. Marinate in refrigerator at least 1 hour or, for hotter flavor, up to 24 hours, turning occasionally.

Prepare grill. Drain chicken, discarding marinade. Place chicken on oiled grid. Grill, covered, over medium-hot coals 25 to 30 minutes or until chicken is no longer pink, turning 3 to 4 times. Serve with dressing.

*Makes 4 servings*

# Pineapple-Scallop Bites

- ½ cup *French's*® Napa Valley Style Dijon Mustard
- ¼ cup orange marmalade
- 1 cup canned pineapple cubes (24 pieces)
- 12 sea scallops (8 ounces), cut in half crosswise
- 12 strips (6 ounces) uncooked turkey bacon, cut in half crosswise*

*\*Or substitute regular bacon for turkey bacon. Simmer 5 minutes in enough boiling water to cover; drain well before wrapping scallops.*

**1.** Soak 12 (6-inch) bamboo skewers in hot water 20 minutes. Combine mustard and marmalade in small bowl. Reserve ½ cup mixture for dipping sauce.

**2.** Hold 1 pineapple cube and 1 scallop half together. Wrap with 1 bacon strip. Thread onto skewer. Repeat with remaining pineapple, scallops and bacon.

**3.** Place skewers on oiled grid. Grill over medium heat 6 minutes, turning frequently and brushing with remaining mustard mixture. Serve hot with reserved dipping sauce.

*Makes 6 servings*

**Prep Time:** 25 minutes
**Cook Time:** 6 minutes

# Honeyed Pork and Mango Kabobs

½ cup honey

¼ cup frozen apple juice concentrate, thawed

3 tablespoons *Frank's® RedHot®* Cayenne Pepper Sauce

¼ teaspoon ground allspice

1 teaspoon grated lemon peel

1 pound pork tenderloin, cut into 1-inch cubes

1 large (12 ounces) ripe mango, peeled and cut into ¾-inch cubes, divided

½ cup frozen large baby onions, partially thawed

**1.** Combine honey, juice concentrate, *Frank's RedHot* Sauce and allspice in small saucepan. Bring to a boil over medium heat. Reduce heat to low; cook, stirring, 5 minutes. Stir in lemon peel. Remove from heat. Pour ¼ cup marinade into small bowl; reserve.

**2.** Place pork in large resealable plastic food storage bag. Pour remaining marinade over pork. Seal bag; refrigerate 1 hour. Prepare grill.

**3.** To prepare dipping sauce, place ¼ cup mango cubes in blender or food processor. Add reserved ¼ cup marinade. Cover; process until puréed. Transfer to serving bowl; set aside.

**4.** Alternately thread pork, remaining mango cubes and onions onto metal skewers. Place skewers on oiled grid. Grill,* over medium-low coals, 12 to 15 minutes or until pork is no longer pink. Serve kabobs with dipping sauce.

*Makes 6 servings (¾ cup sauce)*

*Or, broil 6 inches from heat 10 to 12 minutes or until pork is no longer pink.

**Note:** You may substitute 1½ cups fresh or frozen peach cubes (2 to 3 peaches) for fresh mango.

**Prep Time:** 30 minutes
**Marinate Time:** 1 hour
**Cook Time:** about 20 minutes

# Greek-Style Grilled Feta

1 package (8 ounces) feta cheese, sliced in half horizontally
24 (¼-inch) slices small onion
½ green bell pepper, thinly sliced
½ red bell pepper, thinly sliced
½ teaspoon dried oregano leaves
¼ teaspoon garlic pepper or black pepper
24 (½-inch) slices French bread

**1.** Spray 14-inch-long sheet of foil with nonstick cooking spray. Cut feta into 24 slices. Place onion slices in center of foil and top with feta slices. Sprinkle with bell pepper slices, oregano and garlic pepper.

**2.** Seal foil using Drugstore Wrap technique.* Place foil packet on grid upside down and grill on covered grill over hot coals 15 minutes. Turn packet over; grill on covered grill 15 minutes more.

**3.** Open packet carefully and serve immediately with slices of French bread. *Makes 8 servings*

*Place the food in the center of an oblong piece of heavy-duty foil, leaving at least a two-inch border around the food. Bring the two long sides together above the food; fold down in a series of locked folds, allowing for heat circulation and expansion. Fold the short ends up and over again. Press folds firmly to seal the foil packet.*

# Szechuan Wings

1 package (about 1¾ pounds) PERDUE® Fresh OVEN STUFFER® Roaster Wingettes or Chicken Wingettes
6 tablespoons white vinegar
6 tablespoons chili sauce
6 tablespoons soy sauce
2 tablespoons canola oil
2 tablespoons minced fresh gingerroot
1½ tablespoons sugar
1½ tablespoons crushed red pepper
1½ teaspoons salt

Place wingettes in large bowl. In small bowl, combine remaining ingredients; set aside ¼ cup. Pour soy sauce mixture over wingettes; cover and refrigerate 1 hour or longer.

Prepare lightly greased grill for cooking. Remove wingettes to grill and discard marinade. Grill wingettes, uncovered, 5 to 6 inches over medium-hot coals 25 to 30 minutes or until wingettes are no longer pink and juices run clear, turning and basting frequently with reserved soy sauce mixture. *Makes 3 to 4 servings*

Greek-Style Grilled Feta

# Grilled Vegetable Pizzas

2 tablespoons olive oil

1 clove garlic, minced

1 red bell pepper, cut into quarters

4 slices red onion, cut ¼ inch thick

1 medium zucchini, halved lengthwise

1 medium yellow squash, halved lengthwise

1 cup purchased pizza sauce

¼ teaspoon red pepper flakes

2 (10-inch) prepared pizza crusts

2 cups (8 ounces) shredded fontinella or mozzarella cheese

¼ cup sliced fresh basil leaves

Prepare grill for direct cooking.

Combine oil and garlic in small bowl; brush over bell pepper, onion, zucchini and squash. Place vegetables on grid. Grill on covered grill over medium heat 10 minutes or until crisp-tender, turning halfway through grilling time. Remove vegetables from grill.

Slice bell pepper lengthwise into ¼-inch strips. Cut zucchini and squash crosswise into ¼-inch slices. Separate onion slices into rings.

Combine pizza sauce and red pepper flakes in small bowl. Top crusts with equal amounts of pizza sauce mixture, cheese and grilled vegetables.

Place pizzas, one at a time, on grid. Grill, covered, over medium-low heat 5 to 6 minutes or until cheese is melted and crust is hot.

Sprinkle pizzas with basil; cut into wedges. Serve warm or at room temperature.     *Makes 8 appetizer servings*

# Chicken Kabobs with Thai Dipping Sauce

1 pound boneless skinless
chicken breasts, cut into
1-inch cubes
1 small cucumber, seeded and
cut into small chunks
1 cup cherry tomatoes
2 green onions, cut into
1-inch pieces
⅔ cup teriyaki baste & glaze
sauce
⅓ cup *Frank's® RedHot®*
Cayenne Pepper Sauce
⅓ cup peanut butter
3 tablespoons frozen orange
juice concentrate,
undiluted
2 cloves garlic, minced

Thread chicken, cucumber, tomatoes and onions alternately onto metal skewers; set aside.

To prepare Thai Dipping Sauce, combine teriyaki baste & glaze sauce, **Frank's RedHot** Sauce, peanut butter, orange juice concentrate and garlic; mix well. Reserve ⅔ cup sauce for dipping.

Brush skewers with some of remaining sauce. Place skewers on oiled grid. Grill over hot coals 10 minutes or until chicken is no longer pink in center, turning and basting often with remaining sauce. Serve skewers with reserved Thai Dipping Sauce. Garnish as desired.

*Makes 6 appetizer servings*

**Prep Time:** 15 minutes
**Cook Time:** 10 minutes

## GRILLING TIP

*Spray metal skewers with nonstick cooking spray before threading ingredients onto the skewers. This will make removing the grilled food a snap. Cleaning the skewers will be much easier too.*

# Turkey Ham Quesadillas

¼ cup picante sauce or salsa

4 (7-inch) regular or whole wheat flour tortillas

½ cup shredded reduced-sodium, reduced-fat Monterey Jack cheese

¼ cup finely chopped turkey ham or lean ham

¼ cup canned diced green chilies, drained *or* 2 tablespoons chopped jalapeño peppers*

Nonstick cooking spray

Additional picante sauce or salsa for dipping (optional)

Fat-free or low-fat sour cream (optional)

*\*Jalapeño peppers can sting and irritate the skin; wear rubber gloves when handling peppers and do not touch eyes. Wash hands after handling.*

**1.** Spread 1 tablespoon picante sauce on each tortilla.

**2.** Sprinkle cheese, turkey ham and chilies equally over half of each tortilla. Fold over uncovered half to make quesadilla; spray tops and bottoms of quesadillas with cooking spray.

**3.** Grill on uncovered grill over medium coals 1½ minutes per side or until cheese is melted and tortillas are golden brown, turning once. Quarter each quesadilla and serve with additional picante sauce and sour cream, if desired.        *Makes 8 appetizer servings*

## FOOD FACT

*Quesadillas are a versatile party food. They are made from flour tortillas with meat or vegetable fillings and topped with shredded cheese. Then they are folded into half moons and grilled until the cheese is melted. For an easy party appetizer, assemble the day before and refrigerate until ready to heat on the grill. Serve with a variety of flavorful salsas.*

Turkey Ham Quesadillas

# Thai Satay Chicken Skewers

1 pound boneless skinless
    chicken breasts
⅓ cup soy sauce
2 tablespoons fresh lime juice
2 cloves garlic, minced
1 teaspoon grated fresh
    ginger
¾ teaspoon red pepper flakes
2 tablespoons water
¾ cup canned unsweetened
    coconut milk
1 tablespoon creamy peanut
    butter
4 green onions with tops, cut
    into 1-inch pieces

**1.** Slice chicken crosswise into ⅜-inch-wide strips; place in shallow glass dish.

**2.** Combine soy sauce, lime juice, garlic, ginger and red pepper in small bowl. Reserve 3 tablespoons mixture; cover and refrigerate until preparing peanut sauce. Add water to remaining mixture. Pour over chicken; toss to coat well. Cover; marinate in refrigerator at least 30 minutes or up to 2 hours, stirring mixture occasionally.

**3.** Cover 8 (10- to 12-inch) bamboo skewers with cold water. Soak 20 minutes to prevent them from burning; drain. Prepare grill for direct cooking.

**4.** Meanwhile, for peanut sauce, combine coconut milk, reserved soy sauce mixture and peanut butter in small saucepan. Bring to a boil over medium-high heat, stirring constantly. Reduce heat to low and simmer, uncovered, 2 to 4 minutes or until sauce thickens. Keep warm.

**5.** Drain chicken; reserve marinade from dish. Weave 3 to 4 chicken pieces accordion style onto each skewer, alternating with green onion pieces placed crosswise on skewer. Brush reserved marinade from dish over chicken and onions. Discard remaining marinade.

**6.** Place skewers on grid. Grill skewers on uncovered grill over medium-hot coals 6 to 8 minutes or until chicken is no longer pink in center, turning halfway through grilling time. Serve with warm peanut sauce for dipping. *Makes 8 appetizer servings*

Thai Satay Chicken Skewers

# Grilled Red Bell Pepper Dip

1 red bell pepper, stemmed, seeded and halved

1 cup fat-free or low-fat ricotta cheese

4 ounces fat-free cream cheese

¼ cup grated Parmesan cheese

1 clove garlic, minced *or*
    1 clove Grilled Garlic (page 31)

½ teaspoon Dijon mustard

¼ teaspoon salt

¼ teaspoon herbes de Provence

Mini pita pockets, Melba toast, pretzels or fresh vegetables

**1.** Grill bell pepper halves skin-side down on covered grill over medium coals 15 to 25 minutes or until skin is charred, without turning. Remove from grill and place in plastic bag until cool enough to handle, about 10 minutes. Remove and discard skin with paring knife.

**2.** Place bell pepper in food processor. Add cheeses, garlic, mustard, salt and herbes de Provence; process until smooth. Serve with mini pita pockets or vegetables for dipping. *Makes about 2 cups*

## GRILLING TIP

*Do not crowd pieces of food on the grill. Food will cook more evenly with a ¾-inch space between pieces. When food is crowded together, it tends to steam and does not have as much grilled and smokey flavor.*

# Herbed Croutons with Savory Bruschetta

½ cup regular or reduced-fat mayonnaise

¼ cup *French's*® Napa Valley Style Dijon Mustard

1 tablespoon finely chopped green onion

1 clove garlic, minced

¾ teaspoon dried oregano leaves

1 long thin loaf (18 inches) French bread, cut crosswise into ½-inch-thick slices

Savory Bruschetta (recipe follows)

Combine mayonnaise, mustard, onion, garlic and oregano in small bowl; mix well. Spread herbed mixture on one side of each slice of bread.

Place bread, spread sides up, on grid. Grill over medium-low coals 1 minute or until lightly toasted. Spoon Savory Bruschetta onto herbed croutons. Serve warm.

*Makes 6 appetizer servings*

**Tip:** Leftover croutons may be served with dips or cut up and served in salads.

**Prep Time:** 10 minutes
**Cook Time:** 1 minute

## Savory Bruschetta

1 pound ripe plum tomatoes, cored, seeded and chopped

1 cup finely chopped fennel bulb or celery

¼ cup chopped fresh basil leaves

3 tablespoons *French's*® Napa Valley Style Dijon Mustard

3 tablespoons olive oil

3 tablespoons balsamic vinegar

2 cloves garlic, minced

½ teaspoon salt

Combine ingredients in medium bowl; toss well to coat evenly.

*Makes 3 cups*

**Prep Time:** 15 minutes

Herbed Croutons
with Savory Bruschetta

# Stuffed Portobello Mushrooms

4 portobello mushrooms
(4 ounces each)
¼ cup olive oil
2 cloves garlic, pressed
6 ounces crumbled goat
cheese
2 ounces prosciutto or thinly
sliced ham, chopped
¼ cup chopped fresh basil
Mixed salad greens

Remove stems and gently scrape gills from underside of mushrooms; discard stems and gills. Brush mushroom caps with combined oil and garlic. Combine cheese, prosciutto and basil in medium bowl. Grill mushrooms, top side up, on covered grill over medium KINGSFORD® Briquets 4 minutes. Turn mushrooms over; fill caps with cheese mixture, dividing equally. Cover and grill 3 to 4 minutes longer until cheese mixture is warm. Remove mushrooms from grill; cut into quarters. Serve on mixed greens. *Makes 8 appetizer servings*

# Spicy Mustard Kielbasa Bites

1 pound whole kielbasa or
smoked Polish sausage
1 cup *French's*® Zesty Deli
Mustard
¾ cup honey
1 tablespoon *Frank's*® *RedHot*®
Cayenne Pepper Sauce

**1.** Place kielbasa on grid. Grill over medium heat 10 minutes or until lightly browned, turning occasionally. Cut into bite-sized pieces; set aside.

**2.** Combine mustard and honey in large saucepan. Bring to a boil over medium heat. Stir in kielbasa and *Frank's RedHot* Sauce. Cook until heated through. Transfer to serving bowl. Serve with party toothpicks.

*Makes 8 servings*

**Tip:** Refrigerate leftover honey-mustard mixture. This makes a tasty dip for chicken nuggets, cooked chicken wings or mini hot dogs.

**Prep Time:** 15 minutes
**Cook Time:** 10 minutes

# Grilled Garlic

**1 or 2 heads garlic
Olive oil**

Peel outermost papery skin from garlic heads. Brush heads with oil. Grill heads at edge of grid on covered grill over medium-hot KINGSFORD® Briquets 30 to 45 minutes or until cloves are soft and buttery. Remove from grill; cool slightly. Gently squeeze softened garlic head from root end so that cloves slip out of skins into small bowl. Use immediately or cover and refrigerate up to 1 week.

• For a quick appetizer, spread cloves of Grilled Garlic over toasted bread slices, crackers or raw vegetable slices.

• Mash cloves of Grilled Garlic and add to baked potatoes, mashed potatoes, pasta dishes, soups, salad dressings and dips.

• Spread cloves of Grilled Garlic over bread slices for a flavorful, low-fat sandwich spread. Or, mash cloves and add to mayonnaise.

• Spread cloves of Grilled Garlic onto a pizza crust before adding toppings.

• To season steamed vegetables, mash cloves of Grilled Garlic and stir into melted or softened butter with chopped fresh herbs or spices.

# Grilled Antipasto Platter

16 medium scallops

16 medium shrimp, shelled and deveined

12 mushrooms (about 1 inch diameter)

3 ounces thinly sliced prosciutto or deli-style ham

16 slender asparagus spears

1 jar (6½ ounces) marinated artichoke hearts, drained

2 medium zucchini, cut lengthwise into slices

1 large or 2 small red bell peppers, cored, seeded and cut into 1-inch-wide strips

1 head radicchio, cut lengthwise into quarters (optional)

Lemon Baste (recipe follows)

Lemon wedges

Soak 12 long bamboo skewers in water for at least 20 minutes to keep them from burning. Thread 4 scallops on each of 4 skewers and 4 shrimp on each of another 4 skewers. Thread 6 mushrooms on each of 2 more skewers. Cut prosciutto into 2×1-inch strips. Wrap 2 asparagus spears together with 2 strips of prosciutto; secure with a toothpick. Repeat with remaining asparagus spears. Wrap each artichoke heart in 1 strip of prosciutto; thread on 2 remaining skewers. Place ingredients except radicchio and lemon wedges on a baking sheet. Reserve ¼ cup Lemon Baste. Brush remaining Lemon Baste liberally over ingredients on baking sheet.

Spread medium KINGSFORD® Briquets in a wide single layer over the bed of the grill. Oil hot grid to help prevent sticking. Grill skewers, asparagus bundles, zucchini and red peppers, on an uncovered grill, 7 to 12 minutes until vegetables are tender, seafood firms up and turns opaque and prosciutto around wrapped vegetables is crisp, turning once or twice. Remove each item from grill to a large serving platter as it is done. Pour remaining baste over all. Serve hot or at room temperature. Garnish with radicchio and lemon wedges.

*Makes 8 appetizer servings*

## Lemon Baste

½ cup olive oil

¼ cup fresh lemon juice

½ teaspoon salt

¼ teaspoon black pepper

Whisk together all ingredients in small bowl until well blended.
*Makes about ¾ cup*

Grilled Antipasto Platter

# Parmesan Polenta

4 cups chicken broth
1 small onion, minced
4 cloves garlic, minced
1 tablespoon minced fresh
    rosemary *or* 1 teaspoon
    dried rosemary
½ teaspoon salt
1¼ cups yellow cornmeal
6 tablespoons grated
    Parmesan cheese
1 tablespoon olive oil, divided

**1.** Spray 11×7-inch baking pan with nonstick cooking spray; set aside. Spray one side of 7-inch-long sheet of waxed paper with cooking spray; set aside. Combine chicken broth, onion, garlic, rosemary and salt in medium saucepan. Bring to a boil over high heat; add cornmeal gradually, stirring constantly. Reduce heat to medium and simmer 30 minutes or until mixture has consistency of thick mashed potatoes. Remove from heat and stir in cheese.

**2.** Spread polenta evenly in prepared pan; place waxed paper, sprayed-side down, on polenta and smooth. (If surface is bumpy, it is more likely to stick to grill.) Cool on wire rack 15 minutes or until firm. Remove waxed paper; cut into 6 squares. Remove squares from pan.

**3.** To prevent sticking, spray grid with cooking spray. Prepare coals for grilling. Brush tops of squares with half the oil. Grill oil-side down on covered grill over medium to low coals for 6 to 8 minutes or until golden. Brush with remaining oil and gently turn over. Grill 6 to 8 minutes more or until golden. Serve warm. *Makes 6 servings*

## FOOD FACT

*Polenta is a delicious Italian cornmeal mush that can be served as a hearty breakfast, a first course, a side dish or an entrée with a special sauce. Often flavored with cheese, polenta can be prepared ahead of time and refrigerated up to 2 days before serving. When ready to serve, cut into pieces and brown on the grill until sizzling hot.*

Parmesan Polenta

# Sausage-Bacon-Apricot Kabobs

1 package BOB EVANS®
   Italian Grillin' Sausage
   (approximately 5 links)
1 cup dried apricot halves
8 slices bacon
3 tablespoons apricot
   preserves
3 tablespoons lemon juice
1 tablespoon Dijon mustard
1 teaspoon Worcestershire
   sauce

Precook sausage 10 minutes in gently boiling water. Drain and cut into ¾-inch slices. Alternate sausage and apricots on 8 wooden skewers,* weaving bacon back and forth in ribbonlike fashion between them. Grill or broil over medium-high heat 3 to 4 minutes on each side. Combine preserves, lemon juice, mustard and Worcestershire in small bowl. Brush preserves mixture on kabobs; continue grilling, turning and basting frequently, until bacon is cooked through. Refrigerate leftovers.     *Makes 8 kabobs*

*Soak wooden skewers in water 30 minutes before using to prevent burning.*

## GRILLING TIP

*There are many types of metal skewers made specifically for broiling and grilling kabobs, but many cooks prefer to use bamboo skewers because the wood remains cool during cooking. For best results, soak bamboo skewers in water for about 30 minutes before using to make them more pliable and to prevent them from burning.*

Sausage-Bacon-Apricot Kabobs

# Smoked Focaccia

2 teaspoons sugar

1½ teaspoons active dry yeast

¾ cup warm water (110° to 115°F)

2 tablespoons finely chopped sun-dried tomatoes

1 tablespoon minced fresh basil leaves *or* 1 teaspoon dried basil leaves

1 tablespoon olive oil

½ teaspoon minced garlic

¼ teaspoon salt

1¾ cups bread flour

¼ cup cornmeal

Nonstick cooking spray

1 Grilled Bell Pepper (recipe follows)

¼ teaspoon coarse salt

**1.** Sprinkle sugar and yeast over warm water; stir until yeast is dissolved. Let stand 5 to 10 minutes or until bubbly. Stir in tomatoes, basil, oil, garlic and salt. Add flour, ½ cup at a time, stirring until dough begins to pull away from side of bowl and forms a ball; stir in cornmeal.

**2.** Turn out dough onto lightly floured surface; flatten slightly. Knead gently 5 minutes or until smooth and elastic, adding additional flour to prevent sticking, if necessary. Place dough in large bowl sprayed with nonstick cooking spray and turn dough so all sides are coated. Let rise, covered, in warm place about 1 hour or until doubled in bulk. (Dough may be refrigerated overnight.) Prepare Grilled Bell Pepper.

**3.** Punch down dough; turn onto lightly floured surface and knead 1 minute. Divide dough in half; press each half into 9×7-inch rectangle on large sheet of foil sprayed with cooking spray. Fold edges of foil to form "pan." Dimple surfaces of dough using fingertips; spray tops with cooking spray. Cut bell pepper into strips and arrange on focaccia; sprinkle with coarse salt. Let rise, covered, 30 minutes.

**4.** Grill focaccia on covered grill over medium coals 8 to 12 minutes or until they sound hollow when tapped, keeping on foil "pans." Check bottoms of focaccia after about 6 minutes; move to upper grill rack or over indirect heat to finish if browning too fast.  *Makes 6 servings*

## Grilled Bell Pepper

**1 bell pepper (any color), stemmed, seeded and halved**

Grill bell pepper halves skin-side down on covered grill over medium to hot coals 15 to 25 minutes or until skin is charred, without turning. Remove from grill and place in plastic bag until cool enough to handle, about 10 minutes. Remove skin with paring knife and discard.

Smoked Focaccia

# Raspberry Mushroom Kabobs

1 pound button mushrooms
1 cup (12-ounce jar)
    SMUCKER'S® Red
    Raspberry Preserves
½ cup red wine vinegar
1 tablespoon chopped parsley
1 teaspoon mustard
1 clove garlic, minced
    Salt and pepper, to taste

Remove mushroom stems and reserve for another use. Blanch mushroom caps in boiling salted water for 5 minutes.

Dissolve preserves in red wine vinegar. Stir in parsley, mustard, garlic, salt and pepper. Drain cooked mushrooms and add to sauce to cool. (Recipe can be prepared to this point up to 3 days in advance.)

Thread 3 to 4 mushrooms on each of 12 skewers. Place skewers on preheated grill. Cook for 3 minutes on each side before serving. *Makes 12 kabobs*

## GRILLING TIP

*If you don't have time to make vegetable kabobs, use a grill basket or vegetable grate to cook small vegetables. The basket or grate has small holes to allow the heat to reach the food but keeps them from falling through the grid into the fire. Grates or baskets go on top of the grid and should be oiled and preheated before adding the vegetables.*

# Fresh Grilled Corn Soup

Grilled Corn (recipe follows)
Grilled Onion (recipe
    follows)
1 can (49½ ounces) chicken
    broth (about 6 cups)
2 medium potatoes, peeled
    and cubed
½ teaspoon ground cumin
½ teaspoon chili powder
1½ cups heavy cream or
    half-and-half
⅓ cup chopped fresh cilantro
½ teaspoon hot pepper sauce
    Additional cilantro leaves
        for garnish

Prepare Grilled Corn and Grilled Onion. Cut corn from cobs. Chop onion. Combine corn, onion, broth, potatoes, cumin and chili powder in Dutch oven. Bring to a boil. Reduce heat to medium-low; simmer about 30 minutes until potatoes are tender. Place in food processor in batches. Process until no large pieces remain, but mixture is not completely smooth. Return to Dutch oven; stir in cream, cilantro and pepper sauce. Heat over low heat until warm. *Do not boil.* Ladle into bowls. Garnish with additional cilantro.           *Makes 8 servings (1 cup each)*

**Grilled Corn:** Pull back husks from 4 ears of corn, leaving husks attached. Remove 1 strip of husk from inner portion of each ear and reserve; remove silk. Combine 1½ tablespoons melted butter, 1 teaspoon chopped fresh cilantro, ½ teaspoon ground cumin and ¼ teaspoon chili powder in small bowl; brush onto corn. Bring husks up each ear to cover corn; secure with reserved strips of husk. Grill on covered grill over medium KINGSFORD® briquets 20 to 30 minutes or until tender, turning once or twice.

**Grilled Onion:** Cut 1 medium onion into ½-inch-thick rounds. Insert wooden picks into onion slices from edges to prevent separating into rings. (Soak wooden picks in hot water 15 minutes to prevent burning.) Brush onion slices with olive oil. Grill onion on covered grill over medium KINGSFORD® briquets 20 to 30 minutes or until tender, turning once. Remove picks.

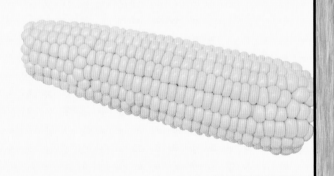

# Grilled Summer Gazpacho

1 red bell pepper, stemmed,
  seeded and halved
4 large (about 2 pounds)
  tomatoes, tops removed
1 small onion, halved
  Nonstick cooking spray
4 cloves garlic, divided
6 (½-inch) slices French bread
1 cup coarsely chopped
  peeled cucumber
1 cup day-old French bread
  cubes, soaked in water
  and squeezed dry
2 to 4 tablespoons chopped
  fresh cilantro
2 tablespoons fresh lemon
  juice
1 tablespoon olive oil
½ teaspoon salt
2 cups ice water
  Additional cilantro leaves
  for garnish

**1.** Prepare coals for grilling. Grill bell pepper halves skin-side down on covered grill over medium to hot coals 15 to 25 minutes or until skin is charred, without turning. Remove from grill and place in plastic bag until cool enough to handle, about 10 minutes. Remove skin; set peppers aside to cool.

**2.** Meanwhile, spray tomatoes and onion halves with cooking spray. Grill tomatoes and onion halves skin-side down on covered grill over medium coals 10 to 20 minutes or until grillmarked and tender, turning as needed. Thread 3 garlic cloves onto water-soaked wooden or bamboo skewer. Spray with cooking spray. Grill garlic on covered grill over medium coals about 8 minutes or until browned and tender. Remove vegetables from grill and let cool on cutting board.

**3.** While vegetables cool, cut remaining garlic clove in half. Spray both sides of French bread slices with cooking spray; rub with garlic clove halves. Grill bread slices on both sides until toasted and golden, watching carefully. Cool; cut into ½-inch croutons and set aside for garnish.

**4.** Gently squeeze cooled tomatoes to remove seeds and release skins. Scrape and discard any excess charring from onion. Coarsely chop bell pepper, tomatoes and onion; add with cucumber to food processor or blender. Cover and process until smooth. Transfer to large bowl.

**5.** Add soaked bread cubes, chopped cilantro, lemon juice, oil and salt to food processor; cover and process until smooth. Combine with grilled vegetable mixture; stir in ice water. Ladle soup into bowls; garnish with garlic croutons and additional cilantro leaves, if desired.

*Makes 6 servings*

# Farmer's Market Grilled Chowder

1 ear fresh corn *or* 1 cup
    frozen corn, thawed
1 small zucchini, cut
    lengthwise into
    ¼-inch-thick slices
1 large potato
1 tablespoon margarine
½ cup chopped onion
2 tablespoons all-purpose
    flour
½ teaspoon salt
½ teaspoon dried thyme leaves
⅛ teaspoon white pepper
1 cup fat-free reduced-sodium
    chicken broth or beer
1 cup low fat (1%) milk
½ cup (2 ounces) shredded
    reduced-fat sharp
    Cheddar cheese

**1.** Remove husks and silk from corn. Place in large bowl and cover with cold water; soak 20 to 30 minutes. Remove; wrap in foil. Grill on covered grill over medium-hot coals 20 to 25 minutes or until hot and tender, turning over halfway through grilling time. Cool; cut kernels from cob. Set aside.

**2.** To grill zucchini, spray zucchini on both sides with cooking spray. Grill on uncovered grill over medium coals 4 minutes or until grillmarked and tender, turning once. Cool; cut into bite-size pieces. Set aside.

**3.** Cut potato in half lengthwise; grill potato halves on covered grill over medium coals 15 to 20 minutes or until potato is tender, turning over once. Cut potato into cubes.

**4.** Melt margarine in large saucepan over medium heat. Add onion; cook and stir 5 minutes or until tender but not brown. Stir in flour, salt, thyme and pepper. Cook and stir about 1 minute.

**5.** Stir broth and milk into flour mixture. Cook and stir over medium heat until mixture begins to bubble; continue cooking about 1 minute more. Stir in corn, zucchini, potato and cheese. Reduce heat to low; simmer, uncovered, until cheese is melted and mixture is hot, stirring constantly. Garnish as desired.

*Makes 4 servings*

Farmer's Market Grilled Chowder

# SUMMER
## SALADS

### Grilled Tri-Colored Pepper Salad

1 each large red, yellow and
    green bell pepper, cut
    into halves or quarters
⅓ cup extra-virgin olive oil
3 tablespoons balsamic
    vinegar
2 cloves garlic, minced
¼ teaspoon salt
¼ teaspoon black pepper
⅓ cup crumbled goat cheese
    (about 1½ ounces)
¼ cup thinly sliced fresh basil
    leaves

**1.** Prepare barbecue grill for direct cooking.

**2.** Place bell peppers, skin-side down, on grid. Grill bell peppers on covered grill over hot coals 10 to 12 minutes or until skin is charred. Place charred bell peppers in paper bag. Close bag; set aside to cool 10 to 15 minutes. Remove skin with paring knife; discard skin.

**3.** Place bell peppers in shallow glass serving dish. Combine oil, vinegar, garlic, salt and black pepper in small bowl; whisk until well combined. Pour over bell peppers. Let stand 30 minutes at room temperature. (Or, cover and refrigerate up to 24 hours. Bring bell peppers to room temperature before serving.)

**4.** Sprinkle bell peppers with cheese and basil just before serving. *Makes 4 to 6 servings*

**Grilled Tri-Colored Pepper Salad**

# Warm Chinese Chicken Salad

1 cup prepared Italian salad
   dressing
2 teaspoons low-sodium soy
   sauce
1 teaspoon minced fresh
   ginger *or* ¼ teaspoon
   dried ground ginger
2 whole chicken breasts, split,
   boned, skinned
8 cups torn mixed greens
¼ cup chopped fresh cilantro
   (optional)
¼ cup diagonally sliced green
   onions
5 fresh California peaches,
   divided
¼ cup toasted sliced almonds
2 tablespoons toasted sesame
   seeds (optional)

For Marinade, in resealable plastic food storage bag, combine salad dressing, soy sauce and ginger. Add chicken; close bag securely, turning to coat well. Refrigerate 30 minutes.

For Salad, arrange greens on 4 serving plates. Sprinkle with cilantro, if desired. Top with green onions. Slice 3 peaches and arrange on lettuce. Remove chicken from marinade, reserving marinade. In small saucepan, bring reserved marinade to a boil. (This can be done on the grill, if desired.) Boil 1 minute. Reserve ½ cup for dressing. Use remaining boiled marinade for basting. Grill or broil chicken until browned and cooked through, basting occasionally with marinade. Halve 2 peaches; baste with marinade and grill about 5 minutes. Slice each chicken breast and arrange chicken and grilled peaches on lettuce. Add almonds and sesame seeds, if desired, to reserved boiled marinade. Pour over salads and serve immediately. *Makes 4 servings*

*Favorite recipe from* **California Tree Fruit Agreement**

## GRILLING TIP

*Marinades that have been in contact with raw or partially cooked fish, poultry or meat carry bacteria and are not safe to eat. When preparing marinades for grilled foods, it is best to divide the marinade in half. Use half of the marinade to marinate the food reserving the other half as a basting sauce or dressing. Always discard marinades after the food is removed or boil the marinade for 1 minute or more before using as a basting sauce or dressing.*

# Fajita-Style Beef Salad

1 package (1.0 ounce)
    LAWRY'S® Taco Spices
    & Seasonings
½ cup water
¼ teaspoon hot pepper sauce
¾ pound top sirloin steak
1 quart salad greens, torn
    into bite-size pieces
1 green bell pepper, chopped
1 onion, thinly sliced
½ cup shredded red cabbage
1 can (8¾ ounces) garbanzo
    beans, drained
1 tomato, cut into wedges
    Tortilla chips
    Spicy Tomato Vinaigrette
    (recipe follows)

In large resealable plastic food storage bag, combine Taco Spices & Seasonings, water and hot pepper sauce; mix well. Add steak; seal bag. Marinate in refrigerator 30 minutes or overnight. Remove steak from marinade; discard used marinade. Grill or broil steak 10 to 12 minutes, or until desired doneness, turning once. Slice into thin strips. In large bowl, toss together salad greens, green pepper, onion, cabbage and garbanzo beans. Place on individual plates or serving platter. Top with beef strips, tomato wedges and tortilla chips. Serve with Spicy Tomato Vinaigrette.

*Makes 6 side-dish or 4 main-dish servings*

**Variation:** Lawry's Spices & Seasonings for Fajitas can be substituted for Taco Spices & Seasonings.

## Spicy Tomato Vinaigrette

 1 cup prepared chunky salsa
½ cup vegetable oil
¼ cup white wine vinegar
 2 tablespoons sliced green onions, including tops
½ teaspoon sugar
½ teaspoon LAWRY'S® Garlic Salt
½ teaspoon LAWRY'S® Seasoned Pepper

In container with stopper or lid, combine all ingredients. Seal top and shake vigorously to mix well. Chill.

*Makes about 2 cups*

# Blackened Chicken Salad

2 cups cubed sourdough bread
Nonstick cooking spray
1 tablespoon paprika
1 teaspoon onion powder
1 teaspoon garlic powder
½ teaspoon dried oregano leaves
½ teaspoon dried thyme leaves
½ teaspoon white pepper
½ teaspoon ground red pepper
½ teaspoon black pepper
1 pound boneless skinless chicken breasts
4 cups bite-size pieces fresh spinach leaves
2 cups bite-size pieces romaine lettuce
2 cups cubed zucchini
2 cups cubed seeded cucumber
½ cup sliced green onions with tops
1 medium tomato, cut into 8 wedges
Ranch Salad Dressing (recipe follows)

**1.** Preheat oven to 375°F. To make croutons, spray bread cubes lightly with cooking spray; place in 15×10-inch jelly-roll pan. Bake 10 to 15 minutes or until browned, stirring occasionally. Set aside.

**2.** Combine paprika, onion powder, garlic powder, oregano, thyme, white pepper, red pepper and black pepper in small bowl; rub on all surfaces of chicken. Broil chicken, 6 inches from heat source, 7 to 8 minutes on each side or until chicken is no longer pink in center. Or, grill chicken, on covered grill over medium-hot coals, 10 minutes on each side or until chicken is no longer pink in center. Cool slightly. Cut chicken into thin strips.

**3.** Combine warm chicken, greens, zucchini, cucumber, green onions, tomato and reserved croutons in large bowl. Drizzle with Ranch Salad Dressing; toss to coat. Serve immediately. *Makes 4 servings*

## Ranch Salad Dressing

¼ cup water
3 tablespoons reduced-calorie cucumber-ranch salad dressing
1 tablespoon reduced-fat mayonnaise or salad dressing
1 tablespoon lemon juice
2 teaspoons minced fresh parsley
⅛ teaspoon salt
⅛ teaspoon black pepper

In small jar with tight-fitting lid, combine all ingredients; shake well. Refrigerate until ready to use; shake before using. *Makes about ½ cup*

# Grilled Potato Salad

1 envelope LIPTON® RECIPE
    SECRETS® Onion
    Soup Mix*
⅓ cup BERTOLLI® Olive Oil
2 tablespoons red wine
    vinegar
1 clove garlic, finely chopped
2 pounds small red or
    all-purpose potatoes,
    cut into 1-inch cubes
1 tablespoon chopped fresh
    basil *or* 1 teaspoon dried
    basil leaves, crushed
    Freshly ground black
    pepper

*Also terrific with LIPTON® RECIPE SECRETS® Onion-Mushroom or Golden Onion Soup Mix.*

**1.** In large bowl, blend soup mix, oil, vinegar and garlic; stir in potatoes.

**2.** Grease 30×18-inch sheet of heavy-duty aluminum foil; top with potato mixture. Wrap foil loosely around mixture, sealing edges airtight with double fold. Place on another sheet of 30×18-inch foil; seal edges airtight with double fold in opposite direction.

**3.** Grill, shaking package occasionally and turning package once, 40 minutes or until potatoes are tender. Spoon into serving bowl and toss with basil and pepper. Serve slightly warm or at room temperature.

*Makes 4 servings*

**Oven Method:** Preheat oven to 450°F. Prepare foil packet as above. Place in large baking pan on bottom rack and bake, turning packet once, 40 minutes or until potatoes are tender. Toss and serve as above.

# BLT Chicken Salad for Two

2 boneless skinless chicken
    breasts
¼ cup mayonnaise or salad
    dressing
½ teaspoon black pepper
4 large lettuce leaves
1 large tomato, seeded and
    diced
3 slices crisp-cooked bacon,
    crumbled
1 hard-cooked egg, sliced
    Additional mayonnaise or
    salad dressing (optional)

**1.** Brush chicken with mayonnaise; sprinkle with pepper. Grill over hot coals 5 to 7 minutes per side or until no longer pink in center. Cool slightly; cut into thin strips.

**2.** Arrange lettuce leaves on serving plates. Top with chicken, tomato, bacon and egg. Spoon additional mayonnaise over top, if desired.

*Makes 2 servings*

Grilled Potato Salad

# Thai Beef Salad

**Dressing**
- 1 cup packed fresh mint or basil leaves, coarsely chopped
- 1 cup olive-oil vinaigrette dressing
- ⅓ cup *Frank's® RedHot®* Cayenne Pepper Sauce
- 3 tablespoons sugar
- 3 tablespoons chopped peeled fresh ginger
- 3 cloves garlic, chopped
- 2 teaspoons *French's®* Worcestershire Sauce

**Salad**
- 1 beef flank steak (about 1½ pounds)
- 6 cups washed and torn mixed salad greens
- 1 cup sliced peeled cucumber
- ⅓ cup chopped peanuts

**1.** Place Dressing ingredients in blender or food processor. Cover; process until smooth. Reserve 1 cup Dressing.

**2.** Place steak in large resealable plastic food storage bag. Pour remaining Dressing over steak. Seal bag; refrigerate 30 minutes.

**3.** Prepare grill. Place steak on grid, reserving marinade. Grill, over hot coals, about 15 minutes for medium-rare, brushing frequently with marinade. Let stand 5 minutes. Slice steak diagonally and arrange over salad greens and cucumber.

**4.** Sprinkle with peanuts and drizzle with reserved 1 cup Dressing. Serve warm. *Makes 6 servings*

## FOOD FACT

*Fresh ginger (also known as gingerroot) has a pungent and spicy flavor. Fresh ginger is completely different from dried ground ginger. To buy, select roots with smooth, unwrinkled skin. Store unpeeled and tightly wrapped in the refrigerator for up to 2 weeks or freeze for up to 2 months. To use fresh ginger, rinse and scrub outer skin before peeling.*

Thai Beef Salad

# Chicken Caesar

¾ cup olive oil

¼ cup fresh lemon juice

¼ cup finely grated Parmesan cheese

1 can (2 ounces) anchovies, drained and chopped

2 teaspoons Dijon mustard

1 clove garlic, minced

½ teaspoon black pepper
    Salt

4 boneless skinless chicken breasts

½ pound green beans, trimmed, cooked and cooled

6 to 8 small new potatoes, cooked, cooled and cut into quarters

¾ cup cooked fresh corn or thawed frozen corn

1 medium carrot, thinly sliced

10 to 12 cherry tomatoes, cut into halves

2 green onions, sliced
    Finely chopped parsley or basil

To make Caesar Dressing, place first 7 ingredients in blender or food processor; process until smooth and creamy. Add salt to taste.

Place chicken in a shallow glass dish. Pour ¼ cup dressing over chicken; turn to coat. Let stand while preparing vegetables, or cover and refrigerate up to 4 hours. Place vegetables in a large bowl; toss with remaining dressing; spoon onto serving plates. Season lightly with salt.

Oil hot grid to help prevent sticking. Grill chicken on covered grill over medium KINGSFORD® Briquets, 6 to 8 minutes, or until chicken is cooked through, turning once. Slice chicken crosswise and serve with vegetables. Sprinkle with parsley or basil. Serve immediately or at room temperature. *Makes 4 servings*

Chicken Caesar

# Grilled Steak Salad

¾ cup Italian salad dressing
¼ cup LA CHOY® Soy Sauce
4 (4-ounce) beef tenderloin
    steaks
8 large mushrooms, stems
    removed
6 cups salad greens

In small bowl, combine salad dressing and soy sauce; mix well. Reserve ¾ cup mixture for dressing. In resealable plastic bag, combine steaks, mushroom caps and ¼ cup remaining soy sauce mixture; marinate 15 minutes. Grill steak over medium-hot heat, basting often with marinade, 5 minutes on each side or to desired doneness. Grill mushrooms last 5 minutes of cooking time. Discard remaining marinade. Serve sliced steak and mushrooms over salad greens and dress with reserved soy sauce mixture. *Makes 4 servings*

# Provençal Grilled Tuna Salad

4 (5- to 6-ounce) tuna steaks,
    ¾ to 1 inch thick
3 tablespoons white wine or
    fish broth
3 tablespoons olive oil
2 tablespoons red wine
    vinegar
½ teaspoon chopped fresh
    rosemary *or* ¼ teaspoon
    dried rosemary leaves
½ teaspoon black pepper
⅛ teaspoon salt
1 clove garlic, minced
    Vegetable cooking spray
6 cups packed torn salad
    greens
1 cup halved cherry tomatoes

Measure thickness of fish to determine cooking time; place in glass dish. To make vinaigrette, combine wine, oil, vinegar, rosemary, pepper and salt in jar with tight-fitting lid. Shake well. Pour 2 tablespoons vinaigrette over fish; add garlic and turn to coat. Marinate 15 to 30 minutes, turning once. Reserve remaining vinaigrette for salad dressing.

Coat grill rack with cooking spray and place on grill to heat 1 minute. Place tuna on grill 4 to 6 inches over hot coals. Cover with lid or tent with foil. Cook, turning once, just until tuna begins to flake easily when tested with fork, about 7 minutes. Discard marinade.

Meanwhile, arrange salad greens on 4 plates. Place hot tuna on greens and add cherry tomatoes. Shake remaining vinaigrette and drizzle over salads. *Makes 4 servings*

**Note:** Halibut, swordfish or shark can be substituted for tuna.

*Favorite recipe from **National Fisheries Institute***

# Thai-Style Salad with Shredded Glazed Chicken

1 head Napa cabbage or
    romaine lettuce, shredded
    (about 6 cups)
1 medium cucumber, peeled,
    halved lengthwise, seeded
    and sliced (about
    1¼ cups)
2 medium carrots, coarsely
    grated (about 1 cup)
2 small oranges, peeled and
    cut into segments
½ cup fresh cilantro leaves
    (optional)
2 Honey-Lime Glazed Chicken
    Breasts, shredded (recipe
    follows)
    Honey-Lime Dressing
    (recipe follows)
¼ cup dry-roasted peanuts,
    chopped

Combine all ingredients except Honey-Lime Dressing and peanuts in large bowl; toss until well blended. Pour Honey-Lime Dressing over salad; toss until well blended. Sprinkle each serving with peanuts just before serving.

*Makes 4 servings*

**Honey-Lime Dressing:** Whisk together 6 tablespoons honey, 3 tablespoons peanut butter, 3 tablespoons lime juice, 2 tablespoons chopped fresh mint, 1 tablespoon minced seeded jalapeño pepper, 1½ teaspoons soy sauce, 1 teaspoon minced garlic and ¾ teaspoon grated lime peel in small bowl until well blended.

## Honey-Lime Glazed Chicken

½ cup honey
2 tablespoons fresh lime juice
2 tablespoons chopped fresh cilantro
1 tablespoon soy sauce
2 teaspoons minced seeded jalapeño pepper
1½ teaspoons minced garlic
6 bone-in chicken breast halves (about 3 pounds)

Combine all ingredients except chicken in small bowl until well blended. Place chicken in shallow baking dish; pour half of marinade over chicken. Cover and refrigerate 2 hours or overnight. Reserve remaining marinade. Grill chicken over medium-hot coals about 15 minutes, turning and basting with reserved marinade, or until chicken is no longer pink in center. Reserve 2 chicken breasts for use in Thai-Style Salad with Shredded Glazed Chicken.

*Favorite recipe from **National Honey Board***

# Salmon, Asparagus and Shiitake Salad

¼ cup cider vinegar

¼ cup extra-virgin olive oil

Grated peel and juice of
1 lemon

4 teaspoons Dijon mustard,
divided

1 clove garlic, minced

¼ teaspoon salt

¼ teaspoon black pepper

2 teaspoons minced fresh
tarragon *or* ¾ teaspoon
dried tarragon leaves

1 pound small salmon fillets,
skinned

1 medium red onion, thinly
sliced

1 pound asparagus, ends
trimmed

¼ pound shiitake mushrooms
or button mushrooms

Additional salt and black
pepper

8 cups lightly packed torn
romaine and red leaf
lettuce

Combine vinegar, oil, peel, juice, 2 teaspoons mustard, garlic, ¼ teaspoon salt and ¼ teaspoon pepper in medium bowl; spoon 3 tablespoons dressing into 2-quart glass dish to use as marinade. Reserve remaining dressing. Add tarragon and 2 teaspoons remaining mustard to marinade in glass dish; blend well. Add salmon; turn to coat. Cover and refrigerate 1 hour. Transfer 3 tablespoons reserved dressing to medium bowl; add onion, tossing to coat. Thread asparagus and mushrooms onto wooden skewers. (Soak skewers in hot water 30 minutes to prevent burning.)

Remove salmon from marinade; discard marinade. Season salmon to taste with additional salt and pepper. Lightly oil hot grid to prevent sticking. Grill salmon over medium-hot KINGSFORD® Briquets 2 to 4 minutes per side or until fish flakes when tested with fork. Grill asparagus and mushrooms over medium-hot briquets 5 to 8 minutes or until crisp-tender. Cut asparagus into 2-inch pieces and slice mushrooms; add to onion mixture. Let stand 10 minutes. Toss lettuce with onion mixture in large bowl; arrange lettuce on platter. Break salmon into 2-inch pieces; arrange salmon and vegetables over lettuce. Drizzle with remaining reserved dressing. Serve immediately. *Makes 4 main-dish servings*

# Warm Salad Valencia

1 package (1¼ pounds)
   PERDUE® FIT 'N EASY®
   Fresh Skinless and
   Boneless Chicken Thighs
3 tablespoons olive oil,
   divided
1 teaspoon dried thyme leaves
   Salt and ground black
   pepper to taste
2 red bell peppers, quartered
   and seeded
3 tablespoons orange juice
1 tablespoon grainy Dijon
   mustard
1 tablespoon balsamic vinegar
1 tablespoon fresh lemon
   juice
1 head Boston or Bibb lettuce
1 head frisée or curly chicory
2 oranges, peeled and
   sectioned
2 tablespoons thinly sliced
   scallions

Prepare outdoor grill for cooking or preheat broiler. Rub chicken with 1 tablespoon oil; season both sides with thyme, salt and black pepper. Grill or broil chicken 6 to 8 inches from heat source 25 to 35 minutes until cooked through, turning once. Slice chicken, reserving juices; set aside. Place bell peppers on edge of grill or on broiler pan. Cook 5 to 10 minutes until tender, turning occasionally. Remove peppers from heat; slice and set aside.

Meanwhile, in small saucepan on side of grill or over low heat, combine orange juice, mustard, vinegar and lemon juice. Whisk in remaining 2 tablespoons oil and any juices from chicken; bring to a simmer. Season mixture with salt and pepper to taste.

To serve on dinner plates, arrange greens and orange sections; top with chicken and pepper slices. Drizzle dressing over salad. Sprinkle with scallions and serve immediately.                    *Makes 5 servings*

# Grilled Corn Salad

4 ears fresh corn, husked and
silks removed
¼ cup CRISCO® Oil,* divided
½ red bell pepper, seeds and
ribs removed, and finely
chopped
3 scallions or green onions,
trimmed and finely
chopped, white and
2-inches of green tops
3 tablespoons chopped
cilantro or parsley
3 tablespoons lime juice
3 tablespoons maple syrup
½ teaspoon salt
¼ teaspoon freshly ground
black pepper

*Use your favorite Crisco Oil product.

**1.** Prepare grill or heat broiler. Rub corn with 2 tablespoons oil. Grill or broil corn for 7 minutes or until ears are lightly brown. Turn with tongs to brown all sides. Remove from grill. Cool; cut kernels off with sharp knife. Place in mixing bowl.

**2.** Combine corn with red bell pepper, scallions and cilantro. Combine remaining 2 tablespoons oil with lime juice, maple syrup, salt and pepper. Toss with corn mixture. Serve at room temperature. *Makes 4 servings*

**Note:** The salad can be made up to 2 days in advance and refrigerated, tightly covered. Let stand at room temperature to take chill off before serving.

**Prep Time:** 15 minutes
**Total Time:** 25 minutes

# Pasta Chicken Breast Salad

8 ounces rotelle pasta
2 (3 ounces each) boneless
skinless chicken breasts
2 teaspoons lemon pepper
½ head iceberg lettuce
5 fresh spinach leaves
½ cup halved red grapes
½ cup halved strawberries*
Fat-free raspberry
vinaigrette dressing

*Other seasonal fruit may be substituted.

Cook pasta as directed on package. Drain and rinse with cold water; set aside. Sprinkle chicken breasts with lemon pepper and broil or grill over medium heat for 10 minutes, turning once.

Meanwhile, tear lettuce and spinach into bite-size pieces; place on dinner plates. Top with pasta, grapes and strawberries. Slice chicken breasts crosswise and place on top. Serve with dressing. *Makes 2 servings*

*Favorite recipe from* **North Dakota Wheat Commission**

# Thai Pork Salad

8 cups lightly packed
    shredded cabbage or
    packaged coleslaw mix
1 cup lightly packed cilantro
    leaves, coarsely chopped
30 large mint leaves, coarsely
    chopped
6 grilled pork loin chops
    (from Garlic-Pepper
    Skewered Pork, page
    206) *or* 6 grilled
    ½-inch-thick boneless
    pork chops
2 tablespoons vegetable oil
½ large red onion, cut into
    thin slivers
½ cup lightly salted roasted
    cashews or peanuts
½ teaspoon salt
¼ to ½ teaspoon cayenne
    pepper
⅓ cup lime juice
1 tablespoon sugar
    Lime wedges
    Red onion strips
    Cilantro sprigs

Combine cabbage, cilantro and mint in large bowl; set aside. Cut pork chops into ¼-inch-thick strips. Heat oil in large skillet over medium-high heat. Add pork, onion, nuts, salt and cayenne pepper. Cook and stir 2 minutes; remove from heat. Stir in lime juice and sugar. Spoon pork mixture over cabbage; toss well to coat. Garnish with lime wedges, onion strips and cilantro.

*Makes 5 main-dish servings*

*Favorite recipe from* **The Kingsford Products Company**

## GRILLING TIP

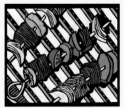

*If you partially cook food in the microwave or on the range, immediately finish cooking the food on the grill. Do not refrigerate or let stand at room temperature before cooking on the grill.*

# Grilled Vegetable & Orzo Salad
## with Citrus Vinaigrette

½ cup thinly sliced shallots or
    green onions
⅓ cup white wine vinegar
¼ cup orange juice
2 tablespoons lemon juice
2 tablespoons extra-virgin
    olive oil
1½ teaspoons grated
    orange peel
1½ teaspoons grated
    lemon peel
1½ teaspoons salt
¼ teaspoon black pepper
10 large mushrooms, cut
    in half
1 package (10 ounces) frozen
    artichoke hearts, thawed
12 ounces orzo pasta, cooked,
    rinsed and drained
2 red or green bell peppers,
    cut in half, stemmed and
    seeded
12 large fresh basil leaves,
    minced (optional)
    Orange peel strips

Combine shallots, vinegar, juices, oil, peels, salt and black pepper in large bowl; whisk until blended. Add mushrooms and artichokes; let stand 30 minutes. Thread artichokes and mushrooms onto wooden skewers; reserve vinaigrette. (Soak wooden skewers in hot water 30 minutes to prevent burning.) Add orzo to reserved dressing; toss to coat. Grill artichokes and mushrooms on covered grill over medium-hot KINGSFORD® Briquets 3 to 5 minutes per side. Grill bell peppers, skin sides down, over medium-hot briquets about 8 minutes until skins on all sides are charred. Place peppers in large resealable plastic food storage bag or paper bag; seal. Let stand 5 minutes; remove skin. Slice mushrooms and chop peppers; add to pasta with artichokes and basil, if desired, tossing until coated. Serve at room temperature. Garnish with orange peel strips.

*Makes 8 side-dish servings (about 1 cup each)*

**Note:** To make an entrée that serves four, add 1 can (15 ounces) rinsed and drained black beans or 2 cups cubed grilled chicken or sliced grilled sausage.

Grilled Vegetable & Orzo Salad
with Citrus Vinaigrette

# Sausage & Wilted Spinach Salad

¼ cup sherry vinegar or white
    wine vinegar
1 teaspoon whole mustard
    seeds, crushed
½ teaspoon salt
¼ teaspoon black pepper
2 ears corn, husked
1 large red onion, cut into
    ¾-inch-thick slices
4 tablespoons extra-virgin
    olive oil, divided
12 ounces smoked turkey,
    chicken or pork sausage
    links, such as Polish,
    Andouille or New Mexico
    style, cut in half
    lengthwise
2 cloves garlic, minced
10 cups lightly packed spinach
    leaves, torn
1 large avocado, peeled and
    cubed

Combine vinegar, mustard seeds, salt and pepper; set dressing aside. Brush corn and onion with 1 tablespoon oil. Insert wooden picks into onion slices from edges to prevent separating into rings. (Soak wooden picks in hot water 15 minutes to prevent burning.) Grill sausage, corn and onion over medium KINGSFORD® Briquets 6 to 10 minutes until vegetables are crisp-tender and sausage is hot, turning several times. Cut corn kernels from cobs; chop onion and slice sausage. Heat remaining 3 tablespoons oil in small skillet over medium heat. Add garlic; cook and stir 1 minute. Toss spinach, avocado, sausage, corn, onion and dressing in large bowl. Drizzle hot oil over salad; toss and serve immediately.

*Makes 4 servings*

## GRILLING TIP

*Watch food carefully during grilling. Total cooking time will vary with the type of food, the position on the grill, the weather, the temperature of the coals and the degree of doneness you desire.*

# Chili-Crusted Grilled Chicken Caesar Salad

1 to 2 lemons
1 tablespoon minced garlic, divided
1½ teaspoons dried oregano leaves, crushed, divided
1 teaspoon chili powder
1 pound boneless skinless chicken breasts
2 anchovy fillets, minced
1 tablespoon olive oil
1 large head romaine lettuce, cut into 1-inch strips
¼ cup grated Parmesan cheese
4 rounds pita bread or whole wheat rolls

**1.** Grate lemon peel; measure 1 to 2 teaspoons. Juice lemon; measure ¼ cup. Combine lemon peel and 1 tablespoon juice in small bowl. Set ¼ teaspoon garlic aside. Add remaining garlic, 1 teaspoon oregano and chili powder to lemon peel mixture; stir to combine. Rub chicken with lemon peel mixture.

**2.** Combine remaining 3 tablespoons lemon juice, ¼ teaspoon garlic, remaining ½ teaspoon oregano, anchovies and oil in large bowl. Add lettuce; toss to coat. Sprinkle with cheese; toss.

**3.** Spray cold grid with nonstick cooking spray. Prepare grill for direct grilling. Place chicken on grid 3 to 4 inches above medium-hot coals. Grill chicken 5 to 6 minutes. Turn chicken; grill 3 to 4 minutes or until chicken is no longer pink in center.

**4.** Arrange salad on 4 large plates. Slice chicken; fan on each salad. Serve with pita bread. *Makes 4 servings*

Chili-Crusted Grilled
Chicken Caesar Salad

# COOKOUT
## SANDWICHES

### Brats 'n' Beer

1 can or bottle (12 ounces) beer (not dark)
4 bratwurst (about 1 pound)
1 sweet or Spanish onion, thinly sliced and separated into rings
1 tablespoon olive oil
¼ teaspoon salt
¼ teaspoon black pepper
4 hot dog rolls

Prepare coals for direct grilling. Pour beer into heavy medium saucepan with ovenproof handle. (If not ovenproof, wrap heavy-duty foil around handle.) Place saucepan on grill. Pierce bratwurst with knife; add to beer. Simmer, uncovered, over medium coals, 15 minutes, turning once.

Place onion rings on heavy-duty foil. Drizzle with oil; sprinkle with salt and pepper. Fold sides of foil over rings to enclose. Place onion slices on grill. Grill, uncovered, 10 to 15 minutes or until onion slices are tender.

Transfer bratwurst to grill. Remove saucepan from grill; discard beer. Grill bratwurst, 10 minutes or until browned and cooked through, turning once. Place bratwurst in rolls. Top each with onions. Garnish as desired. *Makes 4 servings*

Brat 'n' Beer

# Steak and Grilled Vegetable Wraps

Mango Salsa (recipe follows)
1 red bell pepper, seeded, cored and quartered
1 green bell pepper, seeded, cored and quartered
¾ pound large mushrooms
2 green onions, sliced
¼ cup fresh lemon juice
⅛ teaspoon black pepper
½ to ¾ pound beef flank steak
4 large (10-inch) fat-free flour tortillas
⅓ cup lightly packed fresh cilantro

**1.** Prepare barbecue grill for direct cooking. Prepare Mango Salsa; set aside.

**2.** Grill peppers, skin-side down, over hot coals until blackened. Place in paper bag; seal. Steam 5 minutes; remove skin. Grill mushrooms, covered, over medium coals about 2 minutes on each side or until tender and lightly browned. Cut peppers into ½-inch strips; slice mushrooms. Combine vegetables, onions, lemon juice and black pepper in medium bowl; set aside and keep warm.

**3.** Place steak on grid. Grill, covered, over medium heat 14 to 18 minutes (or, uncovered, 17 to 21 minutes) for medium-rare to medium doneness, turning once. Remove from grill and slice into ½-inch strips. Combine with vegetable mixture. Grill tortillas on both sides about 1 minute or until warmed. Spoon ¼ of meat mixture down center of each tortilla. Roll to enclose filling; serve immediately with Mango Salsa. *Makes 4 servings*

**Mango Salsa:** In medium bowl, combine 2 cups peeled, diced mango, ½ cup diced red bell pepper, ¼ cup diced red onion, 1 serrano pepper, seeded and minced, 2 tablespoons chopped cilantro, 2 teaspoons minced fresh ginger and 1 tablespoon lime juice.

Steak and Grilled Vegetable Wrap

# Grilled Club Sandwiches

1 long thin loaf (18 inches)
    French bread
½ cup mayonnaise
¼ cup *French's®* Zesty Deli
    Mustard
2 tablespoons finely chopped
    red onion
2 tablespoons horseradish
½ pound sliced smoked
    boiled ham
½ pound sliced honey-baked
    deli turkey
1 large ripe tomato, sliced
8 ounces Brie cheese, thinly
    sliced
1 bunch watercress, washed
    and drained

Cut bread in half lengthwise. Combine mayonnaise, mustard, onion and horseradish in small bowl; mix well. Spread mixture on both halves of bread. Layer ham, turkey, tomato, cheese and watercress on bottom half of bread. Cover with top half; press down firmly. Cut loaf crosswise into 1½-inch pieces. Thread two mini sandwiches through crusts onto metal skewer. Repeat with remaining sandwiches.

Place sandwiches on well-oiled grid. Grill over medium-low coals about 5 minutes or until cheese is melted and bread is toasted, turning once. Serve warm.

*Makes 6 servings*

**Prep Time:** 15 minutes
**Cook Time:** 5 minutes

## GRILLING TIP

*The cooking rack or grid should be kept clean and free from any bits of charred food. Scrub the grid with a stiff wire brush while it is still warm to help keep it clean.*

# Grilled Turkey Sandwiches
# with Honey Mustard Slaw

⅓ cup *French's®* Zesty Deli
   Mustard
⅓ cup reduced-fat mayonnaise
⅓ cup plain nonfat yogurt
2 tablespoons honey
1 tablespoon cider vinegar
2 cups each finely shredded
   green and red cabbage
4 carrots, finely shredded
¼ cup thinly sliced red onion
2 pounds thin turkey cutlets
   Lettuce leaves
6 large rolls, split

Combine mustard, mayonnaise, yogurt, honey and vinegar in large measuring cup; mix well. To prepare Honey Mustard Slaw, pour ¾ cup mustard mixture in large bowl. Add cabbage, carrots and onion; toss well to coat evenly. Cover and refrigerate until chilled.

Brush remaining mustard mixture on turkey cutlets. Place cutlets on grid. Grill over hot coals 10 minutes or until turkey is no longer pink in center, turning once. To serve, place lettuce leaves on bottom halves of rolls. Arrange turkey over lettuce. Top with Honey Mustard Slaw. Cover with top halves of rolls.  *Makes 6 servings*

**Prep Time:** 20 minutes
**Cook Time:** 10 minutes

# Italian Grilled Sandwich

1 medium eggplant, cut into
   ½ inch thick slices (about
   1 pound)
1 medium zucchini, cut
   diagonally into ¼-inch-
   thick slices (about
   ¾ pound)
½ cup WISH-BONE® Italian or
   Classic House Italian
   Dressing
1 loaf Italian bread, cut
   lengthwise in half (about
   14 inches)
1 jar (12 ounces) roasted red
   peppers, drained and
   rinsed
1 package (8 ounces) fresh
   mozzarella cheese, sliced

In large, shallow nonaluminum baking dish or plastic food storage bag, combine eggplant, zucchini and Italian dressing. Cover, or close bag, and marinate in refrigerator, turning occasionally, 3 to 24 hours.

Remove vegetables, reserving marinade. Grill or broil vegetables, turning once, until tender. Remove; set aside. Brush reserved marinade on bread. Grill or broil until bread is toasted. Arrange roasted red peppers, vegetables and cheese on bottom half of bread. Top with remaining bread and slice into 4 sandwiches.

*Makes about 4 generous servings*

# Barbecued Pork Tenderloin Sandwiches

½ cup ketchup

⅓ cup packed brown sugar

2 tablespoons bourbon or whiskey (optional)

1 tablespoon Worcestershire sauce

½ teaspoon dry mustard

¼ teaspoon ground red pepper

1 clove garlic, minced

2 whole pork tenderloins (about ¾ pound each), well trimmed

1 large red onion, cut into 6 (¼-inch-thick) slices

6 hoagie rolls or Kaiser rolls, split

**1.** Prepare barbecue grill for direct cooking.

**2.** Combine ketchup, sugar, bourbon, if desired, Worcestershire sauce, mustard, red pepper and garlic in small, heavy saucepan with ovenproof handle; mix well. Set saucepan on one side of grid.* Simmer sauce 5 minutes or until thickened, stirring occasionally. Set aside half of sauce; reserve.

**3.** Place tenderloins on center of grid. Grill tenderloins on uncovered grill over medium-hot coals 8 minutes. Turn tenderloins with tongs; continue to grill, uncovered, 5 minutes. Add onion slices to grid. Brush tenderloins and onion with some remaining sauce. Continue to grill, uncovered, 7 to 10 minutes or until internal temperature of pork reaches 160°F when tested with meat thermometer inserted into the thickest part of tenderloins.**

**4.** Transfer pork to cutting board; cover with foil. Let stand 10 to 15 minutes before carving. Internal temperature will continue to rise 5°F to 10°F during stand time. Carve tenderloins crosswise into thin slices; separate onion slices into rings. Divide meat and onion rings among rolls; drizzle with reserved sauce.

*Makes 6 servings*

*If desired, sauce may be prepared on range-top. Combine ketchup, sugar, bourbon, if desired, Worcestershire sauce, mustard, red pepper and garlic in small saucepan. Bring to a boil over medium-high heat. Reduce heat to low and simmer, uncovered, 5 minutes or until thickened, stirring occasionally.

**If using an instant-read thermometer, do not leave thermometer in tenderloins during grilling since the thermometer is not heatproof.

# Maui Chicken Sandwiches

1 can (8 ounces) DOLE®
    Pineapple Slices
½ teaspoon dried oregano
    leaves, crushed
¼ teaspoon garlic powder
4 skinless, boneless, small
    chicken breasts
½ cup light prepared
    Thousand Island salad
    dressing
½ cup finely chopped jicama
    or water chestnuts
¼ teaspoon ground red
    pepper (optional)
4 whole grain or whole wheat
    sandwich rolls
    DOLE® Red or Green Bell
    Pepper, sliced into rings
    or shredded DOLE®
    Iceberg Lettuce

• Combine undrained pineapple slices, oregano and garlic powder in shallow, non-metallic dish. Add chicken; turn to coat all sides. Cover and marinate 15 minutes in refrigerator.

• Grill or broil chicken and pineapple, brushing occasionally with marinade, 5 to 8 minutes on each side or until chicken is no longer pink in center and pineapple is golden brown. Do not baste during last 5 minutes of cooking. Discard any remaining marinade.

• Combine dressing, jicama and ground red pepper, if desired. Spread on rolls. Top with chicken, pineapple and bell pepper rings. Serve open-face, if desired.

*Makes 4 servings*

**Prep Time:** 10 minutes
**Marinate Time:** 15 minutes
**Cook Time:** 15 minutes

## FOOD FACT

*Jicama, often referred to as the "Mexican potato," is a root vegetable with a sweet, nutty flavor. Jicama can be purchased in Mexican markets or in the produce section of most large supermarkets. Cut leftover jicama into julienned strips and use as dippers with your favorite vegetable dip. Its crisp water chestnut-like texture makes it a perfect accompaniment to any creamy dip.*

Maui Chicken Sandwich

# Grilled Portobello & Pepper Wraps

1 container (8 ounces) sour
    cream
1 teaspoon dill weed
1 teaspoon onion powder
2 tablespoons vegetable oil
1 large clove garlic, minced
2 portobello mushrooms,
    stems removed
1 large green bell pepper,
    quartered
1 large red bell pepper,
    quartered
6 (6-inch) flour tortillas,
    warmed

**1.** Prepare grill for direct cooking. Combine sour cream, dill weed and onion powder in small bowl; set aside. Combine oil and garlic in small bowl; set aside.

**2.** Spray grid with nonstick cooking spray. Place mushrooms and bell peppers on prepared grid. Brush lightly with oil mixture; season with salt and pepper to taste.

**3.** Grill over medium-hot coals 10 minutes or until peppers are crisp-tender, turning halfway through grilling time. Remove mushrooms and peppers to cutting board; cut into 1-inch slices.

**4.** Place on serving platter. Serve with sour cream mixture and tortillas. *Makes 4 to 6 servings*

**Serving Suggestion:** Serve with spicy refried beans.

**Prep and Cook Time:** 18 minutes

## FOOD FACT

*Portobello mushrooms have large pancake-shaped dark brown caps and thick tough stems. They have a firm texture when cooked and a beeflike flavor. Because of their large size and sturdiness, they are a good choice for grilling.*

# Cajun Catfish Sandwiches

Aioli Tartar Sauce (recipe
  follows)
4½ teaspoons paprika
1 tablespoon dried oregano
  leaves
1½ teaspoons salt
¾ teaspoon granulated garlic
½ teaspoon white pepper
½ teaspoon black pepper
½ teaspoon cayenne pepper
4 small catfish fillets
  (1¼ pounds)
  Lemon juice
4 sourdough rolls, split
4 cups finely shredded
  cabbage
  Lemon wedges

Prepare Aioli Tartar Sauce; set aside. Combine paprika, oregano, salt, garlic and peppers until blended. Brush catfish with lemon juice; sprinkle evenly with seasoning mix to coat. Lightly oil grid to prevent sticking. Grill over medium-hot KINGSFORD® Briquets, allowing 10 minutes cooking time for each inch of thickness, turning once. Spread Aioli Tartar Sauce onto insides of rolls. Top each roll with catfish fillet and 1 cup cabbage. Serve with lemon wedges. *Makes 4 sandwiches*

**Aioli Tartar Sauce:** Prepare Grilled Garlic (page 31). Combine ½ cup mayonnaise, 12 mashed cloves Grilled Garlic, 2 teaspoons each lemon juice and chopped parsley and 1 teaspoon chopped, drained capers; blend well.

# Grilled Flank Steak with Horseradish Sauce

1 pound beef flank steak
2 tablespoons reduced-
  sodium soy sauce
1 tablespoon red wine vinegar
2 cloves garlic, minced
½ teaspoon black pepper
1 cup nonfat sour cream
1 tablespoon prepared
  horseradish
1 tablespoon Dijon mustard
¼ cup finely chopped fresh
  parsley
½ teaspoon salt
6 sourdough rolls, split
6 romaine lettuce leaves

**1.** Place flank steak in large resealable plastic food storage bag. Add soy sauce, vinegar, garlic and pepper. Close bag securely; turn to coat. Marinate in refrigerator at least 1 hour.

**2.** Prepare grill. Drain steak; discard marinade. Grill flank steak over medium heat, 14 to 18 minutes, (or, uncovered, 17 to 21 minutes) for medium-rare to medium doneness, turning halfway through grilling time. Cover with foil; let stand 15 minutes. Thinly slice steak across grain.

**3.** Combine sour cream, horseradish, mustard, parsley and salt in small bowl until well blended. Spread rolls with horseradish sauce; layer with sliced steak and lettuce. *Makes 6 servings*

# Blackened Chicken Salad in Pitas

1 tablespoon paprika

1 teaspoon onion powder

½ teaspoon garlic powder

½ teaspoon dried oregano
   leaves

½ teaspoon dried thyme leaves

¼ teaspoon salt

¼ teaspoon white pepper

¼ teaspoon ground red
   pepper

¼ teaspoon black pepper

4 boneless skinless chicken
   breasts (about ¾ pound)

4 pita breads

1 cup bite-size pieces spinach
   leaves

2 small tomatoes, cut into
   8 slices

8 thin slices cucumber

½ cup reduced-fat ranch
   dressing

**1.** Combine paprika, onion powder, garlic powder, oregano, thyme, salt and peppers in small bowl; rub on all surfaces of chicken. Grill chicken on covered grill over medium-hot coals, 10 minutes per side or until chicken is no longer pink in center. Cool slightly. Cut into thin strips.

**2.** Wrap 2 pita breads in paper towels. Microwave at HIGH 20 to 30 seconds or just until warm. Repeat with remaining pita breads.

**3.** Divide spinach, chicken strips, tomato slices, cucumber slices and ranch dressing among pita breads. Fold edges over and secure with wooden picks. Serve warm.

*Makes 4 servings*

# Maple Francheezies

Mustard Spread (recipe
    follows)
¼ cup maple syrup
2 teaspoons garlic powder
1 teaspoon black pepper
½ teaspoon ground nutmeg
4 slices bacon
4 jumbo hot dogs
4 hot dog buns, split
½ cup (2 ounces) shredded
    Cheddar cheese

Prepare Mustard Spread; set aside.

Prepare grill for direct cooking.

Combine maple syrup, garlic powder, pepper and nutmeg in small bowl. Brush syrup mixture onto bacon slices. Wrap 1 slice bacon around each hot dog.

Brush hot dogs with remaining syrup mixture. Place hot dogs on grid. Grill, covered, over medium-high heat 8 minutes or until bacon is crisp and hot dogs are heated through, turning halfway through grilling time. Place hot dogs in buns, top with Mustard Spread and cheese.

*Makes 4 servings*

## Mustard Spread

½ cup prepared yellow mustard
1 tablespoon finely chopped onion
1 tablespoon diced tomato
1 tablespoon chopped fresh parsley
1 teaspoon garlic powder
½ teaspoon black pepper

Combine all ingredients in small bowl; mix well.

*Makes about ¾ cup*

**Maple Francheezie**

Cookout Sandwiches

# Grilled Pork Soft Tacos

4 dried mild red ancho or
  California chiles, seeds
  and stems removed
¼ cup lime juice
3 tablespoons cold water
2 tablespoons olive oil,
  divided
2 cloves garlic, minced and
  divided
½ teaspoon salt, divided
½ teaspoon ground cumin
¼ cup reduced-fat sour cream
1½ pounds boneless pork loin
  chops, about ¾-inch thick
1 large red onion, cut into
  ¾-inch-thick slices
2 poblano or green bell
  peppers, cut in half,
  stemmed and seeded
1 large red bell pepper, cut in
  half, stemmed and
  seeded
6 corn tortillas
  Guacamole (optional)

Cover chiles with boiling water in small bowl. Let stand 10 minutes; drain. Place chiles, lime juice, water, 1 tablespoon oil, 1 clove garlic, ¼ teaspoon salt and cumin in blender; process until smooth. Spoon half of chile mixture into small bowl; stir in sour cream. Cover and refrigerate. Spoon remaining chile mixture into 2-quart glass dish; add remaining clove garlic and ¼ teaspoon salt. Add pork, turning to coat. Cover and refrigerate overnight. Brush onion slices with remaining 1 tablespoon oil. Remove pork from marinade; discard marinade. Grill pork and onion over medium-hot KINGSFORD® Briquets about 4 minutes per side or until pork is barely pink. Grill peppers, skin side down, 8 minutes until skins are charred. Place peppers in large resealable plastic food storage bag; seal. Let stand 5 minutes; remove skins. Grill tortillas until hot. Slice pork, onion and peppers. Spoon sour cream mixture down center of each tortilla; top with pork, vegetables and guacamole, if desired. Fold tortillas around filling.

*Makes 6 tacos*

# Santa Fe Chicken Hero

1 package (about 1 pound)
   PERDUE FIT® 'N EASY®
   Fresh Skinless & Boneless
   Thin-Sliced Chicken or
   Turkey Breast Cutlets
1 tablespoon canola oil
   Salt
   Ground black pepper
   Ground red pepper
   Chili powder
5 to 6 thin slices Monterey
   Jack cheese with chilies
5 to 6 slices French or Italian
   bread
2 tablespoons melted butter
   or margarine
5 to 6 leaves Romaine lettuce
1 tomato, thinly sliced
1 avocado, peeled, pitted,
   sliced and tossed with
   lemon juice
½ cup prepared salsa

Prepare grill for cooking. Rub chicken lightly with oil and season to taste with salt, black pepper, red pepper and chili powder. Grill, uncovered, 5 to 6 inches over medium-hot coals about 1 minute on each side. Top chicken with slices of cheese; grill 1 minute longer or until cheese is melted.

Brush bread with melted butter; grill alongside chicken 1 to 2 minutes on each side until golden brown. To serve, place a lettuce leaf on each toasted bread slice. Evenly divide chicken, slices of tomato and avocado on top. Serve sandwiches open-faced with salsa.

*Makes 4 to 5 servings*

## FOOD FACT

*Dry marinades (also called dry rubs) are mixtures of herbs and spices that are rubbed onto the surface of meat and poultry and allowed to stand before cooking. The flavor of the herbs and spices permeates the meat and generally produces a more intense flavor than a liquid marinade.*

# Open-Faced Mesquite Steak Sandwiches

1¼ cups LAWRY'S® Mesquite
    Marinade with Lime Juice,
    divided
1 pound beef flank steak
8 slices sourdough or French
    bread
4 ounces refried beans
1 red onion, thinly sliced
1 green bell pepper, thinly
    sliced
½ cup chunky-style salsa
4 ounces cheddar cheese,
    thinly sliced

In large resealable plastic food storage bag, combine ¾ cup Mesquite Marinade and steak; seal bag. Marinate in refrigerator at least 30 minutes. Remove steak; discard used marinade. Grill or broil steak 8 to 10 minutes or until desired doneness, turning once and basting often with additional ½ cup Mesquite Marinade. *Do not baste during last 5 minutes of cooking.* Discard any remaining marinade. Thinly slice steak on the diagonal across the grain. Spread bread slices with refried beans; top evenly with steak, onion and bell pepper. Top with salsa and cheese. *Makes 4 servings*

**Serving Suggestion:** Serve warm with assorted crisp raw vegetables and iced tea.

**Hint:** Sandwich may be broiled to melt cheese, if desired.

Open-Faced Mesquite
Steak Sandwiches

# Grilled Vegetable Pitas

1 eggplant (about 1 pound),
    cut into ½-inch-thick
    slices
1 large portobello mushroom
    (5 to 6 ounces)
1 small red bell pepper,
    quartered
1 small yellow or green bell
    pepper, quartered
2 (¼-inch) slices large red
    onion
½ cup low-fat Italian or honey
    Dijon salad dressing,
    divided
4 (8-inch) whole wheat or
    white pita breads
4 ounces reduced-fat
    shredded Italian cheese
    blend

**1.** Brush both sides of eggplant slices, mushroom, bell pepper quarters and onion slices with ⅓ cup dressing. Grill over medium coals or broil 4 to 5 inches from heat source 4 to 5 minutes per side or until vegetables are crisp-tender. Cut into bite-size pieces. Toss with additional dressing.

**2.** Cut pita breads in half; open pockets and fill with vegetable mixture. Top with cheese.    *Makes 4 servings*

## GRILLING TIP

*To keep small pieces of vegetables or meat from falling through the grid either purchase a grill basket or create a disposable basket by punching holes in a disposable foil pan. Spray the pan with nonstick cooking spray before use. Heavy-duty foil will also work in emergencies.*

# Grilled Chicken Croissant
# with Roasted Pepper Dressing

½ cup *French's*® Napa Valley
    Style Dijon Mustard
3 tablespoons olive oil
3 tablespoons red wine
    vinegar
¾ teaspoon garlic powder
¾ teaspoon dried Italian
    seasoning
1 jar (7 ounces) roasted red
    peppers, drained
1 pound boneless skinless
    chicken breasts
  Lettuce leaves
4 croissants, split

Whisk together mustard, oil, vinegar, garlic powder and Italian seasoning in small bowl until well blended. Pour ¼ cup mixture into blender. Add peppers. Cover and process until mixture is smooth; set aside.

Brush chicken pieces with remaining mustard mixture. Place pieces on grid. Grill over hot coals 15 minutes or until chicken is no longer pink in center, turning often. To serve, place lettuce leaves on bottom halves of croissants. Arrange chicken on top of lettuce. Spoon roasted pepper dressing over chicken. Cover with croissant top. Garnish as desired.     *Makes 4 servings*

**Prep Time:** 15 minutes
**Cook Time:** 15 minutes

## GRILLING TIP

*Meats and poultry should be completely thawed before grilling. To thaw chicken, transfer it from the freezer to the refrigerator and allow three to four hours per pound to defrost. Chicken may be thawed in the microwave, following manufacturer's directions. Watch the chicken carefully so that the edges do not begin to cook before the chicken is completely thawed. The chicken must be cooked immediately, because all or part of it will reach room temperature when thawed in the microwave. Bacteria multiply rapidly at room temperature and care must be taken to minimize their growth. Never thaw chicken at room temperature.*

Grilled Chicken Croissant
with Roasted Pepper Dressing

# Zesty Stuffed Bread

1 (14-inch) loaf Italian bread
1½ cups shredded JARLSBERG
 or JARLSBERG LITE™
 cheese
1 (8-ounce) container
 reduced-fat or fat-free
 sour cream
1 cup (4 ounces) diced
 smoked turkey
1 cup thinly sliced Napa
 cabbage
½ cup diced red pepper
2 to 3 tablespoons
 horseradish

Slice bread nearly in half horizontally, so it opens like a book. Pull out soft interior (reserve for another use, such as poultry stuffing).

Combine remaining six ingredients. Stuff bread with mixture and wrap well in heavy-duty aluminum foil.

Grill 8 to 10 inches from coals, turning frequently until bread is crispy and filling is hot about 10 to 15 minutes. Or, bake 20 minutes at 350°F until cheese is softened.

Using serrated knife, cut loaf into 1- or 2-inch-thick slices. Serve with green salad.  *Makes 6 to 12 servings*

# Basil Chicken and Vegetables on Focaccia

¼ cup olive oil
2 cloves garlic, minced
2 teaspoons dried basil leaves
½ teaspoon salt
½ teaspoon black pepper,
 divided
4 boneless skinless chicken
 breasts (1¼ pounds)
1 green bell pepper, stemmed,
 seeded and quartered
1 medium zucchini, cut
 lengthwise into 4 slices
½ cup mayonnaise
¼ teaspoon garlic powder
1 loaf (16 ounces) focaccia or
 Italian bread
2 Italian plum tomatoes,
 sliced

Combine oil, garlic, basil, salt and ¼ teaspoon black pepper in small measuring cup. Place chicken and 2 tablespoons marinade in resealable plastic food storage bag. Place bell pepper, zucchini and remaining 2 tablespoons marinade in another food storage bag. Seal bags; knead to coat. Refrigerate 30 minutes.

Combine mayonnaise, garlic powder and remaining ¼ teaspoon black pepper in small bowl; set aside.

Grill or broil chicken, bell pepper and zucchini 4 inches from heat source 6 to 8 minutes on each side or until chicken is no longer pink in center. (Bell pepper and zucchini may take less time.)

Cut focaccia into quarters. Cut each quarter horizontally in half. Top bottom half of each focaccia quarter with reserved mayonnaise mixture, tomatoes, bell pepper, zucchini and chicken. Top with focaccia tops.

*Makes 4 servings*

# Sundance Sandwich

4 boneless skinless chicken
breasts (1¼ pounds)
1 cup NEWMAN'S OWN®
Balsamic Vinaigrette
Salad Dressing, divided
1 red onion, sliced into
4 rounds
2 yellow bell peppers
1 Ciabatta loaf (Italian slipper
bread) *or* 1 round Tuscan
loaf (1 pound)
1 yellow tomato, sliced
1 red tomato, sliced
8 ounces whole milk fresh
mozzarella, sliced
1 small bunch arugula *or*
4 romaine lettuce leaves

**Pesto**
1 cup packed fresh basil
leaves
¼ cup pine nuts
2 cloves garlic, chopped
¼ cup olive oil
⅓ cup freshly grated
Parmesan cheese
¼ teaspoon salt
⅛ teaspoon coarsely ground
black pepper

Marinate chicken breasts in ¾ cup salad dressing 30 minutes. Marinate red onion rounds in remaining ¼ cup vinaigrette.

Grill or broil peppers until brown on all sides; put in paper bag until skins peel off easily, about 15 minutes. Skin and remove seeds. Cut each in quarters.

To prepare pesto, process basil, pine nuts and garlic in food processor until finely chopped. Add olive oil until blended; add cheese, salt and black pepper.

Cook chicken breasts using grill pan or barbecue over medium-high heat. Cook onion rounds with chicken 10 to 12 minutes, turning once. Thinly slice cooked chicken.

To serve, cut Ciabatta loaf horizontally in half. Spread pesto on cut sides of loaf. Layer yellow and red tomatoes, bell peppers, onions, mozzarella cheese, chicken breast slices and arugula on bread. *Makes 6 servings*

# Southern Barbecue Sandwich

1 pound boneless beef sirloin
  or flank steak*
¾ cup *French's®* Worcestershire
  Sauce, divided
½ cup ketchup
½ cup light molasses
¼ cup *French's®* Classic Yellow®
  Mustard
2 tablespoons *Frank's®*
  *RedHot®* Cayenne Pepper
  Sauce
½ teaspoon hickory salt
4 sandwich buns, split

*You may substitute 1 pound pork tenderloin
for the steak. Cook pork until meat is juicy and
barely pink in center or substitute leftover sliced
steak for the grilled steak. Stir into sauce and
heat through.*

Place steak in large resealable plastic food storage bag.
Pour ½ cup Worcestershire over steak. Seal bag and
marinate meat in refrigerator 20 minutes.

To prepare barbecue sauce, combine ketchup, molasses,
remaining ¼ cup Worcestershire, mustard, *Frank's
RedHot* Sauce and hickory salt in medium saucepan.
Bring to a boil over high heat. Reduce heat to low. Cook
5 minutes until slightly thickened, stirring occasionally.
Set aside.

Place steak on grid, discarding marinade. Grill over hot
coals 15 minutes, turning once. Remove steak from grid;
let stand 5 minutes. Cut steak diagonally into thin slices.
Stir meat into barbecue sauce. Cook until heated through,
stirring often. Serve steak and sauce in sandwich buns.
Garnish as desired.                    *Makes 4 servings*

**Prep Time:** 15 minutes
**Marinate Time:** 20 minutes
**Cook Time:** 25 minutes

## GRILLING TIP

*Grilling is a great way to put a meal on the table in the
summertime without heating up the kitchen. Marinate protein
in the morning before leaving for work or while you are
preparing the rest of the meal.*

Southern Barbecue Sandwich

# Grilled Vegetable Sandwiches with Garlic Mayonnaise

⅓ cup mayonnaise
2 cloves garlic, minced
2 large red bell peppers,
    seeded and quartered
1 small eggplant, cut into
    ¼-inch slices
  Vegetable oil
8 slices country-style bread

**1.** Prepare grill for direct cooking. Blend mayonnaise and garlic in small bowl; set aside.

**2.** Spray grid with nonstick cooking spray. Place bell peppers and eggplant on prepared grid. Brush vegetables with oil and season with salt and pepper to taste.

**3.** Grill vegetables, on covered grill, over medium-hot coals 10 minutes or until fork-tender, turning halfway through grilling time.

**4.** Spread desired amount of garlic mayonnaise on each bread slice. Top 4 slices with equal amounts of grilled vegetables; cover with remaining bread slices. Cut each sandwich in half. *Makes 4 servings*

**Serving Suggestions:** Serve with creamy hot bean soup or cold gazpacho made with garden fresh ingredients.

**Prep and Cook Time:** 25 minutes

Grilled Vegetable Sandwich
with Garlic Mayonnaise

# Jamaican Chicken Sandwich

1 teaspoon Jerk Seasoning (recipe follows)
4 boneless skinless chicken breasts
2 tablespoons reduced-fat mayonnaise
2 tablespoons plain nonfat yogurt
1 tablespoon mango chutney
4 onion rolls, split and toasted
4 lettuce leaves
8 slices peeled mango or papaya

**1.** Prepare Jerk Seasoning. Sprinkle chicken with jerk seasoning and set aside. Spray grid with nonstick cooking spray. Prepare grill for direct cooking.

**2.** Place chicken on grid, 3 to 4 inches from medium-hot coals. Grill 5 to 7 minutes on each side or until no longer pink in center.

**3.** Combine mayonnaise, yogurt and chutney in small bowl; spread on onion rolls.

**4.** Place chicken on onion roll bottoms; top each with lettuce leaf and 2 slices of mango.     *Makes 4 servings*

**Prep Time:** 8 minutes
**Cook Time:** 14 minutes

## Jerk Seasoning

1½ teaspoons salt
1½ teaspoons ground allspice
1 teaspoon sugar
1 teaspoon ground thyme
1 teaspoon black pepper
½ teaspoon garlic powder
½ teaspoon ground red pepper
¼ teaspoon ground cinnamon
¼ teaspoon ground nutmeg

Combine all ingredients in small bowl.

# Italian Sausage & Pepper Pita Wraps

4 (6-inch) hot or mild Italian
  sausages (about
  1¼ pounds)
1 green bell pepper, stemmed,
  seeded and cut
  lengthwise into quarters
1 small onion, sliced
4 pita breads
1 tablespoon olive oil
1 cup prepared marinara
  sauce
½ teaspoon dried basil leaves
¼ teaspoon dried oregano
  leaves
1 cup (4 ounces) shredded
  Italian blend cheese or
  mozzarella cheese

**1.** Prepare grill for direct cooking.

**2.** Place sausage links on center of grid over medium coals; arrange bell pepper and onion around sausages. Grill on covered grill 7 minutes. Turn sausages and vegetables; grill 8 to 9 minutes or until sausages are cooked through and vegetables are crisp-tender.

**3.** Brush pita breads on one side with oil. Place on grid at edge of coals; grill until soft.

**4.** Meanwhile, combine marinara sauce, basil and oregano in small saucepan. Simmer over medium-low heat until hot, about 5 minutes.

**5.** Cut sausages in half lengthwise. Cut bell pepper into strips and separate onion slices into rings.

**6.** Divide sausages, bell pepper and onion among pita breads. Top with sauce and cheese. Fold pita breads in half.                    *Makes 4 servings*

## GRILLING TIP

*To avoid running back and forth from the kitchen to the grill, assemble everything you need for grilling like grill utensils, matches or starter, hot pads, tongs, a basting brush, an instant-read thermometer and a clean plate for cooked food.*

# Moroccan Grilled Turkey
# with Cucumber Yogurt Sauce

Cucumber Yogurt Sauce
(recipe follows)
⅓ cup fresh lime juice
2 cloves garlic, minced
½ teaspoon salt
½ teaspoon curry powder
¼ teaspoon ground cumin
¼ teaspoon cayenne pepper
1 package BUTTERBALL®
    Fresh Boneless Turkey
    Breast Cutlets
3 large pitas, cut in half*

*Pitas may be filled and folded in half.*

Prepare Cucumber Yogurt Sauce.

Prepare grill for medium-direct-heat cooking. Lightly spray unheated grill rack with nonstick cooking spray. Combine lime juice, garlic, salt, curry powder, cumin and cayenne pepper in medium bowl. Dip cutlets in lime juice mixture. Place cutlets on rack over medium-hot grill. Grill 5 to 7 minutes on each side or until meat is no longer pink in center. Place turkey and Cucumber Yogurt Sauce in pitas. *Makes 6 servings*

**Prep Time:** 20 Minutes

## Cucumber Yogurt Sauce

1 cup fat-free yogurt
½ cup shredded cucumber
1 teaspoon grated lime peel
1 teaspoon salt
½ teaspoon ground cumin

Combine yogurt, cucumber, lime peel, salt and cumin in medium bowl. Chill.

Moroccan Grilled Turkey
with Cucumber Yogurt Sauce

# Chicago Fire Italian Sausage Sandwiches

1 package BUTTERBALL®
    Lean Fresh Turkey Hot
    Italian Sausage
5 large hot dog buns
5 teaspoons yellow mustard
5 tablespoons chopped onion
5 tablespoons pickle relish
10 tomato wedges
10 hot sport peppers

Grill sausage according to package directions. Place in buns. Add mustard, onion, relish, tomato wedges and peppers to each sandwich. *Makes 5 sandwiches*

**Prep Time:** 15 minutes

# Pork Pitas with Fruity Mustard Salsa

1 pound boneless pork chops
    or chicken breasts
4 tablespoons *French's®*
    Classic Yellow® Mustard,
    divided
1 cup chopped canned
    peaches, drained
⅓ cup finely chopped red bell
    pepper
1 small green onion, minced
1 tablespoon minced cilantro
    leaves
1 teaspoon *Frank's® RedHot®*
    Cayenne Pepper Sauce
6 large soft pita breads or
    pita pocket bread, heated

Preheat broiler or grill. Brush chops with *2 tablespoons* mustard. Broil or grill 10 to 15 minutes or until no longer pink in center. Set aside.

Combine peaches, bell pepper, onion, remaining *2 tablespoons* mustard, cilantro and *Frank's RedHot* Sauce in medium bowl.

To serve, thinly slice chops. Arrange pork in center of pitas. Spoon salsa on top. Fold in half to serve.

*Makes 6 servings*

**Prep Time:** 15 minutes
**Cook Time:** 10 minutes

Chicago Fire Italian Sausage Sandwich

# Grilled Vegetable & Cheese Sandwiches

2 large zucchini squash, cut lengthwise into eight ¼-inch slices

4 slices sweet onion (such as Vidalia or Walla Walla), cut ¼ inch thick

1 large yellow bell pepper, cut lengthwise into quarters

6 tablespoons prepared light or regular Caesar salad dressing, divided

8 oval slices sourdough bread

6 (1-ounce) slices Muenster cheese

**1.** Prepare barbecue for grilling. Brush both sides of vegetables with ¼ cup dressing. Place vegetables on grid over medium coals. Grill on covered grill 5 minutes. Turn; grill 2 minutes.

**2.** Brush both sides of bread lightly with remaining 2 tablespoons dressing. Place bread around vegetables; grill 2 minutes or until bread is lightly toasted. Turn bread; top 4 pieces of bread with 4 slices of cheese. Tear remaining 2 cheese slices into small pieces; place on bread next to cheese to cover bread. Grill vegetables and bread 1 to 2 minutes more or until cheese is melted, bread is toasted and vegetables are crisp-tender.

**3.** Arrange vegetables over cheese side of bread; top with remaining bread. *Makes 4 servings*

**Serving Suggestion:** Serve with a fresh fruit salad.

**Prep and Cook Time:** 22 minutes

Grilled Vegetable & Cheese Sandwiches

# Grilled Chicken Breast and Peperonata Sandwiches

1 tablespoon olive oil or
   vegetable oil
1 medium red bell pepper, cut
   into strips
1 medium green bell pepper,
   cut into strips
¾ cup onion slices (about
   1 medium onion)
2 cloves garlic, minced
¼ teaspoon salt
¼ teaspoon black pepper
4 boneless skinless chicken
   breasts (1 pound)
4 small French rolls, split and
   toasted

**1.** Heat oil in large nonstick skillet over medium heat until hot. Add bell peppers, onion and garlic; cook and stir 5 minutes. Reduce heat to low; cook and stir about 20 minutes or until vegetables are very soft. Sprinkle with salt and black pepper.

**2.** Grill chicken on covered grill over medium-hot coals 10 minutes on each side or until chicken is no longer pink in center. Or, broil chicken, 6 inches from heat source, 7 to 8 minutes on each side or until chicken is no longer pink in center.

**3.** Place chicken in rolls. Divide bell pepper mixture evenly; spoon over chicken. *Makes 4 servings*

## GRILLING TIP

*An instant-read thermometer is a griller's best friend. For thin cuts of meat or poultry insert the thermometer from the side of the cut. Be sure to cover the indentation on the stem to ensure the thermometer will accurately measure the temperature.*

Grilled Chicken Breast
and Peperonata Sandwich

# BACKYARD
## BURGERS

### Ranchero Onion Burgers

1 pound ground beef
½ cup salsa
½ cup (2 ounces) shredded Monterey Jack cheese
1⅓ cups *French's®* French Fried Onions, divided
½ teaspoon garlic powder
¼ teaspoon ground black pepper
4 hamburger rolls

Combine beef, salsa, cheese, ⅔ *cup* French Fried Onions, garlic powder and pepper in large bowl. Shape into 4 patties.

Place patties on oiled grid. Grill* over medium coals, covered, 8 to 10 minutes (or, uncovered, 13 to 15 minutes) to medium doneness (160°F), turning once. Serve on rolls. Garnish with additional salsa, if desired. Top with remaining ⅔ *cup* onions.          *Makes 4 servings*

*Or, broil 6 inches from heat.*

**Tip:** For extra-crispy warm onion flavor, heat French Fried Onions in the microwave for 1 minute. Or, place in foil pan and heat on the grill 2 minutes.

**Prep Time:** 10 minutes
**Cook Time:** 10 minutes

**Ranchero Onion Burger**

# Greek Burgers

Yogurt Sauce (recipe
    follows)
1 pound ground beef
2 tablespoons red wine
1 tablespoon chopped fresh
    oregano *or* 1 teaspoon
    dried oregano leaves
2 teaspoons ground cumin
½ teaspoon salt
    Dash ground red pepper
    Dash black pepper
4 pita breads
    Lettuce
    Chopped tomatoes

Prepare Yogurt Sauce.

Soak 4 bamboo skewers in water about 20 minutes. Combine ground beef, wine, oregano, cumin, salt, red pepper and black pepper in medium bowl; mix lightly. Divide mixture into eight equal portions; form each portion into an oval, each about 4 inches long. Cover; chill 30 minutes.

Preheat grill. Insert skewers lengthwise through centers of ovals, placing 2 on each skewer. Grill, covered, about 8 to 10 minutes (or, uncovered, 13 to 15 minutes) to medium doneness (160°F), turning once. Fill each pita bread with equal amount of lettuce, meat and chopped tomatoes. Serve with Yogurt Sauce.   *Makes 4 servings*

## Yogurt Sauce

2 cups plain yogurt
1 cup chopped red onion
1 cup chopped cucumber
¼ cup chopped fresh mint *or* 1 tablespoon plus
    1½ teaspoons dried mint leaves
1 tablespoon chopped fresh marjoram *or* 1 teaspoon
    dried marjoram leaves

Combine ingredients in small bowl. Cover; chill up to 4 hours before serving.

# Blue Cheese Burgers with Red Onion

2 pounds ground beef chuck

2 cloves garlic, minced

1 teaspoon salt

½ teaspoon black pepper

4 ounces blue cheese

⅓ cup coarsely chopped
   walnuts, toasted

1 torpedo (long) red onion *or*
   2 small red onions, sliced
   into ⅜-inch-thick rounds

2 baguettes (each 12 inches
   long)
   Olive or vegetable oil

Combine beef, garlic, salt and pepper in medium bowl. Shape meat mixture into 12 oval patties. Mash cheese and blend with walnuts in small bowl. Divide cheese mixture equally; place onto centers of 6 meat patties. Top with remaining meat patties; tightly pinch edges together to seal in filling.

Oil hot grid to help prevent sticking. Grill patties and onion on covered grill, over medium KINGSFORD® Briquets, 7 to 12 minutes for medium doneness (160°F), turning once. Cut baguettes into 4-inch lengths; split each piece and brush cut sides with olive oil. Move cooked burgers to edge of grill to keep warm. Grill bread, oil side down, until lightly toasted. Serve burgers on toasted baguettes. *Makes 6 servings*

## GRILLING TIP

*For hamburgers, steaks and fish use the direct cooking method. Arrange the coals in a single layer directly under the food.*

# Mediterranean Burgers

1½ pounds ground beef
¼ cup (1 ounce) shredded
    mozzarella cheese
2 tablespoons grated
    Parmesan cheese
2 tablespoons chopped
    kalamata olives
1 tablespoon chopped fresh
    parsley
1 tablespoon diced tomato
2 teaspoons dried oregano
    leaves
1 teaspoon black pepper
4 hamburger buns, split

Prepare grill for direct cooking.

Shape beef into eight ¼-inch-thick burger patties.

Combine cheeses, olives, parsley, tomato, oregano and pepper in small bowl. Place ¼ of cheese mixture on top of 1 burger patty; spread to within ½ inch of edge. Top cheese mixture with another burger patty; seal edges to enclose filling. Repeat with remaining cheese mixture and burger patties.

Place burgers on grid. Grill, covered, over medium heat 8 to 10 minutes (or, uncovered, 13 to 15 minutes) for medium doneness (160°F), turning once.

Remove burgers from grill and place burgers between buns. *Makes 4 servings*

# Cowboy Burgers

1 pound ground beef
½ teaspoon LAWRY'S®
    Seasoned Salt
½ teaspoon LAWRY'S®
    Seasoned Pepper
2 tablespoons plus
    2 teaspoons butter or
    margarine
1 large onion, thinly sliced
1 package (1.0 ounce)
    LAWRY'S® Taco Spices
    & Seasonings
4 slices cheddar cheese
4 Kaiser rolls
    Lettuce leaves
    Tomato slices

In medium bowl, combine ground beef, Seasoned Salt and Seasoned Pepper; shape into four patties. Grill or broil about 5 to 6 minutes on each side for medium (160°F). Meanwhile, in medium skillet, heat butter. Add onion and Taco Spices & Seasonings and cook over medium-high heat until onion is soft and transparent. Top each patty with onions and cheese. Return to grill or broiler until cheese is melted. Place each patty on roll; top with lettuce and tomato. *Makes 4 servings*

**Serving Suggestion:** Serve with baked beans.

Mediterranean Burger

# Mexicali Burgers

Guacamole (recipe follows)
1 pound ground beef
⅓ cup crushed tortilla chips
⅓ cup prepared salsa or
    picante sauce
3 tablespoons finely chopped
    fresh cilantro
2 tablespoons finely chopped
    onion
1 teaspoon ground cumin
4 slices Monterey Jack or
    Cheddar cheese
4 kaiser rolls or hamburger
    buns, split
Lettuce leaves (optional)
Sliced tomatoes (optional)

To prevent sticking, spray grill with nonstick cooking spray. Prepare coals for grilling. Meanwhile, prepare Guacamole.

Combine beef, tortilla chips, salsa, cilantro, onion and cumin in medium bowl until well blended. Shape mixture into 4 burgers. Place burgers on grill, 6 inches from medium coals. Grill, covered, 8 to 10 minutes (or, uncovered, 13 to 15 minutes) for medium doneness (160°F), turning once. Place 1 slice cheese on each burger during last 1 to 2 minutes of grilling. If desired, place rolls, cut side down, on grill to toast lightly during last 1 to 2 minutes of grilling. Place burgers between rolls; top burgers with Guacamole. Serve with lettuce and tomatoes. Garnish as desired. *Makes 4 servings*

## Guacamole

1 ripe avocado, seeded
1 tablespoon salsa or picante sauce
1 teaspoon fresh lime or lemon juice
¼ teaspoon garlic salt

Place avocado in medium bowl; mash with fork until avocado is slightly chunky. Add salsa, lime juice and garlic salt; blend well. *Makes about ½ cup*

**Mexicali Burger**

# Polynesian Burgers

¼ cup LAWRY'S® Teriyaki
  Marinade with Pineapple
  Juice
1 pound ground beef
½ cup chopped green bell
  pepper
4 onion-flavored hamburger
  buns
1 can (5¼ ounces) pineapple
  slices, drained
  Lettuce leaves

In medium bowl, combine Teriyaki Marinade, ground beef and bell pepper; mix well. Let stand 10 to 15 minutes. Shape into 4 patties. Grill or broil burgers 8 to 10 minutes for medium doneness (160°F), turning halfway through grilling time. Serve burgers on onion buns topped with pineapple slices and lettuce.

*Makes 4 servings*

**Serving Suggestion:** Serve with assorted fresh fruits.

**Hint:** For extra teriyaki flavor, brush buns and pineapple slices with additional fresh Teriyaki Marinade; grill or broil until buns are lightly toasted and pineapple is heated through.

## FOOD FACT

*To make the ultimate tender burger, handle ground meat as little as possible. Form patties quickly with as few pats as possible. Wetting your hands with cold water will help to keep meat from sticking to your hands. Keep the patties covered tightly in the refrigerator until just before grilling.*

Polynesian Burger

# Wisconsin Cheese Stuffed Burgers

3 pounds ground beef
½ cup dry bread crumbs
2 eggs
1¼ cups (5 ounces) of your
    favorite shredded
    Wisconsin cheese,
    shredded Pepper Havarti
    cheese, crumbled Blue
    cheese or crumbled Basil
    & Tomato Feta cheese

In a large mixing bowl, combine beef, bread crumbs and eggs; mix well, but lightly. Divide mixture into 24 balls; flatten each on waxed paper to 4 inches across. Place 1 tablespoon cheese on each of 12 patties. Top with remaining patties, carefully pressing edges to seal. Grill patties 4 inches from coals, turning only once, 6 to 9 minutes on each side for medium doneness (160°F). To keep cheese between patties as it melts, do not flatten burgers with spatula while grilling. *Makes 12 servings*

**Caution:** Cheese filling may be very hot if eaten immediately after cooking.

*Favorite recipe from* **Wisconsin Milk Marketing Board**

# Hawaiian-Style Burgers

1½ pounds ground beef
⅓ cup chopped green onions
2 tablespoons Worcestershire
    sauce
⅛ teaspoon black pepper
⅓ cup pineapple preserves
⅓ cup barbecue sauce
6 pineapple slices
6 hamburger buns, split and
    toasted

**1.** Combine beef, onions, Worcestershire and pepper in large bowl. Shape into six 1-inch-thick patties.

**2.** Combine preserves and barbecue sauce in small saucepan. Bring to a boil over medium heat, stirring often.

**3.** Grill patties over medium coals, covered, 8 to 10 minutes (or, uncovered, 13 to 15 minutes) for medium doneness (160°F), turning and brushing often with sauce. Place pineapple on grill; grill 1 minute or until browned, turning once.

**4.** To serve, place patties on buns with pineapple.
*Makes 6 servings*

**Broiling Directions:** Arrange patties on rack in broiler pan. Broil 4 inches from heat 10 to 12 minutes for medium doneness (160°F), turning and brushing often with sauce. Broil pineapple 1 minute, turning once.

# A Perfect Burger

Basil Aioli (recipe follows)
Grilled Onion Relish (recipe follows)
1⅓ pounds lean ground beef
1 cup (4 ounces) shredded Cheddar cheese
4 hamburger buns
Tomato slices
Mixed greens or lettuce leaves

Prepare Basil Aioli and Grilled Onion Relish. Form beef into 4 equal patties. Lightly oil grid to prevent sticking. Grill beef on covered grill over medium KINGSFORD® Briquets 8 minutes. Turn; grill 7 to 8 minutes longer for medium (160°F) or to desired doneness. Top with cheese. Place buns, cut sides down, over briquets to toast. Serve burgers on toasted buns with Basil Aioli, Grilled Onion Relish, sliced tomato and greens. *Makes 4 servings*

**Basil Aioli:** Mash 6 cloves Grilled Garlic (page 31) until smooth; stir together with ¼ cup mayonnaise, 2 tablespoons chopped fresh basil and 2 teaspoons fresh lemon juice until blended. Season to taste with salt and pepper. Makes about ½ cup.

**Grilled Onion Relish:** Cut 2 medium yellow onions into ½-inch-thick slices. Secure with wooden picks. (Soak wooden picks in hot water 15 minutes.) Brush onions with olive oil. Grill over medium KINGSFORD® briquets on covered grill 25 minutes, turning once. Cool; chop onions. In small saucepan, combine 3 tablespoons balsamic vinegar and 2 tablespoons brown sugar; heat until sugar is dissolved. Stir in onions, dash cayenne pepper, and salt and pepper to taste. Makes about 1 cup.

## FOOD FACT

*Aioli is a garlic mayonnaise used as a condiment or sauce. Delicious on all types of meat, poultry and fish, prepare aioli easily by grilling garlic bulbs while cooking other items on the grill. The garlic will then be ready to combine with mayonnaise for a condiment that can be kept in the refrigerator for future meals.*

# The All-American Burger

Burger Spread (recipe
  follows)
1½ pounds ground beef
  2 tablespoons chopped fresh
    parsley
  2 teaspoons onion powder
  2 teaspoons Worcestershire
    sauce
  1 teaspoon garlic powder
  1 teaspoon salt
  1 teaspoon black pepper
  4 hamburger buns, split

Prepare Burger Spread; set aside.

Prepare grill for direct cooking.

Combine beef with parsley, onion powder, Worcestershire sauce, garlic powder, salt and pepper in medium bowl; mix lightly, but thoroughly. Shape mixture into four ½-inch-thick burgers.

Place burgers on grid. Grill, covered, over medium heat 8 to 10 minutes (or, uncovered, 13 to 15 minutes) for medium doneness (160°F), turning halfway through grilling time.

Remove burgers from grill. Place burgers between buns; top each burger with Burger Spread.    *Makes 4 servings*

## Burger Spread

½ cup ketchup
¼ cup prepared mustard
2 tablespoons chopped onion
1 tablespoon relish or chopped pickles
1 tablespoon chopped fresh parsley

Combine all ingredients in small bowl; mix well.

*Makes 1 cup*

# Mini Mexican Burger Bites

1½ pounds ground beef
½ cup finely chopped red,
    yellow or green bell
    pepper
2 tablespoons *French's®*
    Worcestershire Sauce
1 teaspoon *Frank's® RedHot®*
    Cayenne Pepper Sauce
1 teaspoon dried oregano
    leaves
¼ teaspoon salt
12 mini dinner rolls
    Shredded Cheddar cheese

**1.** Gently combine all ingredients except rolls and cheese in large bowl. Shape into 12 mini patties. Broil or grill patties 4 to 6 minutes for medium doneness (160°F internal temperature), turning once.

**2.** Arrange burgers on rolls and top with Cheddar cheese. Top with shredded lettuce, if desired.

*Makes 6 servings*

**Prep Time:** 5 minutes
**Cook Time:** 8 minutes

# Lipton® Onion Burgers

1 envelope LIPTON® RECIPE
    SECRETS® Onion
    Soup Mix*
2 pounds ground beef
½ cup water

*Also terrific with LIPTON® RECIPE
SECRETS® Beefy Onion, Onion-Mushroom,
Beefy Mushroom, Savory Herb with Garlic or
Ranch Soup Mix.*

**1.** In large bowl, combine all ingredients; shape into 8 patties.

**2.** Grill or broil until done.

*Makes about 8 servings*

**Prep Time:** 10 minutes
**Cook Time:** 12 minutes

Mini Mexican Burger Bites

# Ranch Burgers

1¼ pounds lean ground beef
¾ cup prepared HIDDEN
    VALLEY® The Original
    Ranch® Dressing
¾ cup dry bread crumbs
¼ cup minced onions
1 teaspoon salt
¼ teaspoon black pepper
    Sesame seed buns
    Lettuce, tomato slices and
      red onion slices
      (optional)
    Additional HIDDEN
      VALLEY® The Original
      Ranch® Dressing

In large bowl, combine beef, salad dressing, bread crumbs, onions, salt and pepper. Shape into 6 patties. Grill over medium coals, covered, 8 to 10 minutes (or, uncovered, 13 to 15 minutes) for medium doneness (160°F), turning once. Place on sesame seed buns with lettuce, tomato and red onion slices, if desired. Serve with a generous amount of additional salad dressing.

*Makes 6 servings*

# Curried Beef Burgers

1 pound lean ground beef
¼ cup mango chutney,
    chopped
¼ cup grated apple
1½ teaspoons curry powder
½ teaspoon salt
    Dash black pepper
1 large red onion, sliced
    ¼ inch thick

Preheat grill.

Combine ground beef, chutney, apple, curry powder, salt and pepper in medium bowl; mix lightly. Shape into four patties.

Grill over medium coals, covered, 8 to 10 minutes (or, uncovered, 13 to 15 minutes (160°F), turning once. Grill onions 5 minutes or until lightly charred, turning once. Serve with burgers.

*Makes 4 servings*

Ranch Burger

# Cheesy Spinach Burgers

1 envelope LIPTON® RECIPE
    SECRETS® Onion Soup
    Mix
2 pounds ground beef
1 package (10 ounces) frozen
    chopped spinach, thawed
    and squeezed dry
1 cup shredded mozzarella or
    Cheddar cheese (about
    4 ounces)

**1.** In large bowl, combine all ingredients; shape into 8 patties.

**2.** Grill or broil over medium heat 11 to 13 minutes for medium (160°F), turning once. Serve, if desired, on hamburger buns. *Makes 8 servings*

# Swiss Burgers

1½ pounds ground beef
¾ cup shredded Swiss cheese
    (about 3 ounces)
1 can (8 ounces) sauerkraut,
    heated and drained
½ cup WISH-BONE®
    Thousand Island or Just
    2 Good Thousand Island
    Dressing

Shape ground beef into 6 patties. Grill or broil over medium heat 11 to 13 minutes for medium (160°F), turning once. Top evenly with cheese, sauerkraut and Thousand Island dressing. Serve, if desired, with rye or pita bread. *Makes about 6 servings*

# All-American Onion Burger

1 pound ground beef
2 tablespoons *French's*®
 Worcestershire Sauce
1⅓ cups *French's*® French Fried
 Onions, divided
½ teaspoon garlic salt
¼ teaspoon ground black
 pepper
4 hamburger rolls

Combine beef, Worcestershire, ⅔ *cup* French Fried Onions, garlic salt and pepper. Form into 4 patties. Place patties on grid. Grill over hot coals about 10 minutes or until meat thermometer inserted into beef reaches 160°F, turning once. Top with remaining ⅔ *cup* onions. Serve on rolls. *Makes 4 servings*

**Luscious Oniony Cheeseburger:** Place 1 slice cheese on each burger before topping with French Fried Onions.

**Tangy Western Burger:** Top each burger with 1 tablespoon barbecue sauce and 1 strip crisp bacon before topping with French Fried Onions.

**California Burger:** Combine 2 tablespoons each mayonnaise, sour cream and *French's*® Zesty Deli Mustard in small bowl; spoon over burgers. Top each burger with avocado slices, sprouts and French Fried Onions.

**Salisbury Steak Burger:** Prepare 1 package brown gravy mix according to directions. Stir in 1 can (4 ounces) drained sliced mushrooms. Spoon over burgers and top with French Fried Onions.

**Pizza Burger:** Top each burger with pizza sauce, mozzarella cheese and French Fried Onions.

**Chili Burger:** Combine 1 can (15 ounces) chili without beans, 2 tablespoons *Frank's RedHot* and 2 teaspoons each chili powder and ground cumin. Cook until heated through. Spoon over burgers and top with French Fried Onions.

**Prep Time:** 10 minutes
**Cook Time:** 10 minutes

# Pizza Burgers

1 pound lean ground beef
1 cup (4 ounces) shredded
    mozzarella cheese
1 tablespoon minced onion
1½ teaspoons chopped fresh
    oregano *or* ½ teaspoon
    dried oregano leaves
1 tablespoon chopped fresh
    basil *or* 1 teaspoon dried
    basil leaves
½ teaspoon salt
    Dash black pepper
    Prepared pizza sauce,
    heated
4 English muffins

Preheat grill. Combine ground beef, cheese, onion, oregano, basil, salt and pepper in medium bowl; mix lightly. Shape into four patties.

Grill over medium heat, covered, 8 to 10 minutes (or, uncovered, 11 to 13 minutes) for medium (160°F), turning once. Top with pizza sauce. Serve on English muffins.

*Makes 4 servings*

# Zesty Onion Burgers

1½ pounds ground beef
1⅓ cups *French's®* French Fried
    Onions, divided
3 tablespoons *French's®* Zesty
    Deli Mustard
1 tablespoon prepared
    horseradish
¾ teaspoon garlic salt
¼ teaspoon ground black
    pepper
    Lettuce leaves
    Tomato slices
6 kaiser rolls

Combine beef, ⅔ *cup* French Fried Onions, mustard, horseradish, garlic salt and ground pepper in large bowl. Shape into 6 patties.

Place patties on oiled grid. Grill* over medium coals, covered, 8 to 10 minutes for medium doneness (160°F), turning once.

Arrange lettuce, tomatoes and burgers on rolls. Top with remaining ⅔ *cup* onions. *Makes 6 servings*

*Or, broil 6 inches from heat.*

**Prep Time:** 10 minutes
**Cook Time:** 10 minutes

Pizza Burger

# Southwest Pesto Burgers

**Cilantro Pesto**
- 1 large clove garlic
- 4 ounces fresh cilantro, stems removed and rinsed
- 1½ teaspoons bottled minced jalapeño pepper *or* 1 tablespoon bottled sliced jalapeño pepper,* drained
- ¼ teaspoon salt
- ¼ cup vegetable oil

**Burgers**
- 1¼ pounds ground beef
- ¼ cup plus 1 tablespoon Cilantro Pesto, divided
- ½ teaspoon salt
- 4 slices pepper Jack cheese
- 2 tablespoons light or regular mayonnaise
- 4 kaiser rolls, split
- 1 ripe avocado, peeled and sliced
- Salsa

*Jalapeño peppers can sting and irritate the skin; wear rubber gloves when handling peppers and do not touch eyes. Wash hands after handling peppers.*

**1.** For pesto, with motor running, drop garlic through feed tube of food processor; process until minced. Add cilantro, jalapeño pepper and salt; process until cilantro is chopped.

**2.** With motor running, slowly add oil through feed tube; process until thick paste forms. Transfer to container with tight-fitting lid. Store in refrigerator up to 3 weeks.

**3.** To complete recipe, prepare barbecue grill for direct cooking.

**4.** Combine beef, ¼ cup pesto and salt in large bowl; mix well. Form into 4 patties. Place patties on grid over medium coals. Grill, covered, 8 to 10 minutes (or, uncovered, 11 to 13 minutes) for medium doneness (160°F), turning once. Add cheese to patties during last 1 minute of grilling.

**5.** While patties are cooking, combine mayonnaise and remaining 1 tablespoon pesto in small bowl; mix well. Top patties with mayonnaise mixture. Serve on rolls with avocado and salsa.                *Makes 4 servings*

**Serving Suggestion:** Serve with refried beans.

**Make-Ahead Time:** up to 3 weeks in refrigerator
**Final Prep and Cook Time:** 20 minutes

## FOOD FACT

*Traditional pesto is made from fresh basil, garlic, pine nuts, Parmesan cheese and olive oil. The ingredients are mashed together to form a sauce. Today pesto may also describe numerous variations made from one herb like cilantro or mint mixed with garlic, oil and a few other ingredients to make flavorful sauces for meat, poultry and vegetables.*

**Southwest Pesto Burger**

# Blue Cheese Burgers

1¼ pounds lean ground beef
1 tablespoon finely chopped
    onion
1½ teaspoons chopped fresh
    thyme *or* ½ teaspoon
    dried thyme leaves
¾ teaspoon salt
    Dash black pepper
4 ounces blue cheese,
    crumbled

**1.** Preheat grill.

**2.** Combine ground beef, onion, thyme, salt and pepper in medium bowl; mix lightly. Shape into eight patties.

**3.** Place cheese in center of four patties to within ½ inch of outer edge; top with remaining patties. Press edges together to seal.

**4.** Grill over medium heat, covered, 8 to 10 minutes (or, uncovered, 11 to 13 minutes) for medium doneness (160°F), turning once. Serve with lettuce, tomatoes and Dijon mustard on whole wheat buns, if desired.

*Makes 4 servings*

# Backyard Barbecue Burgers

1½ pounds ground beef
⅓ cup barbecue sauce, divided
1 onion, peeled and sliced
1 to 2 tomatoes, sliced
1 to 2 tablespoons olive oil
6 kaiser rolls, split
    Green or red leaf lettuce

**1.** Prepare grill for direct grilling. Combine ground beef and 2 tablespoons barbecue sauce in large bowl. Shape into six 1-inch-thick patties.

**2.** Place patties on grid directly above medium coals. Grill, covered, 8 to 10 minutes (or, uncovered, 11 to 13 minutes) for medium doneness (160°F), turning and brushing often with remaining barbecue sauce.

**3.** Meanwhile, brush onion and tomato slices with oil. Place on grid. Grill onion* slices about 10 minutes and tomato slices about 2 to 3 minutes.

**4.** Just before serving, place rolls, cut side down, on grid and grill until toasted. Serve patties on toasted rolls with grilled onions, tomatoes and lettuce.     *Makes 6 servings*

*\*Onion slices may be cooked in 2 tablespoons oil in large skillet over medium heat 10 minutes until tender and slightly brown.*

# Scandinavian Burgers

1 pound lean ground beef
¾ cup shredded zucchini
⅓ cup shredded carrots
2 tablespoons finely minced
    onion
1 tablespoon fresh chopped
    dill *or* 1 teaspoon dried
    dill weed
½ teaspoon salt
   Dash black pepper
1 egg, beaten
¼ cup beer
4 whole wheat or rye rolls
    (optional)

Preheat grill.

Combine ground beef, zucchini, carrots, onion, dill, salt and pepper in medium bowl; mix lightly. Stir in egg and beer. Shape into four patties.

Grill over medium heat, covered, 8 to 10 minutes (or, uncovered, 11 to 13 minutes) for medium doneness (160°F), turning once. Serve on whole wheat buns or rye rolls, if desired. *Makes 4 servings*

# Italian Sausage Turkey Burgers

1 pound ground turkey
1 pound Italian turkey
    sausage
8 hamburger buns
8 tablespoons bottled
    marinara sauce
8 slices low-fat mozzarella
    cheese

**1.** Preheat charcoal grill for direct-heat cooking.

**2.** In large bowl combine ground turkey and Italian sausage. Shape mixture into 8 burgers approximately 3½ inches in diameter. Grill burgers 5 to 6 minutes per side or until 165°F is reached on meat thermometer and meat is no longer pink in center.

**3.** To serve, place burgers on bottom halves of buns. Top each burger with 1 tablespoon marinara sauce, 1 slice mozzarella cheese and other half of bun.

*Makes 8 servings*

*Favorite recipe from* **National Turkey Federation**

# Grilled Feta Burgers

½ **pound lean ground beef sirloin**

½ **pound ground turkey breast**

2 **teaspoons grated lemon peel**

1 **teaspoon dried oregano leaves**

1 **teaspoon olive oil**

¼ **teaspoon salt**

⅛ **teaspoon black pepper**

1 **ounce feta cheese**

  **Cucumber Raita (recipe follows)**

4 **slices tomato**

4 **whole wheat hamburger buns**

**1.** Combine sirloin, turkey, lemon peel, oregano, oil, salt and pepper; mix well and shape into 8 patties. Make small depression in each of 4 patties and place ¼ of the cheese in each depression. Cover each with remaining 4 patties, sealing edges to form burgers.

**2.** Grill burgers 10 to 12 minutes (160°F) or until thoroughly cooked, turning once. Serve with Cucumber Raita and tomato slice on whole wheat bun.   *Makes 4 burgers*

## Cucumber Raita

1 **cup plain nonfat yogurt**

½ **cup finely chopped cucumber**

1 **tablespoon minced fresh mint leaves**

1 **clove garlic, minced**

¼ **teaspoon salt**

Combine all ingredients in small bowl. Cover and refrigerate until ready to use.

## GRILLING TIP

*When cooking with ground meats, be sure to cook to an internal temperature of 160°F for ground beef, pork and lamb and 165°F for ground turkey and chicken.*

Grilled Feta Burger

# Swiss Burger

1 package (about 1¼ pounds) PERDUE® Fresh Ground Turkey, Ground Turkey Breast Meat or Ground Chicken
½ cup thinly sliced scallions
1 teaspoon Worcestershire sauce
4 ounces fresh white mushrooms, thinly sliced
2 teaspoons olive oil
½ teaspoon salt
Ground pepper to taste
4 to 5 pieces Swiss cheese
Dijon mustard
4 to 5 Kaiser rolls
6 to 8 tablespoons sour cream

Prepare outdoor grill or preheat broiler. In large bowl, combine ground turkey, scallions and Worcestershire sauce. Shape mixture into 4 or 5 patties.

**To grill**
When coals are medium-hot, place burgers on hottest area of cooking surface of grill; cook 1 to 2 minutes on each side to brown. Move burgers to edge of grill; cook 4 to 6 minutes longer on each side until thoroughly cooked, juices run clear and burgers spring back to the touch (165°F).

**To broil**
Place burgers on rack in broiling pan 4 inches from heat source. Broil 4 to 6 minutes on each side until burgers are thoroughly cooked and spring back to the touch (165°F).

While burgers are cooking, toss mushrooms with oil and sprinkle lightly with salt and pepper. Place mushrooms on sheet of heavy-duty aluminum foil. Grill or broil along with burgers during last 1 to 2 minutes of cooking time.

When burgers are cooked through, place a piece of Swiss cheese on each; cook 1 minute longer or just enough to melt cheese. To serve, spread mustard on bottom halves of rolls; cover with a burger and an equal portion of mushrooms. Top each with a generous dollop of sour cream and remaining roll half. *Makes 4 to 5 servings*

# All-American Turkey Burgers

1 pound ground turkey
½ cup chopped onion
¼ cup ketchup
1 clove garlic, minced
⅛ teaspoon pepper
4 kaiser rolls, sliced
4 leaves lettuce
4 slices tomato
4 slices onion

**1.** Preheat charcoal grill for direct-heat cooking.

**2.** In medium bowl combine turkey, onion, ketchup, garlic and pepper. Shape turkey mixture into 4 burgers, approximately 3½ inches in diameter.

**3.** Grill burgers 5 to 6 minutes per side until 165°F is reached on meat thermometer and meat is no longer pink in center.

**4.** To serve, place each burger on bottom half of roll; top with lettuce, tomato and onion and top half of roll.

*Makes 4 servings*

*Favorite recipe from* **National Turkey Federation**

# Grilled Salsa Turkey Burger

3 ounces lean ground turkey
1 tablespoon mild or medium
    salsa
1 tablespoon crushed baked
    tortilla chips
1 (1-ounce) reduced-fat
    Monterey Jack cheese
    slice (optional)
1 whole wheat hamburger
    bun, split
1 lettuce leaf
  Additional salsa

**1.** Combine turkey, 1 tablespoon salsa and chips in small bowl; mix lightly. Shape into patty. Lightly oil grid or broiler rack to prevent sticking.

**2.** Grill over medium-hot coals or broil 4 to 6 inches from heat 6 minutes on each side or until no longer pink in center, turning once. Top with cheese during last 2 minutes of grilling time, if desired. Place bun, cut sides down, on grill during last 2 minutes of grilling time to toast until lightly browned.

**3.** Cover bottom half of bun with lettuce; top with burger, additional salsa and top half of bun.

*Makes 1 serving*

# Bistro Burgers with Blue Cheese

1 pound ground turkey or
  beef
¼ cup chopped fresh parsley
2 tablespoons minced chives
¼ teaspoon dried thyme leaves
2 tablespoons *French's*® Napa
  Valley Style Dijon
  Mustard
  Lettuce and tomato slices
4 crusty rolls, split in half
2 ounces blue cheese,
  crumbled
1⅓ cups *French's*® French Fried
  Onions

**1.** In large bowl, gently mix meat, herbs and mustard. Shape into 4 patties.

**2.** Grill or broil patties 10 minutes or until no longer pink in center (165°F). Arrange lettuce and tomatoes on bottom half of rolls. Place burgers on top. Sprinkle with blue cheese and French Fried Onions. Cover with top half of rolls. Serve with additional mustard.

*Makes 4 servings*

**Tip:** Toast onions in microwave 1 minute for extra crispness.

**Prep Time:** 10 minutes
**Cook Time:** 10 minutes

# Chutney Turkey Burgers

1 pound ground turkey
½ cup purchased chutney,
  divided
½ teaspoon salt
½ teaspoon pepper
⅛ teaspoon hot pepper sauce
½ cup nonfat yogurt
1 teaspoon curry powder
4 hamburger buns

**1.** Preheat charcoal grill for direct-heat cooking.

**2.** In medium bowl combine turkey, ¼ cup chutney, salt, pepper and hot pepper sauce. Shape turkey mixture into 4 burgers, approximately 3½ inches in diameter. Grill turkey burgers 5 to 6 minutes per side until 165°F is reached on meat thermometer and meat is no longer pink in center.

**3.** In small bowl combine yogurt, curry powder and remaining ¼ cup chutney.

**4.** To serve, place burgers on bottom halves of buns; spoon yogurt mixture over burgers and cover with top halves of buns.

*Makes 4 servings*

*Favorite recipe from **National Turkey Federation***

# Apple Turkey Burgers

1 pound ground turkey
1 Granny Smith apple, peeled,
    cored and grated
½ teaspoon ground coriander
½ teaspoon salt
¼ teaspoon black pepper
1 (8-ounce) can jellied
    cranberry sauce
½ teaspoon dry mustard
⅛ teaspoon cinnamon
⅛ teaspoon nutmeg
4 hamburger buns

**1.** Preheat charcoal grill for direct-heat cooking.

**2.** In medium bowl, combine turkey, apple, coriander, salt and pepper. Evenly divide turkey mixture into 4 burgers, approximately 3½ inches in diameter. Grill turkey burgers 5 to 6 minutes per side or until 165°F on meat thermometer and meat is no longer pink in center.

**3.** In small bowl, combine cranberry sauce, mustard, cinnamon and nutmeg.

**4.** To serve, place 1 burger on bottom half of each bun. Spoon sauce over burgers and top with other half of bun.

*Makes 4 servings*

*Favorite recipe from* **National Turkey Federation**

# Santa Monica Burgers

1 package (about 1¼ pounds)
    PERDUE® Fresh Ground
    Turkey, Ground Turkey
    Breast Meat or Ground
    Chicken
4 strips crisp bacon, crumbled
¼ cup chopped tomato
¼ cup chopped onion
1 teaspoon salt
¼ teaspoon ground pepper
4 to 5 sourdough rolls

In mixing bowl, combine turkey, bacon, tomato, onion, salt and pepper. Form into 4 or 5 burgers and grill following package directions. Serve on split, lightly toasted rolls, garnished with Guaco-Mayo (recipe below), if desired.

*Makes 4 servings*

**Guaco-Mayo:** In food processor or blender, combine 1 small ripe avocado, ½ cup mayonnaise, 2 tablespoons chopped onion, 2 tablespoons lemon juice and 1 pickled jalapeño pepper. Purée; stir in 1 chopped mild chile and ¼ cup peeled, seeded and chopped tomato.

Apple Turkey Burgers

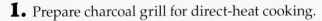

# Turkey Burgers with Cilantro Pesto

1 pound ground turkey
½ cup chopped onion
¼ cup chunky salsa
1 jalapeño pepper, seeded
  and minced
1 teaspoon chopped garlic
½ teaspoon *each* dried
  oregano leaves and salt
4 hamburger buns, split and
  toasted
Cilantro Pesto (recipe
  follows)

**1.** Prepare charcoal grill for direct-heat cooking.

**2.** In medium bowl combine turkey, onion, salsa, jalapeño, garlic, oregano and salt. Shape mixture into four burgers, approximately 4½ inches in diameter.

**3.** Grill 5 to 6 minutes per side until meat thermometer registers 165°F and meat is no longer pink in center.

**4.** To serve, place cooked burgers on bottom halves of buns; top each burger with 2 tablespoons Cilantro Pesto and top halves of buns.                    *Makes 4 servings*

*Favorite recipe from* **National Turkey Federation**

## Cilantro Pesto

1 large clove garlic
1 cup packed cilantro leaves
¼ cup *each:* chopped walnuts and Parmesan cheese
¼ teaspoon salt
¼ cup olive oil

**1.** In food processor, fitted with metal blade with motor running, drop garlic through feed tube to finely chop. Add cilantro, walnuts, cheese and salt. Process 45 seconds or until smooth. Scrape sides of bowl.

**2.** With motor running, slowly add olive oil and process until well blended. Cover and refrigerate several hours.

*Makes ⅔ cup*

*Favorite recipe from* **National Turkey Federation**

**Turkey Burger with Cilantro Pesto**

# All-American Stuffed Turkey Burger

1 pound ground turkey
¼ cup uncooked quick oats
1 egg
½ teaspoon garlic powder
  Dash pepper
½ cup chopped onion
¼ cup dill pickle relish,
  drained
2 tablespoons ketchup
2 teaspoons prepared
  mustard
2 slices (1 ounce each)
  reduced-calorie low-
  sodium process American
  cheese, cut into 4 equal
  strips
  Lettuce leaves (optional)
  Tomato slices (optional)

**1.** Preheat grill for direct-heat grilling.

**2.** In medium bowl, combine turkey, oats, egg, garlic powder and pepper. Divide turkey mixture in half. On 2 (11×10-inch) pieces wax paper, shape each half of turkey mixture into a patty 6 inches in diameter.

**3.** Sprinkle onion and relish over one patty, leaving ½-inch border around outside edge; top with ketchup and mustard. Arrange cheese strips, spoke-fashion, over ketchup and mustard. Carefully invert second patty over cheese. Remove top piece wax paper. Press edges together to seal.

**4.** Lightly grease cold grill rack and position over hot coals. Invert turkey burger onto grill rack; remove wax paper. Grill burger 8 minutes per side or until internal temperature of 165°F is reached on meat thermometer. To turn burger, slide flat cookie sheet under burger and invert onto second flat cookie sheet, then carefully slide burger back onto grill rack.*

**5.** To serve, cut burger into quarters. Serve with lettuce and tomato, if desired.          *Makes 4 servings*

*Can use greased wire grill basket, if desired.

*Favorite recipe from* **National Turkey Federation**

## GRILLING TIP

*Remember, hot coals create a hot grill, grid, tools and food. Always wear heavy-duty fireproof mitts to protect your hands.*

**All-American Stuffed Turkey Burger**

# Curried Walnut Grain Burgers

2 eggs
⅓ cup plain yogurt
2 teaspoons Worcestershire
    sauce
2 teaspoons curry powder
½ teaspoon salt
¼ teaspoon ground red
    pepper
1⅓ cups cooked couscous or
    brown rice
½ cup finely chopped walnuts
½ cup grated carrot
½ cup minced green onions
⅓ cup fine, dry plain bread
    crumbs
4 sesame seed hamburger
    buns
    Honey mustard
    Thinly sliced cucumber or
    apple
    Alfalfa sprouts

**1.** Combine eggs, yogurt, Worcestershire sauce, curry, salt and red pepper in large bowl; beat until blended. Stir in couscous, walnuts, carrot, green onions and bread crumbs. Shape into 4 (1-inch-thick) patties.

**2.** Coat grill rack with nonstick cooking spray; place rack on grill over medium-hot coals (350° to 400°F). Place burgers on rack and grill 5 to 6 minutes per side or until done. Serve on buns with mustard, cucumber and sprouts. *Makes 4 servings*

**Note:** Burgers may be broiled 4 inches from heat source for 5 to 6 minutes per side or until done.

**Prep and Cook Time:** 25 minutes

## GRILLING TIP

*The coals are ready when they are about 80% ash gray during the daylight and glowing at night.*

**Curried Walnut Grain Burger**

# Cheesy Lamburger

¼ cup (1 ounce) shredded
    Cheddar cheese
2 tablespoons sweet pickle
    relish
2 tablespoons finely chopped
    onion
1 tablespoon finely chopped
    green bell pepper
1 teaspoon Dijon mustard
1 pound lean ground
    American lamb
4 multi-grain hamburger
    buns, toasted
4 lettuce leaves
4 slices tomato

Prepare grill. Combine cheese, relish, onion, bell pepper and mustard in small bowl. Shape lamb into 8 thin patties about 4 inches in diameter. Spoon cheese mixture onto centers of 4 patties. Top each with another patty, pressing edges to seal filling inside. Place burgers on grid. Grill 4 inches over medium coals 5 minutes on each side or to desired doneness. Serve on buns with lettuce and tomato. *Makes 4 servings*

**Variation:** Substitute dill pickle relish and Monterey Jack or Swiss cheese for the sweet relish and Cheddar.

**Prep Time:** 15 minutes
**Cook Time:** 10 to 15 minutes

*Favorite recipe from* **American Lamb Council**

# Grilled Salmon Burgers

1 pound fresh boneless,
    skinless salmon
2 tablespoons sliced green
    onions
1 teaspoon LAWRY'S® Garlic
    Pepper
½ teaspoon LAWRY'S®
    Seasoned Salt
2 tablespoons LAWRY'S®
    Citrus Grill Marinade
    with Orange Juice

In food processor, combine all ingredients; process on pulse setting until salmon is well minced and mixed. Form into 4 patties. Broil or grill, 4 to 5 inches from heat source, 3 to 4 minutes on each side, or until cooked through. *Makes 4 servings*

**Serving Suggestion:** Serve on warm toasted hamburger buns.

# The Other Burger

1 pound ground pork, about 80% lean
1 teaspoon ground black pepper
¼ teaspoon salt

Gently mix together ground pork and seasonings. Shape into 4 burgers, each about ¾-inch thick. Place over moderately hot coals in kettle-style grill. Cover and grill for 5 minutes; turn and finish grilling 4 to 5 minutes more or until no longer pink in center. Serve immediately, on sandwich buns if desired. *Makes 4 servings*

**Eastern Burger:** To Other Burger basic mix, add 2 tablespoons dry sherry, 1 tablespoon grated gingerroot and 2 teaspoons soy sauce.

**Veggie Burger:** To Other Burger basic mix, add 1 grated carrot, 3 tablespoons chopped fresh parsley and 3 drops hot pepper sauce.

**South-of-the-Border Burger:** To Other Burger basic mix, add ¼ teaspoon each ground cumin, oregano, seasoned salt and crushed red chiles.

**Italian Burger:** To Other Burger basic mix, add 1 crushed garlic clove, 2 teaspoons each red wine and olive oil and 1 teaspoon crushed fennel seed.

**Prep Time:** 10 minutes
**Cook Time:** 10 minutes

*Favorite recipe from **National Pork Board***

# Fresh Rockfish Burgers

8 ounces skinless rockfish or
    scrod fillet
1 egg white *or* 2 tablespoons
    egg substitute
¼ cup dry bread crumbs
1 green onion, finely chopped
1 tablespoon finely chopped
    fresh parsley
2 teaspoons fresh lime juice
1½ teaspoons capers
1 teaspoon Dijon mustard
¼ teaspoon salt
⅛ teaspoon black pepper
    Nonstick cooking spray
4 grilled whole wheat
    English muffins or
    hamburger buns
4 leaf lettuce leaves
8 slices red or yellow tomato
    Additional Dijon mustard
    for serving (optional)

**1.** Finely chop rockfish and place in medium bowl. Add egg white, bread crumbs, onion, parsley, lime juice, capers, mustard, salt and pepper; gently combine with fork. Shape into 4 patties.

**2.** Spray heavy grillproof cast iron skillet or griddle with nonstick cooking spray; place on grid over hot coals to heat. Spray tops of burgers with additional cooking spray. Place burgers in hot skillet; grill on covered grill over hot coals 4 to 5 minutes or until burgers are browned on both sides, turning once. Serve on English muffins or buns with lettuce, tomato slices and Dijon mustard, if desired. *Makes 4 servings*

## GRILLING TIP

*Watch foods carefully during grilling. Set a timer to remind you when it's time to check the food on the grill.*

**Backyard Burgers**

**Fresh Rockfish Burger**

# BLAZING
## BEEF

### Peppercorn Steaks

4 beef top loin (New York
   Strip) or beef ribeye
   steaks, ¾ inch thick
2 tablespoons olive oil
1 to 2 teaspoons cracked red
   or black peppercorns *or*
   freshly ground pepper
1 teaspoon minced garlic
1 teaspoon dried herbs, such
   as rosemary or parsley
Salt

**1.** Combine oil, peppercorns, garlic and herbs in small bowl. Rub mixture on both sides of each steak. Cover and refrigerate.

**2.** Prepare grill for direct cooking.

**3.** Place steaks on grid over medium heat. Grill, covered, 10 to 12 minutes for medium-rare to medium doneness, turning occasionally. Season with salt after cooking.

*Makes 4 servings*

### GRILLING TIP

*Always use tongs or a spatula when handling meat. Piercing meat with a fork allows delicious juices to escape and makes meat less moist.*

**Peppercorn Steaks**

# Beef Kabobs with Apricot Glaze

1 can (15¼ ounces)
    DEL MONTE® Apricot
    Halves
1 tablespoon cornstarch
1 teaspoon Dijon mustard
½ teaspoon dried basil leaves
1 pound boneless beef top
    sirloin steak, cut into
    1½-inch cubes
1 small green bell pepper, cut
    into ¾-inch pieces
4 medium mushrooms, cut
    in half
4 to 8 skewers*

*To prevent burning of wooden skewers, soak skewers in water for 10 minutes before assembling kabobs.

**1.** Drain apricot syrup into small saucepan. Blend in cornstarch until dissolved. Cook over medium heat, stirring constantly, until thickened. Stir in mustard and basil. Set aside.

**2.** Thread beef, apricots, bell pepper and mushrooms alternately onto skewers; brush with apricot syrup mixture. Grill kabobs over hot coals (or broil) about 5 minutes on each side or to desired doneness, brushing occasionally with additional syrup mixture. Garnish, if desired. *Makes 4 servings*

**Prep and Cook Time:** 25 minutes

# Grilled Jerk Steak

4 teaspoons TABASCO®
    brand Pepper Sauce
2 teaspoons salt
1 teaspoon garlic powder
1 teaspoon dried thyme leaves
¼ teaspoon ground allspice
2 pounds boneless beef top
    loin steaks, ¾ inch thick

Combine all ingredients except steaks in small bowl. Rub mixture on both sides of each steak. Cover and refrigerate at least 1 hour or overnight. Preheat grill or broiler. Place steak on rack in grill or broiler pan. Grill steaks 10 to 12 minutes for medium-rare or to desired doneness, turning once. *Makes 4 servings*

**Beef Kabobs with Apricot Glaze**

# Beef with Dry Spice Rub

3 tablespoons firmly packed
brown sugar
1 tablespoon yellow mustard
seeds
1 tablespoon whole coriander
seeds
1 tablespoon black
peppercorns
4 cloves garlic
1½ to 2 pounds beef top round
steak (London Broil),
about 1½ inches thick
Vegetable or olive oil
Salt

Place sugar, mustard seeds, coriander seeds, peppercorns and garlic in blender or food processor; process until seeds and garlic are crushed. Rub beef with oil; pat on spice mixture. Season generously with salt.

Lightly oil hot grid to prevent sticking. Grill beef on covered grill over medium-low KINGSFORD® Briquets 16 to 20 minutes for medium rare or to desired doneness, turning once. Let stand 5 minutes before cutting across the grain into thin diagonal slices.  *Makes 6 servings*

# Dinner on the Grill

1 cup LA CHOY® Lite Soy
Sauce
1 cup fat-free Italian salad
dressing
2 tablespoons minced fresh
parsley
1 tablespoon garlic powder
1 to 1½ pounds boneless beef
top sirloin steak, ¾ inch
thick
2 *each:* medium zucchini and
yellow squash, cut into
quarters lengthwise
2 sweet onions, cut into
½-inch slices
1 small eggplant, cut into
½-inch slices
¼ cup grated reduced-fat
Parmesan cheese

**Chill**
**1.** In a large bowl, combine La Choy Soy Sauce, salad dressing, parsley and garlic powder; mix well.

**2.** Place steak in large container; cover with *half* the marinade. Cover; refrigerate 1 to 2 hours, turning occasionally.

**3.** Add *remaining* ingredients *except* cheese to *remaining* marinade; coat vegetables. Marinate 30 minutes.

**Grill**
**1.** Preheat grill. Remove steak from marinade; discard used marinade. Place steak and *all* vegetables over medium-hot heat. Cook steak 6 to 7 minutes on each side or to desired doneness.

**2.** Cook vegetables 3 to 4 minutes or until crisp-tender; turning occasionally. Discard any *remaining* marinade.

**3.** Sprinkle with cheese before serving.
*Makes 4 servings*

# Mini Beef & Colorado Potato Kabobs

2 COLORADO Sangre red
   potatoes, baked
1 green bell pepper, cut into
   ¾-inch cubes
1 small onion, cut into
   wedges
½ pound beef tenderloin, cut
   into ¾-inch cubes
   Bamboo skewers

Marinade
   ¼ cup olive oil
   ¼ cup balsamic vinegar
   1 tablespoon snipped fresh
      thyme
   1 tablespoon snipped fresh
      basil
   1 tablespoon snipped fresh
      parsley
   1 clove garlic, minced
   ½ teaspoon sugar
   ½ teaspoon salt
   ½ teaspoon black pepper

Quarter baked potatoes lengthwise. Cut crosswise into ¾-inch chunks; set aside. Blanch bell pepper and onion in boiling water 1 to 2 minutes; drain. For marinade, combine olive oil, vinegar, herbs, garlic, sugar, salt and black pepper in medium bowl. Place beef, bell pepper and onion in marinade. Toss to coat well. Cover and chill several hours or overnight. Soak bamboo skewers in hot water 5 minutes. Thread beef, potatoes, bell pepper and onion on skewers. Grill over medium high heat 5 to 7 minutes, turning once. If desired, broil 5 to 6 inches from heat source 5 to 7 minutes or to desired doneness.

*Makes 4 servings*

*Favorite recipe from* **Colorado Potato Administrative Committee**

## FOOD FACT

*Seasoning blends are the easiest way to perk up grilled meats, poultry or seafood. Either purchase your favorite seasoning blend or create your own by mixing together your favorite herbs and spices along with salt and pepper. Pat or rub onto sides of raw meat just before grilling.*

# Marinated Flank Steak with Pineapple

1 can (15¼ ounces)
   DEL MONTE® Sliced
   Pineapple In Its Own
   Juice
¼ cup teriyaki sauce
2 tablespoons honey
1 pound beef flank steak

**1.** Drain pineapple, reserving 2 tablespoons juice. Set aside pineapple for later use.

**2.** Combine reserved juice, teriyaki sauce and honey in shallow 2-quart dish; mix well. Add meat; turn to coat. Cover and refrigerate at least 30 minutes or overnight.

**3.** Remove meat from marinade, reserving marinade. Grill meat over hot coals (or broil), brushing occasionally with reserved marinade. Cook about 4 minutes on each side for rare; about 5 minutes on each side for medium; or about 6 minutes on each side for well done. During last 4 minutes of cooking, grill pineapple until heated through.

**4.** Slice meat across grain; serve with pineapple. Garnish, if desired.                *Makes 4 servings*

**Note:** Marinade that has come into contact with raw meat must be discarded or boiled for several minutes before serving with cooked food.

**Prep and Marinate Time:** 35 minutes
**Cook Time:** 10 minutes

## FOOD FACT

*Flank steak is a boneless cut of beef that weighs 1 to 2 pounds. Because flank has thin long fibers, be sure to slice across the grain. Serve the juicy tender slices as delicious entrées, fabulous salad toppings and wonderful sandwich fillings. You'll be the hero of the grill with one fabulous, tasty and easy-to-prepare beef cut.*

**Marinated Flank Steak with Pineapple**

# Vietnamese Grilled Steak Wraps

1 beef flank steak (about
    1½ pounds)
  Grated peel and juice of
    2 lemons
6 tablespoons sugar, divided
2 tablespoons dark sesame oil
1¼ teaspoons salt, divided
½ teaspoon black pepper
¼ cup water
¼ cup rice vinegar
½ teaspoon crushed red
    pepper
6 (8-inch) flour tortillas
6 red leaf lettuce leaves
⅓ cup lightly packed fresh
    mint leaves
⅓ cup lightly packed fresh
    cilantro leaves
  Star fruit slices
  Red bell pepper strips
  Orange peel strips

Cut beef across the grain into thin slices. Combine lemon peel, juice, 2 tablespoons sugar, sesame oil, 1 teaspoon salt and black pepper in medium bowl. Add beef; toss to coat. Cover and refrigerate at least 30 minutes. Combine water, vinegar, remaining 4 tablespoons sugar and ¼ teaspoon salt in small saucepan; bring to a boil. Boil 5 minutes without stirring until syrupy. Stir in crushed red pepper; set aside.

Remove beef from marinade; discard marinade. Thread beef onto metal or wooden skewers. (Soak wooden skewers in hot water 30 minutes to prevent burning.) Grill beef over medium-hot KINGSFORD® Briquets about 3 minutes per side until cooked through. Grill tortillas until hot. Place lettuce, beef, mint and cilantro on tortillas; drizzle with vinegar mixture. Roll tortillas to enclose filling. Garnish with star fruit, bell pepper and orange peel strips. *Makes 6 wraps*

**Vietnamese Grilled Steak Wrap**

# Beef Tenderloin with Dijon-Cream Sauce

3 tablespoons balsamic
    vinegar*
2 tablespoons olive oil
1 beef tenderloin roast (about
    1½ to 2 pounds)
    Salt
3 tablespoons mustard seeds
1½ tablespoons white
    peppercorns
1½ tablespoons black
    peppercorns
    Dijon-Cream Sauce (page
    168)

*Substitute 2 tablespoons red wine vinegar plus 1½ teaspoons sugar for the balsamic vinegar.

Combine vinegar and oil in a cup; rub onto beef. Season generously with salt. Let stand 15 minutes. Meanwhile, coarsely crush mustard seeds and peppercorns in a blender or food processor or by hand with a mortar and pestle. Roll beef in crushed mixture, pressing it into the surface to coat.

Oil hot grid to help prevent sticking. Grill beef on a covered grill over medium KINGSFORD® Briquets 16 to 24 minutes (depending on size and thickness) until a meat thermometer inserted in the center almost registers 145°F for medium-rare. (Cook until 160°F for medium or 170°F for well done; add another 5 minutes for every 10°F.) Turn halfway through cooking. Let stand 5 to 10 minutes before slicing. Slice and serve with a few spoonfuls of sauce. *Makes 6 servings*

**continued on page 168**

## GRILLING TIP

*When choosing a beef tenderloin roast for the grill, purchase a center-cut piece or a piece cut from the thicker end, as it will grill more evenly. Test doneness with an instant-read thermometer. Remove roast from the grill just before it reaches the desired temperature. The internal temperature can rise 5° to 10°F as the roast stands.*

**Beef Tenderloin
with Dijon-Cream Sauce**

## Dijon-Cream Sauce

1 can (14½ ounces) beef broth
1 cup whipping cream
2 tablespoons butter, softened
1½ to 2 tablespoons Dijon mustard
1 to 1½ tablespoons balsamic vinegar*
  Coarsely crushed black peppercorns and mustard
    seeds for garnish

*Substitute 2 teaspoons red wine vinegar plus 1 teaspoon sugar for the balsamic vinegar.

Bring beef broth and whipping cream to a boil in a saucepan. Boil gently until reduced to about 1 cup; sauce will be thick enough to coat a spoon. Remove from heat; stir in butter, a little at a time, until all the butter is melted. Stir in mustard and vinegar, adjusting amounts to taste. Sprinkle with peppercorns and mustard seeds.

*Makes about 1 cup*

# Grilled Flank Steak

½ cup soy sauce
3 tablespoons packed brown sugar
3 tablespoons lime juice
2 tablespoons dry sherry (optional)
1 tablespoon grated fresh ginger *or* 1 teaspoon ground ginger
3 cloves garlic, minced
1 beef flank steak (1½ to 2 pounds)

Stir together soy sauce, sugar, lime juice, sherry, if desired, ginger and garlic until sugar is dissolved. Reserve ¼ cup marinade for basting. Place beef in large resealable plastic food storage bag; add remaining marinade. Seal bag; turn to coat evenly. Marinate in refrigerator several hours or overnight. Remove beef from marinade; discard marinade. Grill beef on covered grill over medium-hot KINGSFORD® Briquets 12 to 14 minutes until medium-rare or to desired doneness, turning once and basting with reserved ¼ cup marinade. Slice steak diagonally across grain into thin slices.

*Makes 6 to 8 servings*

# Karrie's Bistro Beef Dinner

¾ cup prepared Italian salad
    dressing
¼ cup LA CHOY® Soy Sauce
4 (4-ounce) boneless beef
    tenderloin steaks
8 large mushrooms, stems
    removed
1 bag (5 ounces) mixed salad
    greens
1 large tomato, cut into
    wedges
2 hard boiled eggs, quartered
    (optional)
1 pint deli prepared potato
    salad (optional)
    Croutons (optional)

In a small bowl, combine salad dressing and soy sauce; mix well. In a resealable plastic food storage bag, combine steaks and ¼ *cup* soy mixture; marinate *10* minutes. Place steak on grid over medium-hot heat. Grill, basting occasionally with marinade, 5 minutes on each side or to desired degree of doneness. Grill mushroom caps last 5 minutes of cooking time. Discard remaining marinade. To serve, arrange salad greens on large platter; top with steaks and remaining ingredients. Drizzle with about ⅓ cup dressing; serve with remaining dressing.

*Makes 4 servings*

# Onion-Marinated Steak

2 large red onions
¾ cup plus 2 tablespoons
    WISH-BONE® Italian
    Dressing*
1 (2- to 3-pound) boneless
    beef top sirloin steak

*\* Also terrific with Wish-Bone® Robusto Italian or Just 2 Good Italian Dressing.*

Cut 1 onion in half; refrigerate one half. Chop remaining onion to equal 1½ cups. In blender or food processor, process 1 cup Italian dressing and chopped onion until puréed.

In large, shallow nonaluminum baking dish or plastic bag, pour 1¾ cups dressing-onion marinade over steak; turn to coat. Cover, or close bag, and marinate in refrigerator, turning occasionally, 3 to 24 hours. Refrigerate remaining ½ cup marinade.

Remove steak from marinade, discarding marinade. Grill or broil steak, turning and brushing frequently with refrigerated marinade, until steak is done.

Meanwhile, in saucepan, heat remaining 2 tablespoons Italian dressing and cook remaining onion half, cut into thin rings, stirring occasionally, 4 minutes or until tender. Serve over steak.

*Makes 8 servings*

# Ginger Beef and Pineapple Kabobs

1 cup LAWRY'S® Thai Ginger
    Marinade with Lime Juice,
    divided
1 can (16 ounces) pineapple
    chunks, juice reserved
1½ pounds beef top sirloin
    steak, cut into 1½-inch
    cubes
2 red bell peppers, cut into
    chunks
2 medium onions, cut into
    wedges

In large resealable plastic food storage bag, combine ½ cup Thai Ginger Marinade and 1 tablespoon pineapple juice; mix well. Add steak; seal bag. Marinate in refrigerator at least 30 minutes. Remove steak; discard used marinade. Alternately thread steak, vegetables and pineapple onto skewers. Grill or broil skewers 10 to 15 minutes or until desired doneness, turning once and basting often with additional ½ cup Thai Ginger Marinade. Do not baste during last 5 minutes of cooking. Discard any remaining marinade. *Makes 6 servings*

**Serving Suggestion:** Serve kabobs with a light salad and bread.

## GRILLING TIP

*Watch foods carefully during grilling. Total cooking time will vary with the type of food, position on the grill, weather, temperature of the coals and degree of doneness you desire.*

## Steak Provençal

4 beef sirloin, tenderloin or
ribeye steaks (about
11 ounces each)
5 tablespoons I CAN'T
BELIEVE IT'S NOT
BUTTER!® Spread
2 large cloves garlic, finely
chopped
1½ cups chopped tomatoes
(about 2 medium)
1 to 2 tablespoons rinsed and
chopped large capers
¼ teaspoon salt
¼ teaspoon ground black
pepper
2 tablespoons chopped fresh
parsley

Grill or broil steaks to desired doneness.

Meanwhile, in 10-inch skillet, melt I Can't Believe It's Not Butter! Spread and cook garlic over medium heat, stirring occasionally, 30 seconds. Add tomatoes, capers, salt and pepper. Cook, stirring occasionally, 3 minutes or until tomatoes are cooked and mixture is saucy. Stir in parsley. Serve over hot steaks.           *Makes 4 servings*

## It's the Berries Grilled Steak

¼ cup LA CHOY® Soy Sauce
4 boneless beef strip steaks,
½-inch-thick
½ cup Knott's® Light
Blackberry Preserves
¼ cup red wine vinegar
½ cup blackberries, fresh or
frozen, thawed

**1.** In medium bowl, combine soy sauce and steaks. Cover and refrigerate 30 minutes to 1 hour, turning several times during marinating.

**2.** In small saucepan, combine preserves and vinegar; mix well. Heat until preserves have dissolved. Reserve ½ cup sauce.

**3.** Remove steaks from refrigerator 15 minutes before grilling. Discard used marinade. Preheat grill. Over hot coals, grill steaks on one side 4 minutes; baste with blackberry sauce while grilling. Turn and grill to desired doneness. Place steaks on serving dish and ladle *2 tablespoons* reserved blackberry sauce over each steak. Evenly divide blackberries over steaks.

*Makes 4 (3-ounce) servings*

**Steak Provençal**

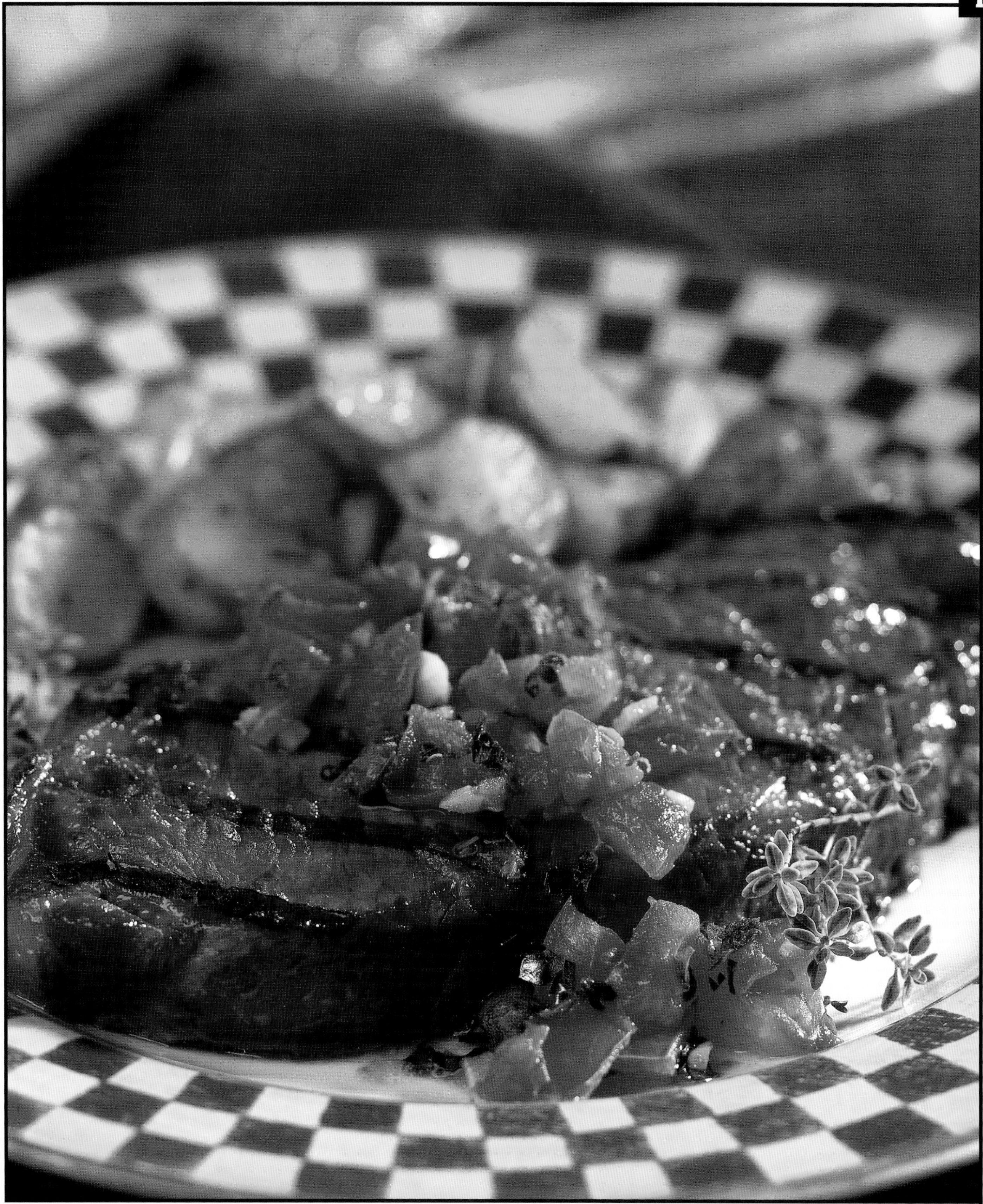

# Korean Beef Short Ribs

2½ **pounds flanken-style beef**
**short ribs, cut ⅜ to**
**½ inch thick***
¼ **cup water**
¼ **cup soy sauce**
¼ **cup chopped green onions**
1 **tablespoon sugar**
2 **teaspoons dark sesame oil**
2 **teaspoons grated fresh**
**ginger**
2 **cloves garlic, minced**
½ **teaspoon black pepper**
1 **tablespoon sesame seeds,**
**toasted**

*\*Flanken-style ribs may be ordered from your butcher. They are cross-cut short ribs sawed through the bones, ⅜ to ½ inch thick.*

**1.** Place ribs in large resealable plastic food storage bag. Combine water, soy sauce, green onions, sugar, oil, ginger, garlic and pepper in small bowl; pour over ribs. Seal bag tightly, turning to coat. Marinate in refrigerator at least 4 hours or up to 24 hours, turning occasionally.

**2.** Prepare barbecue grill for direct cooking.

**3.** Drain ribs; reserve marinade. Place ribs on grid. Grill ribs, on covered grill, over medium-hot coals 5 minutes. Brush tops lightly with reserved marinade; turn and brush again. Discard remaining marinade. Continue to grill, covered, 5 to 6 minutes for medium or until desired doneness is reached. Sprinkle with sesame seeds.

*Makes 4 to 6 servings*

## FOOD FACT

*A marinade with fresh ginger helps to tenderize less-tender cuts of meat. However, the maximum time to marinate meats with a marinade using fresh ginger is 24 hours. A longer marinating time will over tenderize the meat and give it a mushy texture.*

# Satay Skewers with Sesame

1½ cups dry roasted peanuts
⅔ cup seasoned rice vinegar
½ cup light corn syrup
½ cup soy sauce
2 tablespoons sesame oil
2 tablespoons minced fresh ginger
2 tablespoons chopped fresh cilantro
½ teaspoon LAWRY'S® Garlic Powder with Parsley
½ teaspoon crushed red pepper flakes (optional)
1 pound beef sirloin steak or 1 pound boneless, skinless chicken, cut into strips
Skewers

In food processor, combine peanuts, rice vinegar and corn syrup; process until peanuts are puréed. Add soy sauce, sesame oil, ginger, cilantro, Garlic Powder with Parsley and red pepper flakes, if desired. Pulse until mixture is blended; cover. Refrigerate at least 1 hour. Thread meat onto skewers; brush with half of the sauce. Grill or broil to desired doneness, turning and brushing frequently with sauce. In small saucepan, boil remaining sauce 1 minute. Use for dipping sauce.

*Makes 4 servings*

**Serving Suggestion:** Serve with hot cooked white rice and iced tea.

**Hint:** If using wooden skewers, soak in water 30 minutes before using to prevent scorching.

## FOOD FACT

*Saté (also satay) is a dish popular in Indonesia and Malaysia. It consists of pieces or strips of meat, poultry or seafood that have been marinated and then threaded onto skewers for grilling. Saté is generally served with a spicy peanut sauce.*

**Satay Skewers with Sesame**

# Marinated Grilled Steaks

1¼ cups dry red wine *or* ¼ cup lemon juice and ¾ cup orange juice

¼ cup CRISCO® Oil*

1 small onion, peeled and chopped

2 tablespoons chopped fresh parsley

1 tablespoon jarred minced garlic *or* 2 large garlic cloves, peeled and minced

2 bay leaves, crumbled

1 tablespoon Italian seasoning

1 teaspoon salt

½ teaspoon freshly ground black pepper

4 (6- to 8-ounce) beef steaks *or* 1 beef flank steak (1 to 2 pounds)

*Use your favorite Crisco Oil product.*

**1.** Combine wine, oil, onion, parsley, garlic, bay leaves, Italian seasoning, salt and pepper in a large resealable plastic food storage bag. Add steaks. Marinate 30 minutes to 1 hour, depending on the size of steak and time available.

**2.** Prepare grill or heat broiler.

**3.** Remove meat from marinade. Discard marinade. Grill meat to desired doneness. Turn with tongs. Allow steaks to rest 5 minutes before carving. Serve immediately.                    *Makes 4 servings*

**Tip:** Always brush the cool grill grids with Crisco® Oil or spray with Crisco® No-Stick Spray before turning on the grill so that food will not stick.

**Prep Time:** 10 minutes
**Total Time:** 1½ hours

## FOOD FACT

*While the flavor of meat marinated in wine will continue to improve with time, do not marinate foods in lemon or lime juice for more than the time specified. The citric acid will turn the meats gray.*

# London Broil Dijon

2 tablespoons olive or
   vegetable oil
2 large heads garlic,
   separated into cloves and
   peeled
1 can (14½ ounces) reduced-
   sodium beef broth
½ cup water
1 sprig fresh oregano or
   parsley
4½ teaspoons Dijon mustard
2 pounds beef top round
   steak (London broil),
   about 1½ inches thick
Salt and black pepper

Heat oil in medium saucepan; add garlic and sauté over medium-low heat, stirring frequently, until garlic just starts to brown in spots. Add broth, water and oregano. Simmer until mixture is reduced by about one third. Process broth mixture, in batches, in blender or food processor until smooth. Return to saucepan; whisk in mustard. Set aside. Season meat with salt and pepper.

Oil hot grid to help prevent sticking. Grill beef on covered grill over medium-low KINGSFORD® Briquets 10 to 14 minutes for medium-rare doneness; 12 to 16 minutes for medium doneness, turning once or twice. Let stand 5 minutes before slicing. Cut across grain into thin, diagonal slices. Gently rewarm sauce and serve as accompaniment. *Makes 6 servings*

# Grilled Caribbean Steaks

6 tablespoons brown sugar
2 tablespoons plus
   1½ teaspoons paprika
2 tablespoons granulated
   sugar
1 tablespoon kosher salt
1 tablespoon chili powder
1¼ teaspoons granulated garlic
   or garlic powder
1¼ teaspoons dried oregano
   leaves
1¼ teaspoons dried basil leaves
¾ teaspoon dried thyme leaves
¾ teaspoon celery seed
¼ teaspoon cayenne pepper
2 beef T-bone steaks (12 to
   16 ounces each), 1 inch
   thick

To prepare spice mix, combine all ingredients except steaks in small bowl; mix well. Measure out ¼ cup spice mix, reserving remaining for other uses.* Rub steaks with ¼ cup spice mix, using 1 tablespoon per side. Refrigerate steaks, covered, overnight. Grill steaks on covered grill over medium KINGSFORD® Briquets 12 to 14 minutes for medium-rare or to desired doneness, turning once. *Makes 4 to 6 servings*

*Recipe for spice mix makes 1¼ cups. Store leftover spice mix in covered container in cool, dry place. Use with beef, pork or chicken.*

# Guadalajara Beef and Salsa

1 bottle (12 ounces) Mexican
   dark beer*

¼ cup soy sauce

2 cloves garlic, minced

1 teaspoon ground cumin

1 teaspoon chili powder

1 teaspoon hot pepper sauce

4 beef sirloin steaks or
   boneless top loin strip
   steaks (4 to 6 ounces
   each)

Salt and black pepper

Red, green and yellow bell
   peppers, cut lengthwise
   into quarters, seeded
   (optional)

Salsa (recipe follows)

Flour tortillas (optional)

Lime wedges

*Substitute any beer for Mexican dark beer.*

Combine beer, soy sauce, garlic, cumin, chili powder and hot pepper sauce in large shallow glass dish or large heavy plastic food storage bag. Add beef; cover dish or close bag. Marinate in refrigerator up to 12 hours, turning beef several times. Remove beef from marinade; discard marinade. Season with salt and pepper.

Oil hot grid to help prevent sticking. Grill beef and bell peppers, if desired, on covered grill over medium KINGSFORD® Briquets 8 to 12 minutes, turning once. Beef should be of medium doneness and peppers should be tender. Serve with salsa, tortillas, if desired, and lime.

*Makes 4 servings*

## Salsa

2 cups coarsely chopped seeded tomatoes

2 green onions with tops, sliced

1 clove garlic, minced

1 to 2 teaspoons minced seeded jalapeño or serrano
   chile pepper, fresh or canned

1 tablespoon olive or vegetable oil

2 to 3 teaspoons lime juice

8 to 10 sprigs fresh cilantro, minced (optional)

½ teaspoon salt or to taste

½ teaspoon sugar or to taste

¼ teaspoon black pepper

Combine tomatoes, green onions, garlic, chile pepper, oil and lime juice in medium bowl. Stir in cilantro, if desired. Season with salt, sugar and black pepper. Adjust seasonings to taste, adding additional lime juice or chile pepper, if desired.

*Makes about 2 cups*

## Charcoal Beef Kabobs

½ cup vegetable oil

¼ cup lemon juice

1½ tablespoons (½ packet)
HIDDEN VALLEY®
The Original Ranch®
Salad Dressing &
Seasoning Mix

2 pounds beef top round or
boneless sirloin steak, cut
into 1-inch cubes

1 or 2 red, yellow or green
bell peppers, cut into
1-inch squares

16 pearl onions *or* 1 medium
onion, cut into wedges

8 cherry tomatoes

Combine oil, lemon juice and dry salad dressing & seasoning mix. Pour over beef cubes in shallow dish. Cover and refrigerate 1 hour or longer. Drain beef; reserve marinade. Thread beef cubes, peppers and onions onto skewers. Grill kabobs on uncovered grill over medium-hot KINGSFORD® Briquets 15 minutes, brushing often with reserved marinade and turning to brown all sides. A few minutes before serving, add cherry tomatoes to ends of skewers.    *Makes 6 servings*

## Peppered Steak with Dijon Sauce

4 boneless beef top loin (New
York strip) steaks, cut
1 inch thick (about
1½ pounds)

1 tablespoon *French's*®
Worcestershire Sauce
Cracked black pepper

⅓ cup mayonnaise

⅓ cup *French's*® Napa Valley
Style Dijon Mustard

3 tablespoons dry red wine

2 tablespoons minced red or
green onion

2 tablespoons minced fresh
parsley

1 clove garlic, minced

**1.** Brush steaks with Worcestershire and sprinkle with pepper to taste; set aside. To prepare Dijon sauce, combine mayonnaise, mustard, wine, onion, parsley and garlic in medium bowl.

**2.** Place steaks on grid. Grill steaks over high heat 15 minutes for medium-rare or to desired doneness, turning often. Serve with Dijon sauce. Garnish as desired.    *Makes 4 servings*

**Tip:** Dijon sauce is also great served with grilled salmon and swordfish. To serve with fish, substitute white wine for red wine and minced dill for fresh parsley.

**Prep Time:** 10 minutes
**Cook Time:** 15 minutes

Charcoal Beef Kabobs

# Ranch-Style Fajitas

2 pounds beef flank or skirt
  steak
½ cup vegetable oil
⅓ cup lime juice
2 packets (1 ounce each)
  HIDDEN VALLEY® The
  Original Ranch® Salad
  Dressing & Seasoning
  Mix
1 teaspoon ground cumin
½ teaspoon black pepper
6 flour tortillas
  Lettuce
  Guacamole, prepared
  HIDDEN VALLEY® The
  Original Ranch® Dressing,
  and picante sauce for
  toppings

Place steak in large baking dish. In small bowl, whisk together oil, lime juice, salad dressing & seasoning mix, cumin and pepper. Pour mixture over steak. Cover and refrigerate several hours or overnight.

Remove steak; place marinade in small saucepan. Bring to a boil. Grill steak over medium-hot coals 8 to 10 minutes or to desired doneness, turning once and basting with heated marinade during last 5 minutes of grilling. Remove steak and slice diagonally across grain into thin slices. Heat tortillas following package directions. Divide steak strips among tortillas; roll up to enclose. Serve with lettuce and desired toppings.          *Makes 6 servings*

## FOOD FACT

*Fajitas originated in Texas. The traditional dish is prepared by marinating beef skirt steak in oil, lime juice, garlic and ground red pepper before grilling. The steak is cut into thin strips and rolled in flour tortillas. Both flank and strip steak have a coarse grain. For the most tender juicy slices, be sure to cut the steak across the grain.*

## Teriyaki Glazed Beef Kabobs

1¼ to 1½ pounds beef top or
    bottom sirloin, cut into
    1-inch cubes
½ cup bottled teriyaki sauce
1 teaspoon Oriental sesame
    oil (optional)
1 clove garlic, minced
8 to 12 green onions
1 or 2 plum tomatoes, cut
    into slices (optional)

Thread beef cubes on metal or bamboo skewers. (Soak bamboo skewers in water for at least 20 minutes to keep them from burning.) Combine teriyaki sauce, sesame oil, if desired, and garlic in small bowl. Brush beef and onions with part of glaze, saving some for grilling; let stand 15 to 30 minutes.

Oil hot grid to help prevent sticking. Grill beef on covered grill over medium KINGSFORD® Briquets 6 to 9 minutes for medium doneness, turning several times and brushing with glaze. Add onions and tomatoes, if desired, to grid 3 to 4 minutes after beef; grill until onions and tomatoes are tender. Remove from grill; brush skewers, onions and tomatoes with remaining glaze.

*Makes 4 servings*

## Jamaican Steak

2 pounds beef flank steak
¼ cup packed brown sugar
3 tablespoons orange juice
3 tablespoons lime juice
3 cloves garlic, minced
1 piece (1½×1 inches) fresh
    ginger, minced
2 teaspoons grated orange
    peel
2 teaspoons grated lime peel
1 teaspoon salt
1 teaspoon black pepper
¼ teaspoon ground cinnamon
⅛ teaspoon ground cloves
    Shredded orange peel
    Shredded lime peel

Score both sides of beef.* Combine sugar, juices, garlic, ginger, grated peels, salt, pepper, cinnamon and cloves in 2-quart glass dish. Add beef; turn to coat. Cover and refrigerate steak at least 2 hours. Remove beef from marinade; discard marinade. Grill beef over medium-hot KINGSFORD® Briquets about 6 minutes per side until medium-rare or to desired doneness. Garnish with shredded orange and lime peels.

*Makes 6 servings*

*To score flank steak, cut ¼-inch-deep diagonal lines about 1 inch apart in surface of steak to form diamond-shaped design.*

**Teriyaki Glazed Beef Kabobs**

# Rosemary Steak

4 boneless beef top loin (New York strip) steaks (about 6 ounces each)
2 tablespoons minced fresh rosemary
2 cloves garlic, minced
1 tablespoon extra-virgin olive oil
1 teaspoon grated lemon peel
1 teaspoon coarsely ground black pepper
½ teaspoon salt
Fresh rosemary sprigs

Score steaks in diamond pattern on both sides. Combine minced rosemary, garlic, oil, lemon peel, pepper and salt in small bowl; rub mixture onto surface of meat. Cover and refrigerate at least 15 minutes. Grill steaks over medium-hot KINGSFORD® Briquets about 4 minutes per side until medium-rare or to desired doneness. Cut steaks diagonally into ½-inch-thick slices. Garnish with rosemary sprigs.    *Makes 4 servings*

# Perfectly Grilled Steak & Potatoes

Olive oil
1½ teaspoons cracked black pepper
2 cloves garlic, pressed
Salt
½ teaspoon dried thyme leaves
4 beef tenderloin steaks or boneless top loin steaks, 1½ inches thick
4 medium potatoes, cut into ½-inch slices
Ground black pepper
Lime wedges

Combine 2 tablespoons oil, cracked pepper, garlic, ½ teaspoon salt and thyme in cup. Brush oil mixture over steaks to coat both sides. Brush potato slices with additional oil; season to taste with additional salt and ground pepper. Lightly oil hot grid to prevent sticking. Grill beef and potatoes on covered grill over medium-hot KINGSFORD® Briquets 10 to 12 minutes or to desired doneness, turning once. Serve steaks with potatoes and lime wedges.    *Makes 4 servings*

# FIRED-UP
## PORK & LAMB

## Grilled Sherry Pork Chops

¼ cup HOLLAND HOUSE®
    Sherry Cooking Wine
¼ cup GRANDMA'S®
    Molasses
2 tablespoons soy sauce
4 pork chops (1 inch thick)

In plastic bowl, combine sherry, molasses and soy sauce; pour over pork chops. Cover; refrigerate 30 minutes. Prepare grill. Drain pork chops; reserve marinade. Grill pork chops over medium-high heat 8 to 10 minutes or until pork is no longer pink in center, turning once and brushing frequently with reserved marinade.* Discard any remaining marinade. *Makes 4 servings*

*Do not baste during last 5 minutes of grilling.*

## Apricot-Mustard Grilled Pork Tenderloin

1 pork tenderloin (about
    1 pound)
5 tablespoons honey mustard
3 tablespoons apricot
    preserves

Season tenderloin with salt and pepper. In small bowl, stir together mustard and preserves. Grill pork over a medium-hot fire, brushing with mustard mixture frequently, turning once or twice until just done, about 15 minutes. *Makes 4 servings*

*Favorite recipe from **National Pork Board***

**Grilled Sherry Pork Chop**

# Margarita Pork Kabobs

1 cup margarita drink mix *or*
   1 cup lime juice,
    4 teaspoons sugar and
    ½ teaspoon salt
1 teaspoon ground coriander
1 clove garlic, minced
1 pound pork tenderloin, cut
   into 1-inch cubes
2 tablespoons margarine,
   melted
1 tablespoon minced fresh
   parsley
2 teaspoons lime juice
⅛ teaspoon sugar
1 large green or red bell
   pepper, cut into 1-inch
   cubes
2 ears corn, cut into 8 pieces

For marinade, combine margarita mix, coriander and garlic in small bowl. Place pork cubes in large resealable plastic food storage bag; pour marinade over pork. Close bag securely; turn to coat. Marinate for at least 30 minutes. Combine margarine, parsley, lime juice and sugar in small bowl; set aside. Thread pork cubes onto four skewers, alternating with pieces of bell pepper and corn. (If using bamboo skewers, soak in water 20 to 30 minutes before using to prevent them from burning.) Grill over hot coals for 15 to 20 minutes or until barely pink in center, basting with margarine mixture and turning frequently. *Makes 4 servings*

*Favorite recipe from* **National Pork Board**

# Grilled Smoked Sausage

1 cup apricot or pineapple
   preserves
1 tablespoon lemon juice
1½ pounds smoked sausage

Heat preserves in small saucepan until melted. Strain; reserve fruit pieces. Combine strained preserve liquid with lemon juice in a small bowl to make glaze.

Oil hot grid to help prevent sticking. Grill whole sausage on uncovered grill over low KINGSFORD® Briquets 10 minutes. Halfway through cooking, baste with glaze; turn and continue grilling until heated through. Remove sausage from grill; baste with glaze. Garnish with fruit pieces. *Makes 4 to 5 servings*

Margarita Pork Kabobs

# Spicy Baby Back Ribs

2 tablespoons olive oil
2 racks pork baby back ribs
   (3½ to 4 pounds)
¼ cup packed brown sugar
2 teaspoons dry mustard
2 teaspoons seasoned salt
1 teaspoon garlic powder
1 teaspoon black pepper
⅓ to ½ cup barbecue sauce
½ teaspoon hot pepper sauce

Prepare grill for indirect cooking.

Pour 1 tablespoon olive oil over each rack of ribs; rub to coat. Combine brown sugar, mustard, salt, garlic powder and pepper in small bowl. Rub mixture evenly over ribs. Place ribs on grid directly over drip pan. Grill, covered, over medium coals 1 hour, turning occasionally.

Meanwhile, combine barbecue sauce and hot pepper sauce in small bowl. Baste ribs with sauce; grill 30 minutes more or until ribs are tender, turning and basting with sauce occasionally. Bring any remaining barbecue sauce to a boil over medium-high heat; boil 1 minute. Serve ribs with remaining sauce.

*Makes 4 servings*

# Ginger Peanut Pork Tenderloin

3 tablespoons soy sauce
1 tablespoon honey
1 tablespoon sesame oil
1 tablespoon creamy peanut
   butter
1 tablespoon minced fresh
   ginger
2 teaspoons TABASCO®
   brand Pepper Sauce
1 large clove garlic, minced
1 teaspoon curry powder
½ teaspoon salt
1½ pounds pork tenderloins

Combine all ingredients except pork in medium bowl. Set aside 2 tablespoons mixture. Add pork tenderloins to bowl; cover and marinate at least 2 hours or overnight, turning occasionally.

Preheat grill to medium, placing rack 5 to 6 inches above coals. Place tenderloins on rack; grill 20 to 25 minutes or until no longer pink in center, turning occasionally and brushing frequently with marinade during first 10 minutes of grilling. Let stand 10 minutes before slicing. Brush reserved 2 tablespoons soy sauce mixture over cooked pork.

*Makes 6 servings*

Spicy Baby Back Ribs

# Hickory Smoked Ham
# with Maple-Mustard Sauce

**Hickory chunks or chips for smoking**
**1 fully cooked boneless ham (about 5 pounds)**
**¾ cup maple syrup**
**¾ cup spicy brown mustard or Dijon mustard**

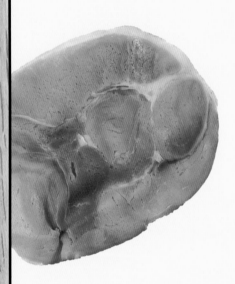

Soak about 4 wood chunks or several handfuls of wood chips in water; drain. If using a canned ham, scrape off any gelatin. If using another type of fully cooked ham, such as a bone-in shank, trim most of the fat, leaving a ⅛-inch layer. (The thinner the fat layer, the better the glaze will adhere to the ham.)

Arrange low KINGSFORD® Briquets on each side of a rectangular metal or foil drip pan. Pour in hot tap water to fill pan half full. Add soaked wood (all the chunks; part of the chips) to the fire.

Oil hot grid to help prevent sticking. Place ham on grid directly above drip pan. Grill ham on covered grill 20 to 30 minutes per pound, until a meat thermometer inserted in the thickest part registers 140°F. If your grill has a thermometer, maintain a cooking temperature of about 200°F. For best flavor, cook slowly over low coals, adding a few briquets to both sides of the fire every hour, or as necessary, to maintain a constant temperature. Add more soaked hickory chips every 20 to 30 minutes.

Meanwhile, prepare Maple-Mustard Sauce by mixing maple syrup and mustard in small bowl; set aside most of the syrup mixture to serve as a sauce. Brush ham with remaining mixture several times during the last 45 minutes of cooking. Let ham stand 10 minutes before slicing. Slice and serve with Maple-Mustard Sauce.

*Makes 12 to 15 servings*

**Note:** Most of the hams available today are fully cooked and need only be heated to a temperature of 140°F. If you buy a partially cooked ham, often labeled "cook before eating," it needs to be cooked to 160°F.

**Note:** Keep the briquet temperature low and replenish the hickory chips every 20 to 30 minutes.

# Honey-Lime Pork Chops

1 envelope LIPTON® RECIPE
SECRETS® Savory Herb
with Garlic Soup Mix*
⅓ cup soy sauce
3 tablespoons lime juice
3 tablespoons honey
1 teaspoon grated fresh
ginger *or* ¼ teaspoon
ground ginger (optional)
4 pork chops, 1½ inches thick

*Also terrific with LIPTON® RECIPE SECRETS®
Garlic Mushroom or Onion Soup Mix.*

**1.** For marinade, blend all ingredients except pork chops.

**2.** In shallow baking dish or plastic bag, pour ½ cup of the marinade over chops; turn to coat. Cover, or close bag, and marinate in refrigerator, turning occasionally, 2 to 24 hours. Refrigerate remaining marinade.

**3.** Remove chops from marinade, discarding marinade. Grill or broil chops, turning once and brushing with refrigerated marinade, until chops are done.

*Makes 4 servings*

# Country Glazed Ribs

3 to 4 pounds pork baby back
ribs, cut into 3- to 4-rib
portions
½ cup *French's*® Bold n' Spicy
Brown Mustard
½ cup packed brown sugar
½ cup finely chopped onion
¼ cup *French's*®
Worcestershire Sauce
¼ cup cider vinegar
1 tablespoon mustard seeds
1 teaspoon ground allspice
Honey Mustard Dip (recipe
follows)

Place ribs in large shallow glass baking pan or resealable plastic food storage bag. To prepare marinade, combine mustard, sugar, onion, Worcestershire, vinegar, mustard seeds and allspice in small bowl; mix well. Pour over ribs, turning to coat all sides. Cover and marinate in refrigerator 1 hour or overnight.

Place ribs on grid, reserving marinade. Grill over medium coals 45 minutes or until ribs are barely pink near bone, turning and basting frequently with marinade. (Do not baste during last 10 minutes of cooking.) Serve with Honey Mustard Dip. Garnish as desired.

*Makes 4 to 6 servings*

## Honey Mustard Dip
½ cup *French's*® Bold n' Spicy Brown Mustard
½ cup honey

Combine mustard and honey in small bowl; mix well.

*Makes 1 cup*

# Pork Tenderloin with Grilled Apple Cream Sauce

1 can (6 ounces) frozen apple
    juice concentrate, thawed
    and divided (¾ cup)
½ cup Calvados or brandy,
    divided
2 tablespoons Dijon mustard
1 tablespoon olive oil
3 cloves garlic, minced
1¼ teaspoons salt, divided
¼ teaspoon black pepper
1½ pounds pork tenderloin
2 green or red apples, cored
1 tablespoon butter
½ large red onion, cut into
    thin slivers
½ cup heavy cream
    Fresh thyme sprigs

Reserve 2 tablespoons juice concentrate. Combine remaining juice concentrate, ¼ cup Calvados, mustard, oil, garlic, 1 teaspoon salt and pepper in glass dish. Add pork; turn to coat. Cover and refrigerate 2 hours, turning pork occasionally. Cut apples crosswise into ⅜-inch rings. Remove pork from marinade; discard marinade. Grill pork on covered grill over medium KINGSFORD® Briquets about 20 minutes, turning 3 times, until meat thermometer inserted in thickest part registers 160°F. Grill apples about 4 minutes per side until tender; cut rings into quarters. Melt butter in large skillet over medium heat. Add onion; cook and stir until soft. Stir in apples, remaining ¼ cup Calvados, ¼ teaspoon salt and reserved 2 tablespoons juice concentrate. Add cream; heat through. Cut pork crosswise into ½-inch slices; spoon sauce over pork. Garnish with fresh thyme.

*Makes 4 servings*

# America's Favorite Pork Chops

4 top loin pork chops
¾ cup Italian dressing
1 teaspoon Worcestershire
    sauce

Place all ingredients in resealable plastic food storage bag; seal bag and place in refrigerator for at least 20 minutes (or as long as overnight). Remove chops from bag, discarding marinade. Grill over medium-hot heat, turning once, until just done, about 8 to 15 minutes total cooking time (depending upon thickness of chops).

*Makes 4 servings*

*Favorite recipe from* **National Pork Board**

**Pork Tenderloin
with Grilled Apple Cream Sauce**

# Mustard-Glazed Ribs

¾ cup beer
½ cup firmly packed dark
   brown sugar
½ cup spicy brown mustard
3 tablespoons soy sauce
1 tablespoon catsup
¾ teaspoon TABASCO® brand
   Pepper Sauce
½ teaspoon ground cloves
4 pounds pork spareribs or
   baby back ribs

Combine beer, sugar, mustard, soy sauce, catsup, TABASCO® Sauce and cloves in medium bowl; mix well. Position grill rack as far from coals as possible. Place ribs on grill over low heat. For spareribs, grill 45 minutes; turn occasionally. Brush with mustard glaze. Grill 30 minutes longer or until meat is cooked through; turn and baste ribs often with mustard glaze. (For baby back ribs, grill 15 minutes. Brush with mustard glaze. Grill 30 minutes longer or until meat is cooked to desired doneness; turn and baste ribs often with mustard glaze.) Heat any remaining glaze to a boil; serve with ribs.

*Makes 4 servings*

# Pork Chops with Orange-Radish Relish

2 cups orange juice
⅓ cup lime juice
⅓ cup packed brown sugar
3 medium oranges, peeled,
   seeded and cut into
   ¼-inch pieces
¼ cup chopped red onion
¼ cup diced radishes
2 tablespoons finely chopped
   fresh cilantro
6 pork chops (about ¾ inch
   thick)
   Salt and black pepper
   Orange curls and radishes
   for garnish

Combine both juices and brown sugar in saucepan. Cook mixture at a low boil, stirring often, about 20 minutes until reduced to about ½ cup and it has a syruplike consistency. Set aside ¼ cup sauce for basting.

Meanwhile, prepare Orange-Radish Relish by combining oranges, onion and diced radishes in colander or strainer and drain well; transfer to bowl. Add cilantro and gently stir in remaining orange syrup. Season pork with salt and pepper.

Oil hot grid to help prevent sticking. Grill pork on covered grill over medium KINGSFORD® Briquets 7 to 10 minutes. (Pork is done at 160°F; it should be juicy and slightly pink in center.) Halfway through cooking, brush with reserved ¼ cup orange syrup and turn once. Serve with Orange-Radish Relish. Garnish with orange curls and radishes.

*Makes 6 servings*

# Peanut Pork Lo Mein

½ recipe Peanut Pork
 Tenderloin (page 208),
 hot and sliced into bite-
 size pieces *or* ¾ pound
 pork tenderloin, grilled
 and sliced into bite-size
 pieces
1 package (12 ounces) fresh
 chow mein noodles or
 linguine
1 red bell pepper, cut into
 thin slivers
1 small red onion, cut into
 thin slivers
1½ cups snow peas, cut in half
 diagonally
2 cloves garlic, minced
8 teaspoons vegetable oil,
 divided
 Salt and freshly ground
 black pepper
2 tablespoons rice vinegar
2 tablespoons oyster sauce
2 tablespoons soy sauce
1 tablespoon dark sesame oil
2 green onions, thinly sliced
 on diagonal

Prepare Peanut Pork Tenderloin. Cook noodles according to package directions; drain and place in large bowl. Meanwhile, place bell pepper, onion, snow peas and garlic in center of 18×12-inch sheet of heavy-duty foil; drizzle with 2 teaspoons vegetable oil and season to taste with salt and black pepper. Bring edges of foil up to form shallow pan. Grill vegetables in foil pan on covered grill over medium KINGSFORD® Briquets about 10 minutes until vegetables are crisp-tender, stirring gently several times. Whisk together vinegar, oyster sauce, soy sauce, sesame oil and remaining 6 teaspoons vegetable oil; pour over noodles, tossing to coat. Arrange noodle mixture on large platter. Top with pork and vegetables; garnish with green onions. Serve immediately.     *Makes 4 servings*

# Honey Pepper Chops

4 top loin pork chops
6 tablespoons honey
3 tablespoons hot pepper
 sauce

Season chops with salt and pepper; grill over medium-hot fire 8 to 10 minutes. Stir together honey and hot pepper sauce; baste chops during grilling. Remove chops from grill and brush with remaining glaze.

*Makes 4 servings*

*Favorite recipe from* **National Pork Board**

# Sausage, Peppers & Onions with Grilled Polenta

5 cups canned chicken broth

1½ cups Italian polenta or
    yellow cornmeal

1½ cups cooked fresh corn or
    thawed frozen corn

2 tablespoons butter or
    margarine

1 cup (4 ounces) freshly
    grated Parmesan cheese

6 Italian-style sausages

2 small or medium red
    onions, sliced into rounds

1 each medium red and green
    bell peppers, cored,
    seeded and cut into
    1-inch-wide strips

½ cup Marsala or sweet
    vermouth (optional)

    Olive oil

To make polenta, bring chicken broth to a boil in large pot. Add polenta and cook at a gentle boil, stirring frequently, about 30 minutes. If polenta starts to stick and burn bottom of pot, add up to ½ cup water. During last 5 minutes of cooking, stir in corn and butter. Remove from heat; stir in Parmesan cheese. Transfer polenta into greased 13×9-inch baking pan; let cool until firm and set enough to cut. (Polenta can be prepared a day ahead and held in refrigerator.)

Prick each sausage in 4 or 5 places with fork. Place sausages, red onions and bell peppers in large shallow glass dish or large heavy plastic food storage bag. Pour Marsala over sausage and vegetables; cover dish or close bag. Marinate in refrigerator up to 4 hours, turning sausages and vegetables several times. (If you don't wish to marinate sausages and vegetables in Marsala, just eliminate this step.)

Oil hot grid to help prevent sticking. Cut polenta into squares, then cut into triangles, if desired. Brush one side with oil. Grill polenta, oiled side down, on a covered grill over medium KINGSFORD® Briquets, about 4 minutes until lightly toasted. Halfway through grilling time, brush top with oil, then turn and continue grilling. Move polenta to edge of grill to keep warm.

When coals are medium-low, drain sausage and vegetables; discard wine. Grill sausage on covered grill 15 to 20 minutes until cooked through, turning several times. After sausage has cooked 10 minutes, place vegetables in center of grid. Grill vegetables 10 to 12 minutes until tender, turning once or twice.

*Makes 6 servings*

**Sausage, Peppers & Onions
with Grilled Polenta**

# Pork Chops with Apple-Sage Stuffing

6 center-cut pork chops
   (3 pounds), about 1 inch
   thick
¾ cup dry vermouth, divided
4 tablespoons minced fresh
   sage *or* 4 teaspoons
   rubbed sage, divided
2 tablespoons soy sauce
1 tablespoon olive oil
2 cloves garlic, minced
½ teaspoon black pepper,
   divided
1 tablespoon butter
1 medium onion, diced
1 apple, cored and diced
½ teaspoon salt
2 cups fresh firm-textured
   white bread crumbs
   Curly endive
   Plum slices

Cut pocket in each chop using tip of thin, sharp knife. Combine ¼ cup vermouth, 2 tablespoons fresh sage (or 2 teaspoons rubbed sage), soy sauce, oil, garlic and ¼ teaspoon pepper in glass dish; add pork chops, turning to coat. Heat butter in large skillet over medium heat until foamy. Add onion and apple; cook and stir about 6 minutes until onion is tender. Stir in remaining ½ cup vermouth, 2 tablespoons sage, ¼ teaspoon pepper and salt. Cook and stir over high heat about 3 minutes until liquid is almost gone. Transfer onion mixture to large bowl. Stir in bread crumbs.

Remove pork chops from marinade; discard marinade. Spoon onion mixture into pockets of pork chops. Close openings with wooden picks. (Soak wooden picks in hot water 15 minutes to prevent burning.) Grill pork chops on covered grill over medium KINGSFORD® Briquets about 5 minutes per side until barely pink in center. Garnish with endive and plum slices.

*Makes 6 servings*

# Texas Barbecued Ribs

1 cup GRANDMA'S®
   Molasses
½ cup coarse-grained mustard
2 tablespoons cider vinegar
2 teaspoons dry mustard
3½ pounds pork baby back ribs
   or spareribs, cut into
   6 sections

Prepare grill for direct cooking. In medium bowl, combine molasses, mustard, cider vinegar and dry mustard. When ready to barbecue, place ribs on grill meaty side up over low coals. Cook 1 to 1¼ hours or until meat is tender and starts to pull away from bone, basting frequently with sauce* during last 15 minutes of cooking. To serve, cut ribs apart carefully with knife and arrange on platter.

*Makes 4 servings*

*\*Do not baste during last 5 minutes of grilling.*

**Pork Chop with Apple-Sage Stuffing**

## Garlic-Pepper Skewered Pork

1 boneless pork loin roast
   (about 2½ pounds)
6 to 15 cloves garlic, minced
⅓ cup lime juice
3 tablespoons firmly packed
   brown sugar
3 tablespoons soy sauce
2 tablespoons vegetable oil
2 teaspoons black pepper
¼ teaspoon cayenne pepper
8 green onions, cut into
   2-inch pieces (optional)

Cut pork crosswise into six ½-inch-thick chops, reserving remaining roast. (Each chop may separate into 2 pieces.) Set chops aside in 13×9×2-inch glass dish. Cut remaining pork roast lengthwise into 2 pieces. Cut each piece into ⅛-inch-thick strips; place in dish with chops. To prepare marinade, combine all remaining ingredients except green onions in small bowl. Pour marinade over pork chops and slices; cover and refrigerate at least 1 hour or overnight. Thread pork slices ribbon style onto metal skewers, alternating pork with green onions. Grill skewered pork slices and chops over medium-hot KINGSFORD® Briquets about 3 minutes per side until no longer pink in center. (Chops may require 1 to 2 minutes longer.) *Do not overcook.* Serve skewered pork immediately. Cover and refrigerate chops for Thai Pork Salad (page 64).

*Makes 4 to 6 servings (plus 6 chops for Thai Pork Salad)*

## Firecracker Barbecue Pork

1 boneless pork loin roast,
   about 2 pounds
¾ cup barbecue sauce
⅓ cup orange marmalade
½ teaspoon hot pepper sauce
1 teaspoon grated
   horseradish (optional)

Season roast with salt and pepper; place over indirect heat in medium-hot grill. Stir together remaining ingredients. Baste roast every 8 to 10 minutes with mixture, until roast is done (internal temperature measured with the meat thermometer 155° to 160°F), about 30 to 45 minutes. Let roast rest for 5 to 8 minutes before slicing to serve. Discard any leftover basting mixture.                    *Makes 4 to 6 servings*

*Favorite recipe from* **National Pork Board**

# Barbecued Ribs

1 cup ketchup
½ cup GRANDMA'S® Molasses
¼ cup cider vinegar
¼ cup Dijon mustard
2 tablespoons Worcestershire
    sauce
1 teaspoon garlic powder
1 teaspoon hickory flavor
    liquid smoke (optional)
¼ teaspoon ground red pepper
¼ teaspoon hot pepper sauce
4 to 6 pounds pork baby
    back ribs

**1.** Prepare grill for direct cooking. While coals are heating, combine all ingredients except ribs in large bowl; mix well. Place ribs on grid over medium coals. Cook ribs 40 to 45 minutes or until they begin to brown; turning occasionally.

**2.** Once ribs begin to brown, begin basting them with sauce. Continue to cook and baste ribs with sauce an additional 1 to 1½ hours or until tender and cooked through.*                         *Makes 4 to 6 servings*

*Do not baste during last 5 minutes of grilling.*

# Peanut Pork Tenderloin

⅓ cup chunky unsweetened
    peanut butter
⅓ cup regular or light canned
    coconut milk
¼ cup lemon juice or dry
    white wine
3 tablespoons soy sauce
3 cloves garlic, minced
2 tablespoons sugar
1 piece (1-inch cube) fresh
    ginger, minced
½ teaspoon salt
¼ to ½ teaspoon cayenne
    pepper
¼ teaspoon ground cinnamon
1½ pounds pork tenderloin

Combine peanut butter, coconut milk, lemon juice, soy sauce, garlic, sugar, ginger, salt, cayenne pepper and cinnamon in 2-quart glass dish until blended. Add pork; turn to coat. Cover and refrigerate at least 30 minutes or overnight. Remove pork from marinade; discard marinade. Grill pork on covered grill over medium KINGSFORD® Briquets about 20 minutes until just barely pink in center, turning 4 times. Cut crosswise into ½-inch slices. Serve immediately.         *Makes 4 to 6 servings*

Barbecued Ribs

# Jamaican Baby Back Ribs

2 tablespoons sugar
2 tablespoons fresh lemon
  juice
1 tablespoon salt
1 tablespoon vegetable oil
2 teaspoons black pepper
2 teaspoons dried thyme
  leaves, crushed
¾ teaspoon each ground
  cinnamon, nutmeg and
  allspice
½ teaspoon ground red
  pepper
6 pounds well-trimmed pork
  baby back ribs, cut into
  3-to 4-rib portions
  Barbecue Sauce (recipe
  follows)

**1.** For seasoning rub, combine all ingredients except ribs and Barbecue Sauce in small bowl; stir well. Spread over all surfaces of ribs; press with fingertips so mixture adheres to ribs. Cover; refrigerate overnight.

**2.** Prepare grill for indirect cooking. While coals are heating, prepare Barbecue Sauce.

**3.** Place seasoned ribs on cooking grid directly over drip pan. Grill, covered, 1 hour, turning occasionally. Baste ribs generously with Barbecue Sauce; grill 30 minutes more or until ribs are tender, turning occasionally.

**4.** Bring remaining Barbecue Sauce to a boil over medium-high heat; boil 1 minute. Serve ribs with remaining sauce. *Makes 6 servings*

## Barbecue Sauce

2 tablespoons butter
½ cup finely chopped onion
1½ cups ketchup
1 cup red currant jelly
¼ cup apple cider
1 tablespoon soy sauce
¼ teaspoon each ground red and black peppers

Melt butter in medium saucepan over medium-high heat. Add onion; cook and stir until softened. Stir in remaining ingredients. Reduce heat to medium-low; simmer 20 minutes, stirring often. *Makes about 3 cups*

# Grilled Asian Pork

¼ cup CRISCO® Oil*

3 tablespoons dark brown
   sugar

2 tablespoons soy sauce

2 teaspoons jarred minced
   garlic *or* 1 large clove
   fresh garlic, peeled and
   minced

1 to 3 teaspoons curry
   powder

½ teaspoon ground ginger

1 pound pork loin, trimmed of
   all fat and sliced
   ¼-inch thick

8 bamboo** or metal skewers

*Use your favorite Crisco Oil product.*

**If using wooden skewers, soak in water 20
minutes before using.*

**1.** Combine oil, brown sugar, soy sauce, garlic, curry and ginger in resealable plastic food storage bag. Add sliced pork; seal bag. Refrigerate 45 minutes.

**2.** While meat is marinating, prepare grill or heat broiler. Thread meat onto skewers. Discard marinade. Grill skewers 3 minutes. Turn gently with tongs. Grill other side 3 minutes or until pork is brown on outside and no longer pink in center. Serve immediately.

*Makes 4 servings*

**Note:** Boneless skinless chicken breasts or lean steak such as flank steak can be marinated and grilled in same manner. For beef, cook to desired degree of doneness. For chicken, grill until chicken is no longer pink in center.

**Prep Time:** 15 minutes
**Total Time:** 1 hour 10 minutes

# Southwestern Kabobs

4 boneless top loin pork
   chops, cut into 1-inch
   cubes

4 tablespoons taco or fajita
   seasoning

½ green bell pepper, seeded
   and cut into 1-inch pieces

½ large onion, peeled, cut into
   1-inch pieces

In a plastic food storage bag or shallow bowl, toss together pork cubes with seasoning until pork is evenly coated. Thread pork cubes, alternating with pepper and onion pieces, onto skewers.* Grill over a medium-hot fire, turning occasionally, until pork is nicely browned.

*Makes 4 servings*

*If using wooden skewers, soak in water for 20 minutes before using.*

*Favorite recipe from **National Pork Board***

# Barbecued Pork Loin

2 teaspoons LAWRY'S®
  Seasoned Salt
1 (3- to 3½-pounds) boneless
  pork loin
1 cup orange juice
¼ cup soy sauce
1 teaspoon LAWRY'S® Garlic
  Powder with Parsley
½ teaspoon LAWRY'S®
  Seasoned Pepper
  Vegetable oil
  Fresh herb sprigs (garnish)

Sprinkle Seasoned Salt onto all sides of meat. In large resealable plastic food storage bag or shallow glass baking dish, place meat; let stand 10 to 15 minutes. In small bowl, combine orange juice, soy sauce, Garlic Powder with Parsley and Seasoned Pepper; mix well. Remove ½ cup marinade for sauce. Pour ¾ cup marinade over meat. Seal bag or cover dish. Refrigerate at least 2 hours or overnight, turning occasionally. Heat grill; brush with vegetable oil. Remove meat from marinade, discard used marinade. Add meat to grill; cook 30 minutes or until internal meat temperature reaches 160°F, turning and brushing frequently with reserved marinade. Remove meat from grill; let stand about 10 minutes before thinly slicing. Meanwhile, in small saucepan, bring additional ½ cup marinade to a boil over medium-high heat; boil 1 minute. *Makes 6 servings*

**Serving Suggestion:** Serve sliced meat with extra heated marinade poured over top. Garnish with fresh herb sprigs. Serve with steamed vegetables.

# Cider Glazed Pork Roast

1 pork loin roast (4 to
  5 pounds), boned
  and tied
½ cup apple cider
¼ cup Dijon-style mustard
¼ cup vegetable oil
¼ cup soy sauce

Insert meat thermometer in center of thickest part of roast. Arrange medium-hot KINGSFORD® Briquets around drip pan. Place roast over drip pan. Cover grill and cook 2½ to 3 hours or until thermometer registers 160°F, adding more briquets as necessary. Combine apple cider, mustard, oil and soy sauce. Brush roast with cider mixture 3 or 4 times during last 30 minutes of cooking. *Makes 6 servings*

Barbecued Pork Loin

# Leg of Lamb with Wine Marinade

1½ cups red wine
1 onion, chopped
1 carrot, chopped
1 rib celery, chopped
2 tablespoons chopped fresh parsley
2 tablespoons olive oil
3 cloves garlic, minced
1 tablespoon dried thyme leaves
1 teaspoon salt
1 teaspoon black pepper
1½ pounds boneless leg of lamb, trimmed

Combine all ingredients except lamb in medium bowl. Place lamb in large resealable plastic food storage bag. Add wine mixture to bag. Close bag securely, turning to coat. Marinate in refrigerator 2 hours or overnight.

Prepare grill for indirect cooking. Drain lamb; reserve marinade.

Place lamb on grid directly over drip pan. Grill, covered, over medium heat about 45 minutes for medium or until internal temperature reaches 145°F when tested with meat thermometer inserted into thickest part of roast. Brush occasionally with reserved marinade. (Do not brush with marinade during last 5 minutes of grilling.)

Transfer roast to cutting board; cover with foil. Let stand 10 to 15 minutes before carving. Internal temperature will continue to rise 5°F to 10°F during stand time.

*Makes 4 servings*

# Garlic-Dijon Butterflied Lamb

½ cup red wine vinegar
¼ cup coarse-grained mustard
8 cloves garlic, minced
2 tablespoons minced fresh rosemary
1 tablespoon olive oil
½ teaspoon salt
½ teaspoon black pepper
4 pounds butterflied boneless leg of lamb

Combine vinegar, mustard, garlic, rosemary, oil, salt and pepper in large glass dish. Add lamb; turn to coat. Cover and refrigerate at least 8 hours or up to 2 days, turning occasionally. Remove lamb from marinade; discard marinade. Grill lamb on covered grill over medium KINGSFORD® Briquets about 25 to 30 minutes until thickest portion is medium-rare or to desired doneness, turning 4 times.

*Makes 8 to 10 servings*

Leg of Lamb with Wine Marinade

# Mediterranean Barbecued Lamb

1 leg of lamb (5 to 6 pounds),
  boned, butterflied and
  trimmed of fat
½ cup olive oil
½ cup *French's*® Napa Valley
  Style Dijon Mustard
¼ cup minced fresh parsley
¼ cup minced fresh marjoram
  or oregano leaves
¼ cup minced fresh thyme
  leaves
2 tablespoons *Frank's*®
  *RedHot*® Cayenne Pepper
  Sauce
2 tablespoons *French's*®
  Worcestershire Sauce
3 cloves garlic, minced
1 tablespoon fennel seeds,
  crushed
  Ratatouille Salsa (recipe
  follows)
  Pita bread, cut in half
  crosswise, or crusty
  French bread slices

Place lamb in large shallow glass dish. Combine oil, mustard, herbs, *Frank's RedHot* Sauce, Worcestershire, garlic and fennel seeds in small bowl; mix well. Rub herb paste onto both sides of lamb. Cover and marinate in refrigerator 1 hour.

Place lamb on grid, reserving herb paste. Grill over medium-high coals about 30 minutes or until lamb is slightly pink in center or cooked to desired doneness, turning and basting often with remaining herb paste. (Do not baste during last 10 minutes of cooking.) Let lamb stand 10 minutes. Cut into thin slices. Serve with Ratatouille Salsa in pita bread. *Makes 10 servings*

**Prep Time:** 15 minutes
**Marinate Time:** 1 hour
**Cook Time:** 30 minutes

## Ratatouille Salsa

1 medium eggplant
1 medium zucchini
1 medium yellow squash
2 tablespoons olive oil
2 tablespoons *French's*® Worcestershire Sauce
4 ripe plum tomatoes, chopped
½ cup oil-cured olives, pitted

Herbed Dressing
  ½ cup olive oil
  3 tablespoons minced fresh basil leaves
  3 tablespoons minced fresh parsley
  3 tablespoons lemon juice
  3 tablespoons *French's*® Worcestershire Sauce
  3 tablespoons *French's*® Napa Valley Style Dijon
    Mustard
  2 tablespoons capers, drained
  2 cloves garlic, minced
  ½ teaspoon salt

Cut eggplant, zucchini and squash lengthwise into ½-inch-thick slices. Combine 2 tablespoons oil and 2 tablespoons Worcestershire in small bowl; mix well. Brush vegetables with oil mixture. Place vegetables on grid. Grill over hot coals about 5 minutes or until vegetables are tender, turning often.

Cut vegetables into large chunks. Place in large bowl with tomatoes and olives. Combine Herbed Dressing ingredients in small bowl; mix well. Pour Herbed Dressing over vegetables; toss to coat evenly. Serve warm or refrigerate until chilled.          *Makes 6 side-dish servings*

**Prep Time:** 20 minutes
**Cook Time:** 5 minutes

## Lamb Brochettes with Plums

2 tablespoons minced fresh
    cilantro
2 tablespoons olive oil
1 tablespoon lemon juice
3 teaspoons cumin, divided
5 medium cloves garlic,
    minced
1½ teaspoons salt, divided
1 teaspoon curry powder
¼ teaspoon ground red
    pepper
¼ teaspoon black pepper
1½ pounds leg of lamb,
    trimmed, cut into 1-inch
    cubes
8 fresh California plums, cut
    into wedges

To prepare marinade, combine cilantro, olive oil, lemon juice, 2 teaspoons cumin, garlic, 1 teaspoon salt, curry powder, red pepper and black pepper in large nonreactive bowl. Add lamb and toss well. Cover with plastic wrap; marinate lamb in refrigerator for 2 hours or overnight. Drain lamb; reserve marinade.

Starting with lamb, alternately thread 4 lamb cubes and 4 plum wedges onto metal skewers.* Brush with reserved marinade; sprinkle with remaining 1 teaspoon cumin and remaining ½ teaspoon salt.

Prepare coals for grilling or preheat broiler and cook, turning skewers occasionally, until lamb is medium-rare, 8 to 10 minutes. Transfer the brochettes to a serving platter or individual plates.

*Makes 6 servings (2 kabobs each)*

*\*If using bamboo skewers, soak in cold water 10 to 15 minutes to prevent burning.*

*Favorite recipe from* **California Tree Fruit Agreement**

# Southwestern Lamb Chops
## with Charred Corn Relish

4 lamb shoulder or blade
  chops (about 8 ounces
  each), cut ¾ inch thick
  and well trimmed
¼ cup vegetable oil
¼ cup lime juice
1 tablespoon chili powder
2 cloves garlic, minced
1 teaspoon ground cumin
¼ teaspoon ground red
  pepper
  Charred Corn Relish (recipe
  follows)
2 tablespoons chopped fresh
  cilantro
  Hot pepper jelly (optional)

Place chops in large resealable plastic food storage bag. Combine oil, lime juice, chili powder, garlic, cumin and ground red pepper in small bowl; mix well. Reserve 3 tablespoons mixture for Charred Corn Relish; cover and refrigerate. Pour remaining mixture over chops. Close bag securely, turning to coat. Marinate in refrigerator at least 8 hours or overnight, turning occasionally.

Prepare grill for direct cooking. Prepare Charred Corn Relish; set aside.

Drain chops; discard marinade. Place chops on grid. Grill, covered, over medium heat 13 to 15 minutes for medium or until desired doneness is reached, turning halfway through grilling time. Sprinkle with cilantro. Serve with Charred Corn Relish and hot pepper jelly, if desired.                *Makes 4 servings*

### Charred Corn Relish

2 large or 3 small ears fresh corn, husked and silk
  removed
½ cup diced red bell pepper
¼ cup chopped fresh cilantro
3 tablespoons reserved lime juice mixture

Place corn on grid. Grill, covered, over medium heat 10 to 12 minutes or until charred, turning occasionally. Cool.

Cut kernels off each cob into large bowl; press cobs with knife to release remaining corn and liquid; discard cobs.

Add bell pepper, cilantro and reserved lime juice mixture to corn; mix well. Let stand at room temperature while grilling chops. Cover and refrigerate if preparing in advance. Bring to room temperature before serving.
*Makes about 1½ cups*

**Southwestern Lamb Chop
with Charred Corn Relish**

# Rosemary-Crusted Leg of Lamb

¼ cup Dijon mustard

2 large cloves garlic, minced

1 boneless butterflied leg of lamb (sirloin half, about 2½ pounds), well trimmed

3 tablespoons chopped fresh rosemary *or* 1 tablespoon dried rosemary, crushed

Fresh rosemary sprigs (optional)

Mint jelly (optional)

**1.** Prepare grill for direct cooking.

**2.** Combine mustard and garlic in small bowl; spread half of mixture over one side of lamb. Sprinkle with half of chopped rosemary; pat into mustard mixture. Turn lamb over; repeat with remaining mustard mixture and rosemary. Insert meat thermometer into center of thickest part of lamb.

**3.** Place lamb on grid. Grill lamb on covered grill over medium coals 35 to 40 minutes or until thermometer registers 160°F for medium or until desired doneness is reached, turning every 10 minutes.

**4.** Meanwhile, soak rosemary sprigs in water. Place rosemary sprigs directly on coals during last 10 minutes of grilling.

**5.** Transfer lamb to carving board; tent with foil. Let stand 10 minutes before carving into thin slices. Serve with mint jelly. *Makes 8 servings*

## FOOD FACT

*Use a meat thermometer to accurately determine the doneness of large cuts of meat cooked on covered grill.*

# Barbecued Leg of Lamb
## with Cucumber Yogurt Dip

1 (5- to 6-pound) leg of lamb,
    bone removed and
    butterflied
1 onion, thinly sliced
½ cup dry white wine
½ cup FILIPPO BERIO®
    Olive Oil
¼ cup lemon juice
2 cloves garlic, thinly sliced
1 tablespoon dried oregano
    leaves
1 bay leaf
    Salt and freshly ground
      black pepper
    Cucumber Yogurt Dip
      (recipe follows)
    Pita bread wedges
2 lemons, cut into wedges

Place lamb in large shallow glass dish. In medium bowl, combine onion, wine, olive oil, lemon juice, garlic, oregano and bay leaf. Pour marinade over lamb; turn to coat both sides. Cover; marinate in refrigerator 3 to 4 hours or overnight, turning occasionally. Remove lamb, reserving marinade.

Brush barbecue grid with olive oil. Grill lamb on covered grill over hot coals 20 minutes, basting occasionally with reserved marinade. Turn with tongs. Grill an additional 20 minutes or until desired doneness is reached. Transfer lamb to warm serving platter. Carve into thin slices; season to taste with salt and pepper. Serve with Cucumber Yogurt Dip, pita bread and lemon wedges.

*Makes 6 to 8 servings*

### Cucumber Yogurt Dip

2 (8-ounce) containers plain yogurt, without gelatin
1 large cucumber, peeled
2 tablespoons FILIPPO BERIO® Olive Oil
1 tablespoon white vinegar
2 cloves garlic, minced
    Salt and white pepper

Line large plastic colander or sieve with large piece of double thickness cheesecloth or large coffee filter. Place colander over deep bowl. Spoon yogurt into colander; cover with waxed paper. Refrigerate until liquid no longer drains from yogurt, about 24 hours. Remove yogurt; place in medium bowl. Discard liquid. Cut cucumber into quarters; remove seeds. Finely chop cucumber; drain on paper towels. Stir cucumber, olive oil, vinegar and garlic into yogurt. Season to taste with salt and pepper. Cover; refrigerate at least 1 hour before serving.

*Makes about 2 cups*

Barbecued Leg of Lamb
with Cucumber Yogurt Dip

# Middle Eastern Souvlaki

3 pounds lean boneless leg
  of lamb, cut into 1-inch
  cubes
1 cup fresh mint leaves,
  coarsely chopped
¾ cup prepared olive oil
  vinaigrette salad dressing
¼ cup *Frank's® RedHot®*
  Cayenne Pepper Sauce
¼ cup *French's®*
  Worcestershire Sauce
1 tablespoon fennel or anise
  seeds, crushed
3 cloves garlic, minced
  Pita bread, cut in half
  crosswise
  Chopped tomatoes
  Sliced onions

Yogurt Sauce
  ¾ cup plain nonfat yogurt
  ½ cup finely chopped
    cucumber
  1 tablespoon *Frank's® RedHot®*
    Cayenne Pepper Sauce
  1 clove garlic, minced

Place lamb cubes in large resealable plastic food storage bag. Combine mint, salad dressing, ¼ cup *Frank's RedHot* Sauce, Worcestershire, fennel seeds and garlic in small bowl; mix well. Pour over lamb. Seal bag and marinate in refrigerator 1 hour.

To prepare Yogurt Sauce, combine yogurt, cucumber, 1 tablespoon *RedHot* Sauce and garlic in small bowl; set aside.

Thread lamb onto metal skewers, reserving marinade. Place skewers on grid. Grill over hot coals 10 to 15 minutes or to desired doneness, turning and basting often with marinade. (Do not baste during last 5 minutes of cooking.) To serve, remove lamb from skewers. Place lamb in pita bread halves. Top with tomatoes, onions and some of the Yogurt Sauce. Garnish as desired.

*Makes 6 to 8 servings*

**Prep Time:** 20 minutes
**Marinate Time:** 1 hour
**Cook Time:** 15 minutes

## FOOD FACT

*Souvlaki is a Greek dish that consists of lamb chunks that have been marinated, then skewered and grilled.*

# Wine & Rosemary Lamb Skewers

1 cup dry red wine
¼ cup olive oil
3 cloves garlic, cut into slivers
1 tablespoon chopped fresh
    thyme *or* 1 teaspoon
    dried thyme leaves,
    crumbled
1 tablespoon chopped fresh
    rosemary *or* 1 teaspoon
    dried rosemary leaves,
    crumbled
2 pounds boneless lamb, cut
    into 1-inch cubes
    Salt and black pepper
4 or 5 sprigs fresh rosemary
    (optional)
    Grilled Bread (recipe follows)

Combine wine, oil, garlic, thyme and rosemary in a shallow glass dish or large heavy plastic food storage bag. Add lamb; cover dish or close bag. Marinate lamb in the refrigerator up to 12 hours, turning several times. Remove lamb from marinade; discard marinade. Thread lamb onto 6 long metal skewers. Season to taste with salt and pepper.

Oil hot grid to help prevent sticking. Grill lamb on covered grill over medium KINGSFORD® Briquets, 8 to 12 minutes, turning once or twice. Remove grill cover and throw rosemary onto coals the last 4 to 5 minutes of cooking, if desired. Move skewers to side of grid to keep warm while bread is toasting. Garnish, if desired.

*Makes 6 servings*

## Grilled Bread

¼ cup olive oil
2 tablespoons red wine vinegar
1 French bread baguette (about 12 inches long), sliced
    lengthwise, then cut into pieces
    Salt and freshly ground black pepper

Mix oil and vinegar in cup; brush over cut surfaces of bread. Season lightly with salt and pepper. Grill bread cut side down on uncovered grill over medium KINGSFORD® Briquets until lightly toasted.

*Makes 6 servings*

# Lamb Chops with Fresh Herbs

⅓ cup vegetable oil
⅓ cup red wine vinegar
2 tablespoons soy sauce
2 tablespoons sherry
1 tablespoon LAWRY'S®
    Seasoned Salt
1 teaspoon LAWRY'S® Garlic
    Powder with Parsley
1 tablespoon lemon juice
1 teaspoon chopped fresh
    oregano
1 teaspoon chopped fresh
    rosemary
1 teaspoon chopped fresh
    thyme
1 teaspoon chopped fresh
    marjoram
1 teaspoon dry mustard
½ teaspoon white pepper
8 lamb loin chops (about
    2 pounds), cut 1 inch
    thick

In large resealable plastic food storage bag, combine all ingredients except chops; mix well. Remove ½ cup marinade for basting. Add chops; seal bag. Marinate in refrigerator at least 1 hour. Remove chops from marinade; discard used marinade. Grill or broil chops until desired doneness, about 8 minutes, turning once and basting often with remaining ½ cup marinade. *Do not baste during last 5 minutes of cooking.* Discard any remaining marinade.

*Makes 4 to 6 servings*

**Serving Suggestion:** Serve with mashed potatoes and fresh green beans.

**Hint:** Substitute ¼ to ½ teaspoon dried herbs for each teaspoon of fresh herbs.

## GRILLING TIP

*To infuse the most flavor of a marinade, allow ¼ cup to ½ cup of marinade for each 1 to 2 pounds of meat and occasionally turn foods over during marinating.*

Lamb Chops with Fresh Herbs

# Mint Marinated Racks of Lamb

2 whole racks (6 ribs each)
    loin lamb chops (about
    3 pounds), well trimmed
1 cup dry red wine
½ cup chopped fresh mint
    leaves
3 cloves garlic, minced
¼ cup Dijon mustard
2 tablespoons chopped fresh
    mint leaves *or*
    2 teaspoons dried mint
    leaves, crushed
⅔ cup dry bread crumbs

Place lamb in large resealable plastic food storage bag. Combine wine, ½ cup mint and garlic in small bowl. Pour over chops. Seal bag tightly; turn to coat. Marinate in refrigerator at least 2 hours or up to 4 hours, turning occasionally.

Prepare grill. Drain lamb, discarding marinade. Pat lamb dry with paper towels. Place lamb in shallow glass dish or on cutting board. Combine mustard and 2 tablespoons mint in small bowl; spread over meaty side of lamb. Pat bread crumbs evenly over mustard mixture. Place lamb, crumb side down, on grid. Grill, covered, over medium coals 10 minutes. Carefully turn; continue to grill, covered, 20 to 22 minutes for medium (160°F) or to desired doneness. Place lamb on carving board. Slice between ribs into individual chops. *Makes 4 servings*

# Lemon Pepper Lamb Kabobs

1½ cups LAWRY'S® Lemon
    Pepper Marinade with
    Lemon Juice, divided
1½ pounds boneless lamb loin
    roast, cut into 1½-inch
    cubes
12 mushrooms
2 green bell peppers, cut into
    chunks
2 onions, cut into wedges
    Skewers

In large resealable plastic food storage bag, combine 1 cup Lemon Pepper Marinade and lamb; seal bag. Marinate in refrigerator at least 30 minutes. Remove lamb from marinade; discard used marinade. Alternately thread lamb and vegetables onto skewers. Grill or broil skewers until desired doneness, about 8 to 10 minutes, turning once and basting often with additional ½ cup Lemon Pepper Marinade. *Do not baste during last 5 minutes of cooking.* Discard any remaining marinade.

*Makes 6 servings*

**Serving Suggestion:** Serve over a bed of couscous with a Greek salad.

**Hint:** If using wooden skewers, soak in water 20 to 30 minutes before using to prevent scorching.

**Mint Marinated Racks of Lamb**

# PATIO
## POULTRY

## Grilled Lemon Chicken Dijon

⅓ cup HOLLAND HOUSE®
　　White with Lemon
　　Cooking Wine
⅓ cup olive oil
2 tablespoons Dijon mustard
1 teaspoon dried thyme leaves
2 whole chicken breasts,
　　skinned, boned and
　　halved

In shallow baking dish combine cooking wine, oil, mustard and thyme. Add chicken and turn to coat. Cover; marinate in refrigerator for 1 to 2 hours.

Prepare grill for direct cooking. Drain chicken, reserving marinade. Grill chicken over medium coals 12 to 16 minutes or until cooked through, turning once and basting with marinade.*　　　　*Makes 4 servings*

*Do not baste during last 5 minutes of grilling.

## Texas Spice Rub

1 tablespoon paprika
1 teaspoon seasoned salt
½ teaspoon brown sugar
¼ teaspoon granulated garlic
⅛ teaspoon cayenne pepper
2 teaspoons water
4 boneless skinless chicken
　　breasts

Combine paprika, salt, sugar, garlic and cayenne. Add water to make paste. Rub on chicken to coat evenly. Grill chicken on covered grill over medium-hot KINGSFORD® Briquets 8 to 10 minutes, turning once, until just cooked through.　　　　*Makes 4 servings*

**Grilled Lemon Chicken Dijon**

# Chicken Teriyaki Kabobs

4 boneless skinless chicken
    breasts (about 1 pound),
    cut into 1-inch cubes
2 medium zucchini, cut into
    ½-inch-thick slices
1 medium-sized green bell
    pepper, cut into 1-inch
    squares
1 small red onion, cut into
    ½-inch cubes
1 cup LAWRY'S® Teriyaki
    Marinade with Pineapple
    Juice, divided
½ teaspoon LAWRY'S®
    Seasoned Pepper
¼ teaspoon LAWRY'S® Garlic
    Powder with Parsley
Skewers

Place chicken and vegetables on skewers, alternating chicken with vegetables. Place in large shallow baking dish. Pour ¾ cup Teriyaki Marinade with Pineapple Juice over kabobs. Turn kabobs over to coat all sides. Cover dish. Refrigerate at least 30 minutes, turning once. Remove skewers from marinade; discard marinade. Sprinkle skewers with Seasoned Pepper and Garlic Powder with Parsley. Grill or broil skewers 10 to 15 minutes or until chicken is no longer pink in center and juices run clear when cut, turning and basting often with remaining ¼ cup Teriyaki Marinade with Pineapple Juice. Do not baste during last 5 minutes of cooking.

*Makes 6 servings*

**Serving Suggestion:** Great served with steamed rice or baked potatoes.

**Hint:** If using wooden skewers, soak in water 20 to 30 before using to prevent scorching.

# Ranch-Style Chicken and Pasta

2 BUTTERBALL® Boneless
    Skinless Chicken Breasts
½ cup prepared ranch salad
    dressing, divided
1 cup uncooked rotini pasta
2 cups broccoli florets
¼ cup diced red bell pepper
2 tablespoons chopped green
    onion

Combine chicken breasts and ¼ cup ranch salad dressing in large bowl; marinate in refrigerator 15 minutes. Cook pasta 8 minutes; add broccoli during last 3 minutes of cooking. Drain pasta and broccoli; set aside. Remove chicken from marinade; discard marinade. Grill chicken 4 to 5 minutes on each side or until no longer pink in center. Combine cooked pasta, broccoli, bell pepper and onion in large bowl. Toss with remaining ¼ cup ranch salad dressing. Serve chicken breasts with ranch-style pasta.

*Makes 2 servings*

**Prep Time:** 30 minutes

Chicken Teriyaki Kabobs

# Asian Grill

4 TYSON® Individually Fresh Frozen® Boneless, Skinless Chicken Breasts
¼ cup orange juice
¼ cup teriyaki sauce
½ teaspoon crushed red pepper flakes
2 red bell peppers, cut into wedges
2 small zucchini, sliced diagonally
4 ounces button or shiitake mushroom caps
1 box UNCLE BEN'S® COUNTRY INN® Rice Pilaf

**PREP:** CLEAN: Wash hands. Remove protective ice glaze from frozen chicken by holding under cool running water 1 to 2 minutes. CLEAN: Wash hands. In small bowl, prepare marinade by combining orange juice, teriyaki sauce and red pepper flakes. Reserve 3 tablespoons marinade; refrigerate until ready to use. Brush remaining marinade over chicken, bell peppers, zucchini and mushrooms.

**COOK:** Grill chicken 20 to 25 minutes or until internal juices of chicken run clear, turning once and brushing occasionally with marinade. (Or insert instant-read meat thermometer in thickest part of chicken. Temperature should read 170°F.) Grill bell peppers, zucchini and mushrooms 5 minutes or until crisp-tender, turning once and brushing occasionally with marinade. Meanwhile, prepare rice according to package directions. Stir in reserved 3 tablespoons marinade.

**SERVE:** Serve grilled chicken and vegetables over rice.

**CHILL:** Refrigerate leftovers immediately.

*Makes 4 servings*

**Prep Time:** 10 minutes
**Cook Time:** 25 minutes

# Barbecued Chicken

¼ cup CRISCO® Oil*
1 medium onion, peeled and chopped
¾ cup ketchup
⅓ cup lemon juice or vinegar
3 tablespoons granulated sugar
3 tablespoons prepared mustard
3 tablespoons Worcestershire sauce
½ teaspoon salt
½ teaspoon freshly ground black pepper
3 pounds bone-in chicken pieces *or* 4 boneless, skinless chicken breasts, flattened to even thickness

*Use your favorite Crisco Oil product.

**1.** Heat oil in small saucepan on medium heat. Add onion. Cook 5 minutes, or until onions are soft. Add ketchup, lemon juice, sugar, mustard, Worcestershire sauce, salt and pepper. Simmer 20 minutes, stirring occasionally.

**2.** Heat grill or broiler while sauce is simmering.

**3.** Rinse chicken. Pat dry. Place on grill over medium heat or about 8 inches from broiler. For whole bone-in pieces: Baste with sauce after about 20 minutes. Turn chicken. Baste again after 15 minutes. Cook 5 minutes longer or until chicken is no longer pink in center, turning and basting as needed. For boneless skinless breasts, baste with sauce immediately. Turn after 5 minutes. Baste again. Grill 3 to 5 minutes, or until chicken is no longer pink in center.**

*Makes 4 servings*

**Cooking times can vary greatly depending on size of chicken pieces and intensity of heat.

**Prep Time:** 25 minutes
**Total Time:** 1 hour

# Herb Garlic Grilled Chicken

¼ cup chopped parsley
1½ tablespoons minced garlic
4 teaspoons grated lemon peel
1 tablespoon chopped fresh mint
1 chicken (2½ to 3 pounds), quartered

Combine parsley, garlic, lemon peel and mint. Loosen skin from breast and thigh portions of chicken quarters by running fingers between skin and meat. Rub some of seasoning mixture evenly over meat under skin, replace skin and rub remaining seasonings over outside of chicken to cover evenly. Arrange medium-hot KINGSFORD® Briquets on one side of covered grill. Place chicken on grid opposite coals. Cover grill and cook chicken 45 to 55 minutes, turning once or twice. Chicken is done when juices run clear. *Makes 4 servings*

# Herbed Butter Chicken

3 tablespoons minced fresh
   basil
2 teaspoons minced fresh
   oregano
2 teaspoons minced fresh
   rosemary
3 tablespoons minced shallots
   or green onion
2 tablespoons butter,
   softened
3 cloves garlic, minced
2 teaspoons grated lemon
   peel
½ teaspoon salt
¼ teaspoon black pepper
4 chicken legs with thighs *or*
   1 whole chicken (about
   3½ pounds), quartered
1 tablespoon olive oil
   Fresh oregano sprigs
   Lemon peel strips

Combine herbs, shallots, butter, garlic, lemon peel, salt and pepper in medium bowl. Loosen chicken skin by gently pushing fingers between the skin and chicken, keeping skin intact. Gently rub herb mixture under skin of chicken, forcing it into the leg section; secure skin with wooden picks. (Soak wooden picks in hot water 15 minutes to prevent burning.) Cover and refrigerate chicken at least ½ hour. Brush chicken with oil. Arrange medium KINGSFORD® Briquets on each side of rectangular metal or foil drip pan. Grill chicken, skin side down, in center of grid on covered grill 20 minutes. Turn chicken and cook 20 to 25 minutes or until juices run clear. Garnish with oregano sprigs and lemon strips.

*Makes 4 servings*

## GRILLING TIP

*Indirect cooking keeps the grill clean and minimizes flare-ups. When cooking with charcoal, place the food on the grid over a metal or disposable foil drip pan with the coals banked on both sides of the pan. When cooking on a gas grill, turn "off" the center burner and turn "on" the two side burners to medium. Place a metal or disposable drip pan directly on the lava rocks in the center of the grill. Place the food on the grid directly over the drip pan.*

**Herbed Butter Chicken**

# Grilled Chile Chicken Quesadillas

2 tablespoons lime juice
3 cloves garlic, minced
1 tablespoon ground cumin
1 tablespoon chili powder
1 tablespoon vegetable oil
1 jalapeño pepper, minced
1 teaspoon salt
6 boneless skinless chicken
   thighs
3 poblano peppers, cut in
   half, stemmed, seeded
2 avocados, peeled and sliced
3 cups (12 ounces) shredded
   Monterey Jack cheese
12 (8-inch) flour tortillas
1½ cups fresh salsa
   Red chiles
   Fresh cilantro sprigs

Combine lime juice, garlic, cumin, chili powder, oil, jalapeño pepper and salt in small bowl; coat chicken with paste. Cover and refrigerate chicken at least 15 minutes. Grill chicken on covered grill over medium-hot KINGSFORD® Briquets 4 minutes per side until no longer pink in center. Grill poblano peppers, skin side down, 8 minutes until skins are charred. Place peppers in large resealable plastic food storage bag; seal. Let stand 5 minutes; remove skin. Cut chicken and peppers into strips. Arrange chicken, peppers, avocados and cheese on half of each tortilla. Drizzle with 2 tablespoons salsa. Fold other half of tortilla over filling. Grill quesadillas on covered grill over medium briquets 30 seconds to 1 minute per side until cheese is melted. Garnish with chiles and cilantro sprigs.  *Makes 12 quesadillas*

# Patio Chicken Kabobs

1 cup HUNT'S® Ketchup
¼ cup LA CHOY® Lite Soy
   Sauce
¼ cup firmly packed brown
   sugar
1 teaspoon crushed red
   pepper flakes
4 ready-to-cook chicken
   kabobs*

*These kabobs are available in the meat department of large supermarkets, or make your own by placing cubed chicken pieces with vegetables on skewers.*

**1.** In small bowl combine *all* ingredients *except* kabobs; blend well.

**2.** Grill kabobs over medium-hot heat, about 10 minutes.

**3.** Baste chicken with marinade; continue cooking and basting for 10 minutes longer or until chicken is no longer pink in center.  *Makes 4 kabobs*

Grilled Chile Chicken Quesadillas

# Chicken with Mediterranean Salsa

¼ cup olive oil

3 tablespoons lemon juice

4 to 6 boneless skinless
chicken breasts

Salt and black pepper

Rosemary sprigs (optional)

Mediterranean Salsa (recipe
follows)

Additional rosemary sprigs
for garnish

Combine olive oil and lemon juice in a shallow glass dish; add chicken. Turn chicken breasts to lightly coat with mixture; let stand 10 to 15 minutes. Remove chicken from dish and wipe off excess oil; season with salt and pepper.

Oil hot grid to help prevent sticking. Place chicken on grid and place a sprig of rosemary on each chicken breast. Grill chicken on a covered grill over medium KINGSFORD® Briquets 10 to 15 minutes until chicken is no longer pink in center, turning once or twice. Serve with Mediterranean Salsa. Garnish, if desired.

*Makes 4 to 6 servings*

## Mediterranean Salsa

2 tablespoons olive oil

2 tablespoons white wine vinegar

1 clove garlic, minced

2 tablespoons finely chopped fresh basil *or* 1 teaspoon
dried basil leaves, crushed

1 tablespoon finely chopped fresh rosemary *or*
1 teaspoon dried rosemary, crushed

1 teaspoon sugar

¼ teaspoon black pepper

10 to 15 kalamata olives,* seeded and coarsely chopped
*or* ⅓ cup coarsely chopped whole pitted ripe olives

½ cup chopped seeded cucumber

¼ cup finely chopped red onion

1 cup chopped seeded tomatoes (about ½ pound)

⅓ cup crumbled feta cheese

*Kalamata olives are brine-cured Greek-style olives. They are available in large supermarkets.*

Combine oil, vinegar, garlic, basil, rosemary, sugar and pepper in a medium bowl. Add olives, cucumber and onion; toss to coat. Cover and refrigerate until ready to serve. Just before serving, gently stir in tomatoes and feta cheese.

*Makes about 2 cups*

**Chicken with Mediterranean Salsa**

# Grilled Chicken with Asian Pesto

4 boneless skinless chicken
    breasts *or* 8 boneless
    skinless thighs *or*
    combination of both
Olive or vegetable oil
Salt and black pepper
Asian Pesto (recipe follows)
Lime wedges

Place chicken between two pieces of waxed paper; pound to ⅜-inch thickness. Brush chicken with oil; season to taste with salt and pepper. Spread about ½ tablespoon Asian Pesto on both sides of each breast or thigh.

Oil hot grid to help prevent sticking. Grill chicken on uncovered grill over medium KINGSFORD® Briquets 6 to 8 minutes until chicken is cooked through, turning once. Serve with additional Asian Pesto and lime wedges.

*Makes 4 servings*

## Asian Pesto

1 cup packed fresh basil
1 cup packed fresh cilantro
1 cup packed fresh mint leaves
¼ cup olive or vegetable oil
2 cloves garlic, chopped
2½ to 3½ tablespoons lime juice
1 tablespoon sugar
1 teaspoon salt
1 teaspoon black pepper

Combine all ingredients in a blender or food processor; process until smooth.

*Makes about ¾ cup*

**Note:** The Asian Pesto recipe makes enough for 6 servings. Leftovers can be saved and used as a spread for sandwiches.

# Magic Carpet Kabobs

1 cup orange juice
½ cup bottled mango chutney, divided
2 tablespoons lemon juice
1 tablespoon grated fresh ginger
2 cloves garlic, pressed
2 teaspoons ground cumin
1 teaspoon grated lemon peel
1 teaspoon grated orange peel
1 teaspoon red pepper flakes
¼ teaspoon salt
4 boneless skinless chicken thighs, cut into chunks
1 medium yellow onion, cut into chunks
4 whole pita bread rounds
½ cup plain low-fat yogurt
¾ cup chopped cucumber
Orange peel strips

Combine orange juice, ¼ cup chutney, lemon juice, ginger, garlic, cumin, grated peels, pepper flakes and salt, blending well; reserve ¼ cup marinade for basting. Combine remaining marinade and chicken in large resealable plastic food storage bag. Seal bag; turn to coat evenly. Marinate in refrigerator overnight. Thread chicken alternately with onion onto 4 long wooden skewers, dividing equally. (Soak wooden skewers in hot water 30 minutes to prevent burning.) Lightly oil grid to prevent sticking. Grill kabobs over medium-hot KINGSFORD® Briquets 10 to 12 minutes until chicken is no longer pink, turning once and basting with reserved marinade. Grill pita breads 1 or 2 minutes until warm. Combine yogurt and remaining ¼ cup chutney. Spoon yogurt mixture down centers of pitas; top with cucumber, dividing equally. Top each with kabob; remove skewer. Garnish with orange peel strips.

*Makes 4 servings*

# Orange-Mint Chicken

1 broiler-fryer chicken (2½ to 3 pounds), cut into halves
2 teaspoons LAWRY'S® Seasoned Salt
½ cup orange marmalade
3 tablespoons butter
3 tablespoons honey
1 teaspoon crushed dried mint leaves
Wedged orange (garnish)
Cilantro (garnish)

Sprinkle Seasoned Salt over chicken. Let stand 10 to 15 minutes. In medium saucepan, combine marmalade, butter, honey and mint. Heat 1 to 2 minutes, stirring frequently. Grill or broil chicken 35 to 45 minutes or until no longer pink in center and juices run clear when cut, turning once and basting often with marmalade mixture. *Do not baste during last 5 minutes of cooking.* Discard remaining marmalade mixture.    *Makes 4 to 6 servings*

**Serving Suggestion:** Serve with wild rice pilaf and garnish with orange wedges and fresh mint, if desired.

# Grilled Chicken Tostados

1 pound boneless skinless
chicken breasts
1 teaspoon ground cumin
¼ cup orange juice
¼ cup plus 2 tablespoons
salsa, divided
1 tablespoon plus 2 teaspoons
vegetable oil, divided
2 cloves garlic, minced
8 green onions
1 can (16 ounces) refried
beans
4 (10-inch) *or* 8 (6- to 7-inch)
flour tortillas
2 cups chopped romaine
lettuce
1½ cups (6 ounces) shredded
Monterey Jack cheese
with jalapeño peppers
1 ripe medium avocado, diced
(optional)
1 medium tomato, seeded
and diced (optional)
Chopped fresh cilantro and
sour cream (optional)

Place chicken in single layer in shallow glass dish; sprinkle with cumin. Combine orange juice, ¼ cup salsa, 1 tablespoon oil and garlic in small bowl; pour over chicken. Cover; marinate in refrigerator at least 2 hours or up to 8 hours, stirring mixture occasionally.

Prepare grill for direct cooking.

Drain chicken; reserve marinade. Brush green onions with remaining 2 teaspoons oil. Place chicken and green onions on grid. Grill, covered, over medium-high heat 5 minutes. Brush tops of chicken with half of reserved marinade; turn and brush with remaining marinade. Turn onions. Continue to grill, covered, 5 minutes or until chicken is no longer pink in center and onions are tender. (If onions are browning too quickly, remove before chicken is done.)

Meanwhile, combine beans and remaining 2 tablespoons salsa in small saucepan; cook, stirring occasionally, over medium heat until hot.

Place tortillas in single layer on grid. Grill, uncovered, 1 to 2 minutes per side or until golden brown. (If tortillas puff up, pierce with tip of knife or flatten by pressing with spatula.)

Transfer chicken and onions to cutting board. Slice chicken crosswise into ½-inch strips. Cut onions crosswise into 1-inch-long pieces. Spread tortillas with bean mixture; top with lettuce, chicken, onions, cheese, avocado and tomato, if desired. Sprinkle with cilantro and serve with sour cream, if desired. *Makes 4 servings*

Grilled Chicken Tostada

# Lemon-Garlic Roasted Chicken

1 chicken (3½ to 4 pounds)
    Salt and black pepper
2 tablespoons butter or
    margarine, softened
2 lemons, cut into halves
4 to 6 cloves garlic, peeled
    and left whole
5 to 6 sprigs fresh rosemary
    Garlic Sauce (page 248)
    Additional rosemary sprigs
    and lemon wedges

Rinse chicken; pat dry with paper towels. Season with salt and pepper, then rub skin with butter. Place lemons, garlic and rosemary in cavity of chicken. Tuck wings under back and tie legs together with cotton string.

Arrange medium-low KINGSFORD® Briquets on each side of rectangular metal or foil drip pan. Pour in hot tap water to fill pan half full. Place chicken, breast side up, on grid directly above drip pan. Grill chicken on covered grill about 1 hour or until meat thermometer inserted in thigh registers 175° to 180°F or until joints move easily and juices run clear when chicken is pierced. Add few briquets to both sides of fire, if necessary, to maintain constant temperature.

While chicken is cooking, prepare Garlic Sauce. When chicken is done, carefully lift from grill to wide shallow bowl so that juices from cavity run into bowl. Transfer juices to small saucepan; bring to a boil. Boil juices 2 minutes; transfer to small bowl or gravy boat. Carve chicken; serve with Garlic Sauce and cooking juices. Garnish with rosemary sprigs and lemon wedges.

*Makes 4 servings*

**continued on page 248**

Lemon-Garlic Roasted Chicken

*Lemon-Garlic Roasted Chicken, continued*

### Garlic Sauce

2 tablespoons olive oil
1 large head of garlic, cloves separated and peeled
2 (1-inch-wide) strips lemon peel
1 can (14½ ounces) reduced-sodium chicken broth
½ cup water
1 sprig *each* sage and oregano *or* 2 to 3 sprigs parsley
¼ cup butter, softened

Heat oil in a saucepan; add garlic cloves and lemon peel. Sauté over medium-low heat, stirring frequently, until garlic just starts to brown in a few spots. Add broth, water and herbs; simmer to reduce mixture by about half. Discard herb sprigs and lemon peel. Transfer broth mixture to a blender or food processor; process until smooth. Return garlic purée to the saucepan and whisk in butter over very low heat until smooth. Sauce can be rewarmed before serving.          *Makes about 1 cup*

**Tip:** The chicken is delicious served simply with its own juices, but the Garlic Sauce is so good you may want to double the recipe.

## Grilled Chicken Breasts with Tropical Salsa

1 package BUTTERBALL®
   Skinless Boneless Chicken
   Breast Fillets
1 cup cubed mango
1 kiwi, diced
2 green onions, chopped
2 tablespoons chopped fresh
   cilantro
1 tablespoon fresh lime juice
½ teaspoon red pepper flakes

Grill chicken fillets 4 to 5 minutes on each side or until internal temperature reaches 170°F and no longer pink in center. Combine mango, kiwi, onions, cilantro, lime juice and red pepper flakes in medium bowl. Serve with chicken.          *Makes 4 servings*

**Prep Time:** 20 minutes

# Sweet and Spicy Chicken Barbecue

1½ cups DOLE® Pineapple
    Orange Juice
1 cup orange marmalade
⅔ cup teriyaki sauce
½ cup firmly packed brown
    sugar
½ teaspoon ground cloves
½ teaspoon ground ginger
4 broiler-fryer chickens,
    halved or quartered
    (about 2 pounds each)
    Salt and pepper
1 can (20 ounces) DOLE®
    Pineapple Slices, drained
4 teaspoons cornstarch

• In saucepan, combine juice, marmalade, teriyaki sauce, brown sugar, cloves and ginger. Heat over medium heat until sugar dissolves; let cool. Sprinkle chicken with salt and pepper. Place chicken in glass baking dish. Pour juice mixture over chicken; turn to coat all sides. Marinate, covered, 2 hours in refrigerator, turning often.

• Preheat oven to 350°F. Light charcoal grill. Drain chicken; reserve marinade. Bake chicken 20 minutes. Arrange chicken on lightly greased grill, 4 to 6 inches above glowing coals. Grill, turning and basting often with reserved marinade, 20 to 25 minutes or until meat near bone is no longer pink. Grill pineapple slices 3 minutes or until heated through.

• In small saucepan, dissolve cornstarch in remaining marinade. Cook over medium heat until sauce boils (at least 1 minute) and thickens. Spoon over chicken. Serve chicken with pineapple. *Makes 8 servings*

# Fresco Marinated Chicken

1 envelope LIPTON® RECIPE
    SECRETS® Savory Herb
    with Garlic Soup Mix*
⅓ cup water
¼ cup BERTOLLI® Olive Oil
1 teaspoon lemon juice or
    vinegar
4 boneless skinless chicken
    breasts (about
    1¼ pounds)

*Also terrific with LIPTON® RECIPE
SECRETS® Golden Onion Soup Mix.*

**1.** For marinade, blend all ingredients except chicken.

**2.** In shallow baking dish or plastic food storage bag, pour ½ cup of the marinade over chicken. Cover, or close bag, and marinate in refrigerator, turning occasionally, up to 3 hours. Refrigerate remaining marinade.

**3.** Remove chicken, discarding marinade. Grill or broil chicken, turning once and brushing with refrigerated marinade until chicken is thoroughly cooked in center. *Makes 4 servings*

# Rosemary's Chicken

4 large boneless skinless
    chicken breasts (about
    1½ pounds)
¼ cup *French's*® Classic Yellow®
    Mustard
¼ cup frozen orange juice
    concentrate, undiluted
2 tablespoons cider vinegar
2 teaspoons dried rosemary
    leaves, crushed
4 strips thick sliced bacon

Place chicken in large resealable plastic food storage bag or glass bowl. To prepare marinade, combine mustard, orange juice concentrate, vinegar and rosemary in small bowl. Pour over chicken. Seal bag or cover bowl and marinate in refrigerator 30 minutes. Wrap 1 strip bacon around each piece of chicken; secure with toothpicks.*

Place chicken on grid, reserving marinade. Grill over medium coals 25 minutes or until chicken is no longer pink in center, turning and basting often with marinade. (Do not baste during last 10 minutes of cooking.) Remove toothpicks before serving. Garnish as desired.

*Makes 4 servings*

*\*Soak toothpicks in water 20 minutes to prevent burning.*

**Prep Time:** 15 minutes
**Marinate Time:** 30 minutes
**Cook Time:** 25 minutes

## GRILLING TIP

*Always wear heavy-duty fireproof mitts to protect your hands from the hot grid, flare-ups and hot food.*

# Pesto Chicken & Pepper Wraps

⅔ cup refrigerated pesto sauce
   or frozen pesto sauce,
   thawed and divided
3 tablespoons red wine
   vinegar
¼ teaspoon salt
¼ teaspoon black pepper
1¼ pounds skinless boneless
   chicken thighs or breasts
2 red bell peppers, cut in half,
   stemmed and seeded
5 (8-inch) flour tortillas
5 thin slices (3-inch rounds)
   fresh-pack mozzarella
   cheese*
5 leaves Boston or red leaf
   lettuce
   Orange slices
   Red and green chiles
   Fresh basil sprigs

*Packaged sliced whole milk or part-skim
mozzarella cheese can be substituted for fresh-
pack mozzarella cheese.

Combine ¼ cup pesto, vinegar, salt and black pepper in medium bowl. Add chicken; toss to coat. Cover and refrigerate at least 30 minutes. Remove chicken from marinade; discard marinade. Grill chicken over medium-hot KINGSFORD® Briquets about 4 minutes per side until chicken is no longer pink in center, turning once. Grill bell peppers, skin sides down, about 8 minutes until skin is charred. Place bell peppers in large resealable plastic food storage bag; seal. Let stand 5 minutes; remove skin. Cut chicken and bell peppers into thin strips. Spread about 1 tablespoon of remaining pesto down center of each tortilla; top with chicken, bell peppers, cheese and lettuce. Roll tortillas to enclose filling. Garnish with orange slices, chiles and basil sprigs.      *Makes 5 wraps*

## GRILLING TIP

*Do not use water to quench flare-ups on a gas grill. Simply close the hood and turn down the heat until the flames subside.*

Pesto Chicken & Pepper Wrap

# Classic Grilled Chicken

1 whole frying chicken*
    (3½ pounds), quartered
¼ cup lemon juice
¼ cup olive oil
2 tablespoons soy sauce
2 large cloves garlic, minced
½ teaspoon sugar
½ teaspoon ground cumin
¼ teaspoon black pepper

*Substitute 3½ pounds chicken parts for whole chicken, if desired. Grill legs and thighs about 35 minutes and breast halves about 25 minutes or until chicken is no longer pink in center, turning once.

Rinse chicken under cold running water; pat dry with paper towels. Arrange chicken in 13×9×2-inch glass baking dish. Combine remaining ingredients in small bowl; pour half of mixture over chicken. Cover and refrigerate chicken at least 1 hour or overnight. Cover and reserve remaining mixture in refrigerator to use for basting. Remove chicken from marinade; discard marinade. Arrange medium KINGSFORD® Briquets on each side of large rectangular metal or foil drip pan. Pour hot tap water into drip pan until half full. Place chicken on grid directly above drip pan. Grill chicken, skin side down, on covered grill 25 minutes. Baste with reserved marinade. Turn chicken; cook 20 to 25 minutes or until juices run clear and chicken is no longer pink in center.

*Makes 6 servings*

# Apricot-Glazed Chicken

½ cup WISH-BONE® Italian
    Dressing*
2 teaspoons ground ginger
    (optional)
1 chicken, cut into serving
    pieces (2½ to 3 pounds)
¼ cup apricot or peach
    preserves

*Also terrific with WISH-BONE® Robusto Italian Dressing.

In large, shallow nonaluminum baking dish or plastic bag, blend Italian dressing and ginger. Add chicken; turn to coat. Cover, or close bag, and marinate in refrigerator, turning occasionally, 3 hours or overnight. Remove chicken, reserving ¼ cup marinade.

In small saucepan, bring reserved marinade to a boil and continue boiling 1 minute. Remove from heat and stir in preserves until melted; set aside.

Grill or broil chicken until chicken is thoroughly cooked near the bone, brushing with preserve mixture during last 5 minutes of cooking.

*Makes 4 servings*

# Southwest Chicken

2 tablespoons olive oil
1 clove garlic, pressed
1 teaspoon chili powder
1 teaspoon ground cumin
1 teaspoon dried oregano
   leaves
½ teaspoon salt
1 pound boneless skinless
   chicken breasts or thighs

Combine oil, garlic, chili powder, cumin, oregano and salt; brush over both sides of chicken to coat. Grill chicken over medium-hot KINGSFORD® Briquets 8 to 10 minutes or until chicken is no longer pink, turning once. Serve immediately or use in Build a Burrito, Taco Salad or other favorite recipes. *Makes 4 servings*

**Note:** Southwest Chicken can be grilled ahead and refrigerated for several days or frozen for longer storage.

**Build a Burrito:** Top warm large flour tortillas with strips of Southwest Chicken and your choice of drained canned black beans, cooked brown or white rice, shredded cheese, salsa verde, shredded lettuce, sliced black olives and chopped cilantro. Fold in sides and roll to enclose filling. Heat in microwave oven at HIGH until heated through. (Or, wrap in foil and heat in preheated 350°F oven.)

**Taco Salad:** For a quick one-dish meal, layer strips of Southwest Chicken with tomato wedges, blue or traditional corn tortilla chips, sliced black olives, shredded romaine or iceberg lettuce, shredded cheese and avocado slices. Serve with salsa, sour cream, guacamole or a favorite dressing.

## FOOD FACT

*Boneless skinless chicken thighs are great for the grill. They contain a little more fat than white meat and will stay moist and tender. Place on oiled grill and cook, turning once, about 8 to 10 minutes per side.*

# Jamaican Jerk Chicken

⅔ cup chopped green onions

3 tablespoons minced fresh
    thyme leaves *or*
      1 tablespoon dried thyme
      leaves

3 tablespoons peanut oil

3 tablespoons soy sauce

2 tablespoons minced fresh
    ginger

1 tablespoon minced garlic

1 habañero pepper, seeded
    and minced *or*
      1 tablespoon minced,
      seeded serrano pepper

1 bay leaf

1 teaspoon freshly ground
    black pepper

1 teaspoon whole coriander

½ teaspoon ground nutmeg

½ teaspoon ground allspice

4 boneless skinless chicken
    breasts (4 to 6 ounces
    each)

To prepare marinade, combine all ingredients except chicken in small bowl; mix well. Place chicken in glass dish. Coat chicken with marinade. Marinate in refrigerator, several hours or overnight. Remove chicken from marinade; discard marinade. Grill chicken on covered grill over medium KINGSFORD® Briquets 4 to 6 minutes per side or until juices run clear.

*Makes 4 servings*

# Mexican Chicken with Spicy Bacon

2 serrano chili peppers
2 cloves garlic
   Dash ground cloves
   Dash ground cinnamon
4 slices bacon, partially
   cooked
1 whole roasting chicken
   (3½ to 4 pounds)
   Cherry tomatoes and
   serrano chili peppers for
   garnish (optional)

Remove stems from peppers. Slit open; remove seeds and ribs. Finely chop peppers and garlic. Place in small bowl. Stir in cloves and cinnamon. Cut bacon into 1-inch pieces.

Lift skin layer of chicken at neck cavity. Insert hand, lifting skin from meat along breast, thigh and drumstick. Using small metal spatula, spread pepper mixture evenly over meat, under skin. Place layer of bacon pieces over pepper mixture. Skewer neck skin to back. Tie legs securely to tail and twist wing tips under back of chicken. Insert meat thermometer in center of thigh muscle, not touching bone.

Arrange medium-hot KINGSFORD® Briquets around drip pan. Place chicken, breast side up, over drip pan. Cover grill and cook about 1 hour or until meat thermometer inserted in thickest part registers 180°F. Garnish with cherry tomatoes and serrano chili peppers, if desired. *Makes 4 servings*

# Tequila Sunrise Chicken

4 boneless skinless chicken
   breasts
⅓ cup lime juice
2 tablespoons KNOTT'S®
   Jalapeño Jelly
2 tablespoons chopped fresh
   cilantro
2 tablespoons tequila
2 tablespoons olive oil
1 teaspoon minced fresh
   garlic
¼ teaspoon salt
¼ teaspoon pepper

**1.** Rinse and pat dry chicken. Arrange chicken in 8×8×2-inch baking dish; set aside.

**2.** In small bowl, combine *remaining* ingredients. Pour half the marinade over chicken and reserve *remaining* marinade for basting. Refrigerate chicken 2 to 8 hours.

**3.** Place chicken on grill over hot coals. Grill chicken until no longer pink and juices run clear, basting frequently with reserved marinade. *Makes 4 servings*

# Wish-Bone® Marinade Italiano

¾ cup WISH-BONE® Italian
Dressing*
2½ to 3 pounds chicken pieces

*Also terrific with Wish-Bone® Robusto Italian
or Just 2 Good Italian Dressing.*

In large, shallow nonaluminum baking dish or plastic bag, pour ½ cup Italian dressing over chicken. Cover, or close bag, and marinate in refrigerator, turning occasionally, 3 to 24 hours.

Remove chicken from marinade; discard marinade. Grill or broil chicken, turning once and brushing frequently with remaining ¼ cup dressing, until chicken is thoroughly cooked and juices run clear.

*Makes about 4 servings*

**Variations:** Substitute 2½ pounds T-bone, top sirloin or top loin steaks; 6 boneless skinless chicken breasts; or 2½ pounds pork chops (about 1 inch thick) in place of chicken pieces.

# Grilled Stuffed Chicken Breasts

6 boneless skinless chicken
breasts
6 tablespoons butter or
margarine, softened
3 tablespoons Dijon-style
mustard, divided
6 slices cooked ham
1 cup (4 ounces) shredded
Swiss cheese
3 tablespoons vegetable oil
1 tablespoon honey
Salt and pepper (optional)

Pound chicken breasts to ¼-inch thickness. In small bowl, blend butter with 2 tablespoons mustard; spread over one side of each chicken breast. Cut ham slices to fit each chicken piece; layer over mustard mixture. Top with shredded cheese. Roll up chicken pieces lengthwise, jelly-roll style; skewer each to enclose ham and cheese. Mix remaining 1 tablespoon mustard with oil and honey; brush over all sides of each roll.

Grill chicken on covered grill over medium-hot KINGSFORD® with Mesquite Charcoal Briquets 25 to 35 minutes, basting often with mustard-honey mixture, until chicken is tender.

*Makes 6 servings*

Wish-Bone® Marinade Italiano

# Citrus Marinated Chicken

1 cup orange juice
¼ cup lemon juice
¼ cup lime juice
2 cloves garlic, pressed or
   minced
4 boneless skinless chicken
   breasts
Salt and black pepper
Citrus Tarragon Butter
   (recipe follows)
Hot cooked couscous with
   green onion slices and
   slivered almonds
   (optional)
Lemon and lime slices and
   Italian parsley for garnish

Combine orange, lemon and lime juices and garlic in a shallow glass dish or large plastic food storage bag. Add chicken; cover dish or close bag. Marinate in refrigerator no more than 2 hours. (Lemon and lime juice will "cook" the chicken if it's left in too long.) Remove chicken from marinade; discard marinade. Season chicken with salt and pepper.

Oil hot grid to help prevent sticking. Grill chicken on a covered grill over medium KINGSFORD® Briquets 6 to 8 minutes until chicken is cooked through, turning once. Serve topped with a dollop of Citrus Tarragon Butter. Serve over couscous. Garnish, if desired.

*Makes 4 servings*

## Citrus Tarragon Butter

½ cup butter, softened
1 tablespoon lemon juice
1 tablespoon orange juice
1 tablespoon finely chopped fresh tarragon
1 teaspoon finely grated orange peel
1 teaspoon finely grated lemon peel

Beat butter in a small bowl until soft and light. Stir in remaining ingredients. Cover and refrigerate until ready to serve.

*Makes about ½ cup*

# Lemon Herbed Chicken

½ cup butter or margarine
½ cup vegetable oil
⅓ cup lemon juice
2 tablespoons finely chopped parsley
2 tablespoons garlic salt
1 teaspoon dried rosemary, crushed
1 teaspoon dried summer savory, crushed
½ teaspoon dried thyme, crushed
¼ teaspoon coarsely cracked black pepper
6 chicken quarters (breast-wing or thigh-drumstick combinations)

Combine butter, oil, lemon juice, parsley, garlic salt, rosemary, summer savory, thyme and pepper in small saucepan. Heat until butter melts. Place chicken in shallow glass dish. Brush with some of sauce. Let stand 10 to 15 minutes.

Oil hot grid to help prevent sticking. Place dark meat pieces on grill 10 minutes before white meat pieces (dark meat takes longer to cook). Grill chicken on uncovered grill over medium-hot KINGSFORD® Briquets 30 to 45 minutes for breast quarters or 50 to 60 minutes for leg quarters. Chicken is done when meat is no longer pink by bone. Turn quarters over and baste with sauce every 10 minutes. *Makes 6 servings*

# Grilled Game Hens, Texas-Style

1 can (8 ounces) tomato sauce
¼ cup vegetable oil
1½ teaspoons chili powder
1 teaspoon paprika
¼ teaspoon garlic powder
¼ teaspoon ground red pepper
4 Cornish game hens (1 to 1½ pounds each), cut into halves

In small bowl, combine all ingredients except game hens. Brush hens generously with tomato mixture. Grill hens on covered grill over medium-hot KINGSFORD® with Mesquite Charcoal Briquets 45 to 50 minutes or until fork-tender, brushing frequently with tomato mixture. *Makes 4 servings*

Lemon Herbed Chicken
and Skewered Vegetables (page 327)

# Turkey Cutlets with Chipotle Pepper Mole

1 package BUTTERBALL®
    Fresh Boneless Turkey
    Breast Cutlets
1 can (14½ ounces) chicken
    broth
¼ cup raisins
4 cloves garlic, minced
1 chipotle chile pepper in
    adobo sauce
2 tablespoons ground
    almonds
2 teaspoons unsweetened
    cocoa
½ cup chopped fresh cilantro
2 tablespoons fresh lime juice
½ teaspoon salt

To prepare chipotle sauce, combine chicken broth, raisins, garlic, chile pepper, almonds and cocoa in medium saucepan. Simmer over low heat 10 minutes. Pour into food processor or blender; process until smooth. Add cilantro, lime juice and salt. Grill cutlets according to package directions. Serve chipotle sauce over grilled cutlets with Mexican polenta.* *Makes 7 servings*

*To make Mexican polenta, cook 1 cup instant cornmeal polenta according to package directions. Stir in ½ teaspoon garlic powder, ½ teaspoon salt and 2 cups taco-seasoned cheese.*

**Prep Time:** 20 minutes

## FOOD FACT

Chipotle chile peppers are dried, smoked jalapeño chiles often found in canned Adobo Sauce, a dark red paste-like sauce. If you like spicy hot food, chipotles in adobo sauce provide a smoky hot flavor you'll truly love.

Turkey Cutlet
with Chipotle Pepper Mole

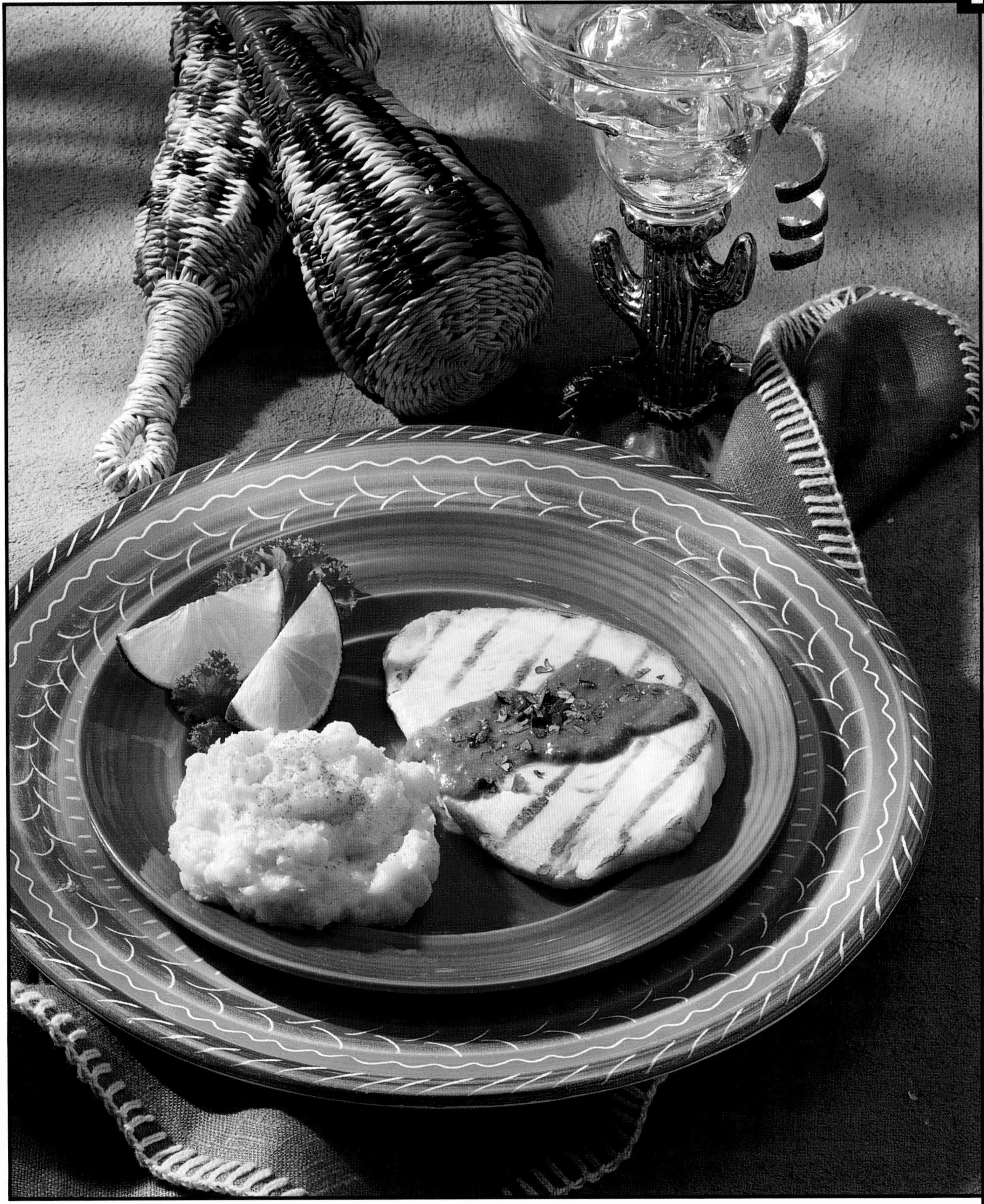

# Turkey Burritos

1 tablespoon ground cumin
1 tablespoon chili powder
1½ teaspoons salt
1½ to 2 pounds turkey
    tenderloin, cut into
    ½-inch cubes
Avocado-Corn Salsa (recipe
    follows, optional)
Lime wedges
Flour tortillas
Sour cream (optional)
Tomato slices for garnish

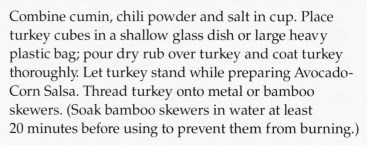

Combine cumin, chili powder and salt in cup. Place turkey cubes in a shallow glass dish or large heavy plastic bag; pour dry rub over turkey and coat turkey thoroughly. Let turkey stand while preparing Avocado-Corn Salsa. Thread turkey onto metal or bamboo skewers. (Soak bamboo skewers in water at least 20 minutes before using to prevent them from burning.)

Oil hot grid to help prevent sticking. Grill turkey on covered grill over medium KINGSFORD® Briquets, about 6 minutes or until turkey is no longer pink in center, turning once. Remove skewers from grill; squeeze lime wedges over skewers. Warm flour tortillas in microwave oven, or brush each tortilla very lightly with water and grill 10 to 15 seconds per side. Top with Avocado-Corn Salsa and sour cream, if desired. Garnish with tomato slices.

*Makes 6 servings*

## Avocado-Corn Salsa

2 small to medium-size ripe avocados, finely chopped
1 cup cooked fresh corn or thawed frozen corn
2 medium tomatoes, seeded and finely chopped
2 to 3 tablespoons chopped fresh cilantro
2 to 3 tablespoons lime juice
½ to 1 teaspoon minced hot green chile pepper
½ teaspoon salt

Gently stir together all ingredients in medium bowl; adjust flavors to taste. Cover and refrigerate until ready to serve.

*Makes about 1½ cups*

**Note:** This recipe is great for casual get-togethers. Just prepare the fixings and let the guests make their own burritos.

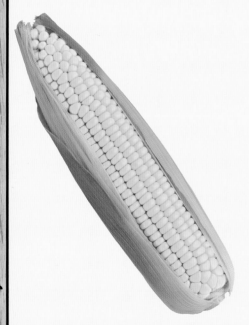

Turkey Burritos

# Butterball® Sweet Italian Sausage with Vesuvio Potatoes

1 package BUTTERBALL®
  Lean Fresh Turkey Sweet
  Italian Sausage
4 baking potatoes, cut
  lengthwise into wedges
2 tablespoons olive oil
½ teaspoon coarse ground
  black pepper
1 can (14½ ounces) chicken
  broth
6 cloves garlic, minced
½ cup dry white wine
6 tablespoons minced fresh
  parsley
2 tablespoons grated
  Parmesan cheese
Salt

Grill sausage according to package directions. Combine potatoes, oil and pepper in large bowl. Spray large nonstick skillet with nonstick cooking spray; add potato mixture. Cook 15 minutes. Add chicken broth and garlic; cook, covered, 10 minutes or until potatoes are tender. Add wine and parsley; cook, uncovered, 5 minutes. Sprinkle with Parmesan cheese. Add salt to taste. Serve with grilled sausage. *Makes 6 servings*

**Prep Time:** 30 minutes

# Turkey Teriyaki

2 tablespoons low-sodium
  soy sauce
2 tablespoons cooking sherry
  or apple juice
1 teaspoon ground ginger
1 tablespoon canola oil
1 teaspoon brown sugar
1 clove garlic, minced
½ teaspoon black pepper
1 pound turkey or chicken
  cutlets

In a small bowl, combine all the ingredients except the turkey and mix well. Place turkey in a resealable plastic food storage bag. Pour soy sauce mixture over the turkey; seal. Refrigerate several hours or overnight.

Remove turkey from bag and discard marinade. Grill 18 to 25 minutes or sauté in 1 teaspoon canola oil in skillet over medium heat until meat is no longer pink. *Makes 4 servings*

*Favorite recipe from* **Canada's Canola Industry**

# Grilled Turkey

Sage-Garlic Baste (recipe
follows)
1 whole turkey (9 to
13 pounds), thawed if
frozen
Salt and black pepper
3 lemons, halved (optional)

Prepare Sage-Garlic Baste. Remove neck and giblets from turkey. Rinse turkey under cold running water; pat dry with paper towels. Season turkey cavity with salt and pepper; place lemons in cavity, if desired. Lightly brush outer surface of turkey with part of Sage-Garlic Baste. Pull skin over neck and secure with skewer. Tuck wing tips under back and tie legs together with cotton string. Insert meat thermometer into thickest part of thigh, not touching bone. Arrange medium-hot KINGSFORD® Briquets on each side of large rectangular metal or foil drip pan. Pour hot tap water into drip pan until half full. Place turkey, breast side up, on grid directly above drip pan. Grill turkey on covered grill 9 to 13 minutes per pound or until thermometer registers 180°F, basting every 20 minutes with remaining Sage-Garlic Baste. Add a few briquets to both sides of fire every hour or as necessary to maintain constant temperature.* Let turkey stand 15 minutes before carving. Refrigerate leftovers promptly. *Makes 8 to 10 servings*

*For larger turkey, add 15 briquets every 50 to 60 minutes.

## Sage-Garlic Baste
Grated peel and juice of 1 lemon
3 tablespoons olive oil
2 tablespoons minced fresh sage *or* 1½ teaspoons
rubbed sage
2 cloves garlic, minced
½ teaspoon salt
¼ teaspoon black pepper

Combine all ingredients in small saucepan; cook and stir over medium heat 4 minutes. Use as baste for turkey or chicken. *Makes about ½ cup*

# Turkey Teriyaki with Grilled Mushrooms

1¼ pounds turkey breast slices,
      tenderloins or medallions
¼ cup sake or sherry wine
¼ cup soy sauce
3 tablespoons granulated
      sugar, brown sugar or
      honey
1 piece (1-inch cube) fresh
      ginger, minced
3 cloves garlic, minced
1 tablespoon vegetable oil
½ pound mushrooms
4 green onions, cut into
      2-inch pieces

Cut turkey into long 2-inch-wide strips.* Combine sake, soy sauce, sugar, ginger, garlic and oil in 2-quart glass dish. Add turkey; turn to coat. Cover and refrigerate 15 minutes or overnight. Remove turkey from marinade; discard marinade. Thread turkey onto metal or wooden skewers, alternating with mushrooms and green onions. (Soak wooden skewers in hot water 30 minutes to prevent burning.) Grill on covered grill over medium-hot KINGSFORD® Briquets about 3 minutes per side until turkey is cooked through.          *Makes 4 servings*

*Do not cut tenderloins or medallions.

# Caribbean Grilled Turkey

1 package BUTTERBALL®
      Fresh Boneless Turkey
      Breast Tenderloins
4 green onions
4 cloves garlic
2 tablespoons peach
      preserves
2 tablespoons fresh lime juice
1 teaspoon salt
1 teaspoon shredded lime
      peel
1 teaspoon bottled hot sauce
1 teaspoon soy sauce
¼ teaspoon black pepper

Lightly spray unheated grill rack with nonstick cooking spray. Prepare grill for medium-direct-heat cooking. In food processor or blender, process onions, garlic, preserves, lime juice, salt, lime peel, hot sauce, soy sauce and pepper until smooth. Spread over tenderloins. Place tenderloins on rack over medium-hot grill. Grill 20 minutes or until meat is no longer pink, turning frequently for even browning.          *Makes 6 servings*

**Prep Time:** 25 minutes

**Turkey Teriyaki
with Grilled Mushrooms**

# SURE-FIRE
## SEAFOOD

### Grilled Fish Florentine

**Marinade**
- ¼ cup vegetable oil
- 2 tablespoons lemon juice
- 2 tablespoons soy sauce
- 1 teaspoon grated lemon peel
- 1 clove garlic, minced
- 4 fresh or frozen red snapper or swordfish fillets or steaks, thawed

**Florentine Sauce**
- 1 tablespoon butter
- ½ cup chopped scallions
- ¼ cup chopped fresh mushrooms
- 1 cup chicken broth
- ⅓ cup HOLLAND HOUSE® White Cooking Wine
- ½ cup whipping cream
- 4 cups chopped fresh spinach
- ¼ teaspoon pepper

**1.** For marinade, in large non-metallic bowl, combine oil, lemon juice, soy sauce, lemon peel and garlic; mix well. Add fish, turning to coat all sides. Cover; refrigerate 2 hours. Prepare grill.

**2.** For Florentine Sauce, melt butter in large skillet over medium heat. Add scallions and mushrooms; cook until softened, about 3 minutes, stirring occasionally. Stir in chicken broth and cooking wine. Bring to a boil; boil until sauce is reduced by half, about 10 minutes. Add whipping cream; simmer over medium heat until sauce is reduced to about ½ cup, about 10 minutes. Strain into food processor bowl. Add spinach; process until smooth. Add pepper; keep warm.

**3.** Drain fish, reserving marinade. Place fish on grill over medium-hot coals. Cook 10 minutes or until fish flakes easily with a fork, turning once and brushing frequently with marinade.* Discard any leftover marinade. Serve fish with Florentine Sauce.

*Makes 4 servings*

*Do not brush with marinade during last 5 minutes of cooking.*

**Grilled Fish Florentine**

# Honey Barbecued Halibut

PAM® No-Stick Cooking
   Spray
2 pounds halibut steaks
½ cup HUNT'S® Original
   Barbecue Sauce
2 tablespoons honey
1 tablespoon WESSON®
   Vegetable Oil
½ teaspoon red wine vinegar

**1.** Spray a 9×9×2-inch baking pan with cooking spray. Place fish in baking pan.

**2.** In a small bowl, combine *remaining* ingredients.

**3.** Pour ⅔ *marinade* over fish. Set aside *remaining* marinade. Turn fish to coat evenly. Cover and marinate in refrigerator at least 2 hours.

**4.** Remove fish from marinade; discard used marinade.

**5.** Cook over hot coals or a preheated broiler 4 minutes per side basting occasionally with *remaining* marinade.

*Makes 8 (5-ounce) servings*

# Grilled Herb Trout

6 whole cleaned trout (each
   at least 10 ounces), head
   removed if desired, boned
   and butterflied
Salt and black pepper
6 bacon slices
6 sprigs dill or tarragon
1 or 2 medium onions, cut
   into wedges
Lemon wedges
Dill or tarragon sprigs for
   garnish

Rinse fish; pat dry with paper towels. Season lightly with salt and pepper. Place 1 slice of bacon and 1 herb sprig in the cavity of each trout; close fish. (There's no need to tie the fish; it will remain closed during cooking.) Place fish in a fish basket, if desired.

Oil hot grid to help prevent sticking. Grill fish on covered grill over medium-hot KINGSFORD® Briquets, 8 to 12 minutes. Halfway through cooking time, turn fish and add onions to grill. Continue grilling until fish turns from transparent to opaque throughout. Serve with lemon. (The bacon does not become crispy; it flavors and bastes the fish during cooking. It can be removed, if desired, just before serving.) Garnish with dill.

*Makes 6 servings*

# Teriyaki Grilled Snapper

2 whole red snappers or
   striped bass (1½ pounds
   each), scaled and gutted
⅓ cup *French's*®
   Worcestershire Sauce
⅓ cup peanut oil
⅓ cup rice vinegar
¼ cup chopped green onion
1 tablespoon Oriental
   sesame oil
1 tablespoon chopped peeled
   fresh ginger
3 cloves garlic, chopped
   Asian Slaw (recipe follows)

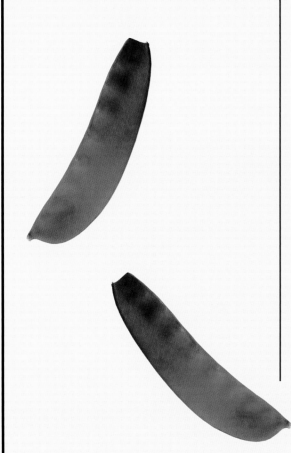

Rinse fish and place in large resealable plastic food storage bag or shallow glass dish. To prepare marinade, place Worcestershire, peanut oil, vinegar, onion, sesame oil, ginger and garlic in blender or food processor. Cover and process until well blended. Reserve ¼ cup marinade for serving. Pour remaining marinade over fish. Seal bag or cover dish and marinate in refrigerator 1 hour.

Place fish in oiled grilling basket, reserving marinade for basting. Grill over medium-high coals 10 to 12 minutes per side or until fish flakes easily with a fork, basting occasionally with basting marinade. (Do not baste during last 5 minutes of cooking.) Discard any unused marinade. Carefully remove bones from fish. Pour reserved ¼ cup marinade over fish. Serve with Asian Slaw. Garnish as desired.                          *Makes 4 servings*

## Asian Slaw

½ small head napa cabbage, shredded (about 4 cups)*
 3 carrots
 2 red or yellow bell peppers, seeded and cut into very
    thin strips
¼ pound snow peas, trimmed and cut into thin strips
⅓ cup peanut oil
¼ cup rice vinegar
 3 tablespoons *French's*® Worcestershire Sauce
 1 tablespoon Oriental sesame oil
 1 tablespoon honey
 2 cloves garlic, minced

*You may substitute 4 cups shredded green cabbage for the napa cabbage.*

Place vegetables in large bowl. Whisk together peanut oil, vinegar, Worcestershire, sesame oil, honey and garlic in small bowl until well blended. Pour dressing over vegetables; toss well to coat evenly. Cover and refrigerate 1 hour before serving.                          *Makes 4 servings*

## Cajun Grilled Shrimp

3 green onions, minced
2 tablespoons lemon juice
3 cloves garlic, minced
2 teaspoons paprika
1 teaspoon salt
¼ to ½ teaspoon black pepper
¼ to ½ teaspoon cayenne
    pepper
1 tablespoon olive oil
1½ pounds shrimp, shelled with
    tails intact, deveined
    Lemon wedges

Combine onions, lemon juice, garlic, paprika, salt and peppers in 2-quart glass dish; stir in oil. Add shrimp; turn to coat. Cover and refrigerate at least 15 minutes. Thread shrimp onto metal or wooden skewers. (Soak wooden skewers in hot water 30 minutes to prevent burning.) Grill shrimp over medium-hot KINGSFORD® Briquets about 2 minutes per side until opaque. Serve immediately with lemon wedges. *Makes 4 servings*

## Asian Swordfish

3 teaspoons dark sesame oil,
    divided
3 tablespoons Chinese rice
    wine or sherry
2 tablespoons soy sauce
2 teaspoons minced fresh
    ginger
2 teaspoons sugar
¼ teaspoon black pepper
1½ pounds swordfish, halibut
    or salmon fillets or
    steaks, ¾ inch thick
1 tablespoon vegetable oil
1 pound fresh mushrooms,
    sliced
2 green onions, sliced
¼ cup cilantro leaves
    Dash salt

Combine 2 teaspoons sesame oil, wine, soy sauce, ginger, sugar and pepper in 2-quart dish. Add swordfish; turn to coat. Cover and refrigerate at least 2 hours. Heat vegetable oil in medium skillet over high heat. Add mushrooms; cook and stir until well browned. Remove from heat; stir in onions, cilantro, salt and remaining 1 teaspoon sesame oil; keep warm. Remove swordfish from marinade; discard marinade. Lightly oil grid to prevent sticking. Grill swordfish over medium-hot KINGSFORD® Briquets about 4 minutes per side until swordfish flakes easily when tested with fork. Spoon mushroom mixture over swordfish.

*Makes 4 to 6 servings*

Cajun Grilled Shrimp

# Baja Fruited Salmon

1 large navel orange, peeled and diced
1 small grapefruit, peeled and diced
1 medium tomato, seeded and diced
¼ cup diced red onion
1 small jalapeño, seeded and finely chopped
2 tablespoons chopped fresh cilantro
2 tablespoons red wine vinegar
1 tablespoon vegetable oil
½ to ¾ teaspoon LAWRY'S® Seasoned Salt
¼ to ½ teaspoon LAWRY'S® Garlic Powder with Parsley
4 salmon steaks, about 5 ounces each
Lemon juice

In medium bowl, combine all ingredients except salmon and lemon juice; mix well. Refrigerate until ready to use. Brush salmon steaks with lemon juice. Grill or broil 5 inches from heat source 5 to 7 minutes on each side or until fish flakes easily with fork. Spoon chilled fruit salsa over salmon. *Makes 4 servings*

**Serving Suggestion:** Serve with pan-fried potatoes. Garnish with lemon slices and parsley.

## GRILLING TIP

*When cooking thick fish steaks, cook fish over high heat on a covered grill. Be sure to brush steaks on both sides with oil and place on an oiled grid. Carefully turn steaks over with a large spatula since they can easily break apart. One way to determine doneness of the fish steak is to press steak with a finger. The fish should break into firm flakes.*

Baja Fruited Salmon

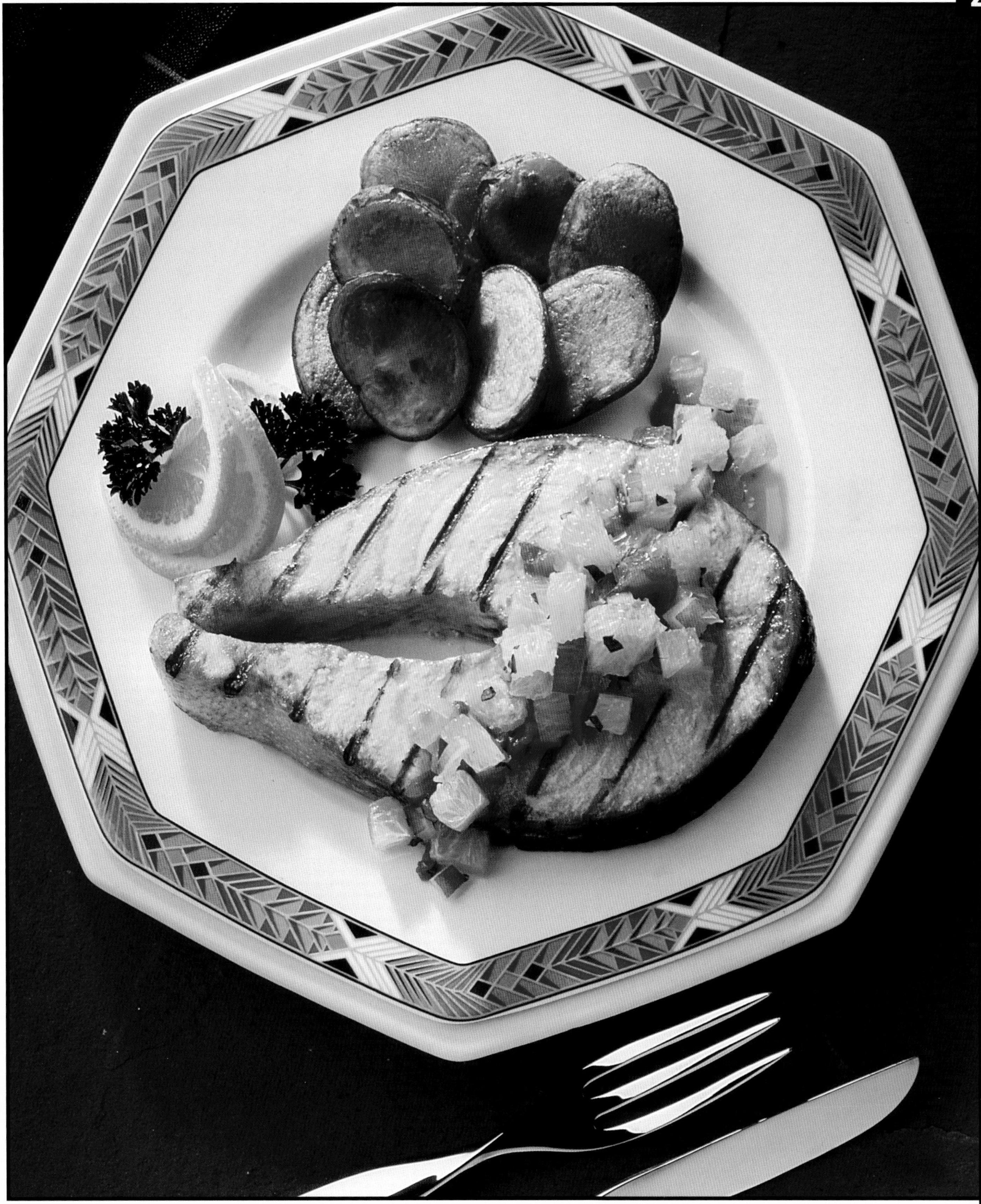

## Broiled Scallops with Honey-Lime Marinade

2 tablespoons honey
4 teaspoons lime juice
1 tablespoon vegetable oil
¼ teaspoon grated lime peel
¼ teaspoon salt
1 dash hot pepper sauce
½ pound bay, calico or sea
    scallops
1 lime, cut into wedges

Combine honey, lime juice, oil, lime peel, salt and hot pepper sauce in large bowl. Rinse scallops and pat dry with paper towel; add to marinade. Marinate scallops in refrigerator, stirring occasionally 1 hour or overnight. Prepare grill or preheat broiler. Thread scallops onto metal skewers. Discard marinade. Grill or broil 4 inches from heat source 4 to 7 minutes or until opaque and lightly browned. Serve with lime wedges.

*Makes 2 servings*

*Favorite recipe from* **National Honey Board**

## Grilled Swordfish Steaks

1 cup uncooked UNCLE
    BEN'S® ORIGINAL
    CONVERTED® Brand
    Rice
4 (1-inch-thick) swordfish
    steaks (about 4 ounces
    each)
3 tablespoons Caribbean jerk
    seasoning
1 can (8 ounces) crushed
    pineapple in juice,
    drained
⅓ cup chopped macadamia
    nuts
1 tablespoon honey

**1.** Cook rice according to package directions.

**2.** During the last 10 minutes of cooking rice, coat both sides of swordfish steaks with jerk seasoning. Lightly spray grid of preheated grill with nonstick cooking spray. Grill swordfish over medium coals 10 to 12 minutes or until fish flakes easily when tested with fork, turning after 5 minutes.

**3.** Stir pineapple, nuts and honey into hot cooked rice; serve with fish.

*Makes 4 servings*

**Tip:** For a nuttier flavor, macadamia nuts can be toasted. Place nuts in small nonstick skillet and heat over medium-high heat about 5 minutes or until lightly browned, stirring occasionally.

**Broiled Scallops
with Honey-Lime Marinade**

# Shrimp Skewers with Tropical Fruit Salsa

½ cup soy sauce
¼ cup fresh lime juice
2 cloves garlic, minced
1½ pounds large shrimp,
    shelled and deveined
Tropical Fruit Salsa (recipe
    follows)
Vegetable oil
Salt and black pepper

Combine soy sauce, lime juice and garlic in shallow glass dish or large heavy plastic food storage bag. Add shrimp; cover dish or close bag. Marinate in refrigerator no longer than 30 minutes.

Meanwhile, prepare Tropical Fruit Salsa. (Salsa should not be made more than two hours before serving.)

Remove shrimp from marinade; discard marinade. Thread shrimp on metal or bamboo skewers. (Soak bamboo skewers in water at least 20 minutes to keep them from burning.) Brush one side of shrimp lightly with oil; season with salt and pepper.

Oil hot grid to help prevent sticking. Grill shrimp, oil side down on covered grill over medium-hot KINGSFORD® Briquets, 6 to 8 minutes. Halfway through cooking time, brush top with oil, season with salt and pepper, then turn and continue grilling until shrimp firm up and turn opaque throughout. Serve with Tropical Fruit Salsa.

*Makes 4 servings*

## Tropical Fruit Salsa

2 mangos*
2 kiwifruit
3 tablespoons finely chopped or finely slivered red onion
3 tablespoons fresh lime juice
1 tablespoon finely chopped fresh mint leaves
1 tablespoon finely chopped fresh cilantro
1 teaspoon sugar
¼ teaspoon salt
¼ teaspoon crushed red pepper flakes

*Substitute 1 papaya or 2 large or 3 medium peaches for mangos.*

Peel fruit. Cut mango into ¼-inch pieces; cut kiwifruit into wedges. Combine with remaining ingredients in medium bowl; adjust flavors to taste. Cover and refrigerate 2 hours. *Makes about 1 cup*

# Grilled Fish with Pineapple Salsa

1 can (20 ounces) pineapple tidbits packed in pineapple juice, drained *or* 1½ cups chopped fresh pineapple

¼ cup chopped pimientos, drained

¼ cup finely chopped red onion or green onions

1 small jalapeño pepper, seeds and ribs removed, and finely chopped

¼ cup CRISCO® Oil,* divided

3 tablespoons rice wine vinegar

2 tablespoons dark brown sugar

¾ teaspoon salt, divided

½ teaspoon freshly ground black pepper, divided

1½ pounds firm-fleshed fish fillets, such as salmon, flounder or halibut

*Use your favorite Crisco Oil product.*

**1.** Combine pineapple, pimientos, red onion, jalapeño, 2 tablespoons oil, vinegar, brown sugar, ¼ teaspoon salt and ¼ teaspoon pepper in glass or stainless steel mixing bowl. Stir well. Refrigerate 30 minutes tightly covered.

**2.** Prepare grill or heat broiler.

**3.** Rinse fish. Pat dry. Brush with remaining 2 tablespoons oil. Sprinkle with remaining ½ teaspoon salt and remaining ¼ teaspoon pepper.

**4.** Grill or broil fish 3 minutes. Turn gently with spatula. Grill 3 minutes or until fish flakes easily with fork. (Fish requires 10 minutes total grilling or broiling time per inch of thickness.) Remove from grill. Top with salsa. Serve immediately. *Makes 4 servings*

**Notes:** The salsa can be made up to 1 day in advance and refrigerated, tightly covered. Boneless skinless chicken breasts, turkey cutlets or thin boneless pork chops can be substituted for fish.

**Tip:** Brush cool grill grid with Crisco® Oil or spray with Crisco® No-Stick Cooking Spray before turning on the grill to keep the fish from sticking.

**Prep Time:** 15 minutes
**Total Time:** 50 minutes

## FOOD FACT

*Mangos are available most of the year in many large supermarkets. They are ripe when they yield to gentle pressure; the color of the skin does not indicate ripeness. Uripe mangos will ripen in a few days when stored at room temperature.*

# Teriyaki Trout

4 whole trout (about
    2 pounds)
¾ cup LAWRY'S® Teriyaki
    Marinade with Pineapple
    Juice
½ cup sliced green onions
2 medium lemons, sliced
    Chopped fresh parsley
    (optional)

Brush the inside and outside of each trout with Teriyaki Marinade with Pineapple Juice; stuff with green onions and lemon slices. Place in shallow glass dish. Reserve ¼ cup Teriyaki Marinade with Pineapple Juice for basting. Pour ½ cup Teriyaki Marinade with Pineapple Juice over trout; cover dish. Marinate in refrigerator at least 30 minutes. Remove trout; discard used marinade. Place trout in oiled hinged wire grill basket; brush with reserved ¼ cup Teriyaki Marinade with Pineapple Juice. Grill 4 to 5 inches from heat source over medium-hot coals 10 minutes or until trout flakes easily with fork, turning and brushing occasionally with reserved marinade. *Do not baste during last 5 minutes of cooking.* Discard used marinade. Sprinkle with parsley, if desired.

*Makes 4 servings*

**Serving Suggestion:** For a delicious side dish, cook sliced bell pepper, onion and zucchini brushed with vegetable oil on grill with trout.

## South Seas Shrimp & Mango

1 pound raw jumbo shrimp,
   shelled and deveined
3 tablespoons *French's®*
   Napa Valley Style Dijon
   Mustard
2 tablespoons olive oil
2 tablespoons fresh orange
   juice
1 tablespoon *Frank's® RedHot®*
   Cayenne Pepper Sauce
1 teaspoon grated
   orange peel
1 large ripe mango, peeled
   and cut into 1-inch pieces
1 red bell pepper, cut into
   1-inch pieces
4 green onions, cut into
   1½-inch pieces

**1.** Place shrimp in large resealable plastic food storage bag. Combine mustard, oil, juice, *Frank's RedHot* Sauce and orange peel in small bowl; pour over shrimp. Seal bag; marinate in refrigerator 20 minutes.

**2.** Alternately thread shrimp, mango, bell pepper and onions onto 4 (10-inch) metal skewers. Place skewers on oiled grid. Grill over high heat 7 minutes or until shrimp are opaque, turning and basting once with mustard mixture. Discard any remaining marinade.

*Makes 4 servings*

**Prep Time:** 15 minutes
**Marinate Time:** 20 minutes
**Cook Time:** 7 minutes

## Lime & Tomato Salmon

½ cup WESSON®
   Vegetable Oil
¼ cup rice vinegar
2 tablespoons *each:*
   LA CHOY® Soy Sauce
   and lime juice
1 tablespoon tequila
   (optional)
4 (8 ounces each) salmon
   steaks, 1-inch thick
   Ground black pepper
½ cup chopped tomatoes
¼ cup chopped cilantro

In a large shallow glass or plastic dish, combine first 5 ingredients; mix well. Add salmon; cover and refrigerate 30 minutes to 1 hour. Place salmon on grill over medium-hot coals. Season with pepper. Grill 4 minutes. Turn steaks and baste with marinade. Cook until just opaque, about 3 minutes. Transfer to plates. Top each steak with equal portions of tomatoes and cilantro.

*Makes 4 servings*

South Seas Shrimp & Mango

# Catfish with Fresh Corn Relish

4 catfish fillets (each about
   6 ounces and at least
   ½ inch thick)
2 tablespoons paprika
½ teaspoon ground red
   pepper
½ teaspoon salt
   Fresh Corn Relish (recipe
   follows)
   Lime wedges
   Grilled baking potatoes
   (optional)
   Tarragon sprigs for garnish

Rinse fish; pat dry with paper towels. Combine paprika, red pepper and salt in cup; lightly sprinkle on both sides of fish.

Oil hot grid to help prevent sticking. Grill fish on covered grill over medium KINGSFORD® Briquets, 5 to 9 minutes. Halfway through cooking time, turn fish over and continue grilling until fish turns from translucent to opaque throughout. (Grilling time depends on the thickness of fish; allow 3 to 5 minutes for each ½ inch of thickness.) Serve with Fresh Corn Relish, lime wedges and potatoes, if desired. Garnish with tarragon sprigs.

*Makes 4 servings*

## Fresh Corn Relish

¼ cup cooked fresh corn or thawed frozen corn
¼ cup finely diced green bell pepper
¼ cup finely slivered red onion
2 tablespoons seasoned (sweet) rice vinegar
1 tablespoon vegetable oil
   Salt and black pepper
½ cup cherry tomatoes, cut into quarters

Toss together corn, green pepper, onion, vinegar and oil in medium bowl. Season with salt and pepper. Cover and refrigerate until ready to serve. Just before serving, gently mix in tomatoes.

*Makes about 1½ cups*

**Catfish with Fresh Corn Relish**

# "Grilled" Tuna with Vegetables in Herb Butter

4 pieces heavy-duty aluminum foil, each 12×18 inches

1 (7-ounce) pouch of STARKIST® Premium Albacore or Chunk Light Tuna

1 cup slivered red or green bell pepper

1 cup slivered yellow squash or zucchini

1 cup pea pods, cut crosswise into halves

1 cup slivered carrots

4 green onions, cut into 2-inch slices

Salt and black pepper to taste (optional)

**Herb Butter**

3 tablespoons butter or margarine, melted

1 tablespoon lemon or lime juice

1 clove garlic, minced

2 teaspoons dried tarragon leaves, crushed

1 teaspoon dried dill weed

On each piece of foil, mound tuna, bell pepper, squash, pea pods, carrots and onions. Sprinkle with salt and black pepper.

For Herb Butter, in small bowl stir together butter, lemon juice, garlic, tarragon and dill. Drizzle over tuna and vegetables. Fold edges of each foil square together to make packets.

**To grill**
Place foil packets about 4 inches above hot coals. Grill for 10 to 12 minutes or until heated through, turning packets over halfway through grill time.

**To bake**
Place foil packets on baking sheet. Bake in preheated 450°F oven for 15 to 20 minutes or until heated through.

**To serve**
Cut an "X" on top of each packet; peel back foil.

*Makes 4 servings*

"Grilled" Tuna with Vegetables
in Herb Butter

# Barbecued Shrimp with Spicy Rice

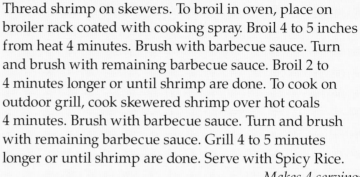

1 pound large shrimp, peeled
and deveined
4 wooden* or metal skewers
Vegetable cooking spray
⅓ cup prepared barbecue
sauce
Spicy Rice (recipe follows)

*Soak wooden skewers in water 20 minutes
before using to prevent burning.*

Thread shrimp on skewers. To broil in oven, place on broiler rack coated with cooking spray. Broil 4 to 5 inches from heat 4 minutes. Brush with barbecue sauce. Turn and brush with remaining barbecue sauce. Broil 2 to 4 minutes longer or until shrimp are done. To cook on outdoor grill, cook skewered shrimp over hot coals 4 minutes. Brush with barbecue sauce. Turn and brush with remaining barbecue sauce. Grill 4 to 5 minutes longer or until shrimp are done. Serve with Spicy Rice.

*Makes 4 servings*

*Favorite recipe from* **USA Rice Federation**

## Spicy Rice

½ cup sliced green onions
½ cup minced carrots
½ cup minced red bell pepper
1 jalapeño or serrano pepper, minced
1 tablespoon vegetable oil
2 cups cooked rice (cooked in chicken broth)
2 tablespoons chopped cilantro
1 tablespoon lime juice
1 teaspoon soy sauce
Hot pepper sauce to taste

Cook onions, carrots, bell pepper and jalapeño pepper in oil in large skillet over medium-high heat until tender crisp. Stir in rice, cilantro, lime juice, soy sauce and pepper sauce; cook until thoroughly heated.

*Makes 4 servings*

**Microwave Directions:** Combine onions, carrots, bell pepper, jalapeño pepper and oil in 2-quart microproof baking dish. Cook on HIGH (100% power) 2 to 3 minutes or until vegetables are tender crisp. Add rice, cilantro, lime juice, soy sauce and pepper sauce. Cook on HIGH 3 to 4 minutes, stirring after 2 minutes, or until thoroughly heated.

*Favorite recipe from* **USA Rice Federation**

# Grilled Tuna with Salsa Salad

1 bag (16 ounces) BIRDS
 EYE® frozen Farm Fresh
 Mixtures Broccoli, Corn
 & Red Peppers
1 can (14½ ounces) diced
 tomatoes with garlic and
 onion*
6 to 8 green onions, sliced
1 to 2 jalapeño peppers, finely
 chopped
1 tablespoon, or to taste,
 lime juice or vinegar
4 tuna steaks, grilled as
 desired

*Or, substitute favorite seasoned diced tomatoes.*

- In large saucepan, cook vegetables according to package directions; drain.

- In large bowl, combine vegetables, tomatoes, onions, peppers and lime juice. Let stand 15 minutes.

- Serve vegetable mixture over tuna.

*Makes 4 servings*

**Prep Time:** 5 minutes
**Cook Time:** 5 to 6 minutes

# Mission Ensenada Fish Tacos

1 package (1.0 ounce)
 LAWRY'S® Chicken Taco
 Spices & Seasonings,
 divided
½ cup sour cream
2 to 3 tablespoons milk
1 tablespoon vegetable oil
1 tablespoon lime juice
1 pound cod or orange
 roughy fillets
6 flour tortillas (taco or fajita
 size), warmed to soften
2 cups shredded cabbage mix
1 can (2.25 ounces) sliced
 black olives, drained
 Fresh lime wedges

In small bowl, combine 2 teaspoons Chicken Taco Spices & Seasonings with sour cream and enough milk to thin to a pouring consistency; set aside. In another small bowl, combine remaining seasonings, oil and lime juice. Brush or spread seasoning paste over entire fish. Grill or broil until fish begins to flake easily, about 10 to 12 minutes. Evenly divide fish and place in center of each tortilla. Top with cabbage and reserved sauce. Garnish with olives and lime wedges. *Makes 6 servings*

**Hint:** Warmed corn tortillas may also be used.

**Variation:** To pan-fry: In medium skillet, heat a small amount of oil until hot. Carefully add fish and cook over medium heat 6 minutes. Turn fish and cook until fish begins to flake easily, 4 to 5 minutes.

**Prep Time:** 15 minutes
**Cook Time:** 10 to 12 minutes

# Grilled Fish with Orange-Chile Salsa

3 medium oranges, peeled
    and sectioned* (about
    1¼ cups segments)
¼ cup finely diced green, red
    or yellow bell pepper
3 tablespoons chopped
    cilantro, divided
3 tablespoons lime juice,
    divided
1 tablespoon honey
1 teaspoon minced, seeded
    serrano pepper *or*
    1 tablespoon minced
    jalapeño pepper
1¼ pounds firm white fish
    fillets, such as orange
    roughy, lingcod, halibut
    or red snapper
    Lime slices (optional)
    Zucchini ribbons, cooked

*Canned mandarin orange segments can be substituted for fresh orange segments, if desired.*

To prepare Orange-Chile Salsa, combine orange segments, bell pepper, 2 tablespoons cilantro, 2 tablespoons lime juice, honey and serrano pepper. Set aside.

Season fish fillets with remaining 1 tablespoon cilantro and 1 tablespoon lime juice. Lightly oil grid to prevent sticking. Grill fish on covered grill over medium KINGSFORD® Briquets 5 minutes. Turn and top with lime slices, if desired. Grill about 5 minutes until fish flakes easily when tested with fork. Serve with Orange-Chile Salsa. Garnish with zucchini ribbons.

*Makes 4 servings*

**Note:** Allow about 10 minutes grilling time per inch thickness of fish fillets.

## GRILLING TIP

*Fish fillets often are thicker at one end than the other. Arrange the fillets so the thin ends are towards the outside of the grill or an area when the heat is less intense.*

**Grilled Fish with Orange-Chile Salsa**

# Thai Seafood Kabobs with Spicy Peanut Rice

1¼ cups UNCLE BEN'S®
ORIGINAL
CONVERTED®
Brand Rice
1 pound medium raw shrimp,
peeled and deveined, with
tails intact
½ pound bay scallops
¼ cup soy sauce
2 tablespoons sesame oil
1 large red bell pepper, cut
into 1-inch squares
6 green onions with tops, cut
into 1-inch pieces
½ cup prepared Thai peanut
sauce*
½ cup chopped peanuts

*Thai peanut sauce can be found in the Asian
section of large supermarkets.

**1.** Cook rice according to package directions.

**2.** Meanwhile, place shrimp and scallops in medium bowl. Combine soy sauce and sesame oil; pour half of mixture over shellfish, tossing to coat. Let stand 15 minutes. Reserve remaining soy sauce mixture for basting.

**3.** Alternately thread shrimp, scallops, bell pepper and green onions onto twelve 12-inch metal skewers. Brush with half the reserved soy sauce mixture. Spoon Thai peanut sauce over each skewer, coating evenly. Grill or broil 8 minutes or until shrimp are pink and scallops are opaque, turning and brushing once with remaining soy sauce mixture and Thai peanut sauce.

**4.** Stir peanuts into cooked rice; place on serving platter. Top with seafood kabobs. Serve immediately.

*Makes 6 servings*

**Serving Suggestion:** Garnish with minced fresh cilantro, if desired.

## GRILLING TIP

*To thread shrimp on a skewer, pierce both the "shoulder" and tail so shrimp forms a U on the skewer.*

Thai Seafood Kabobs
with Spicy Peanut Rice

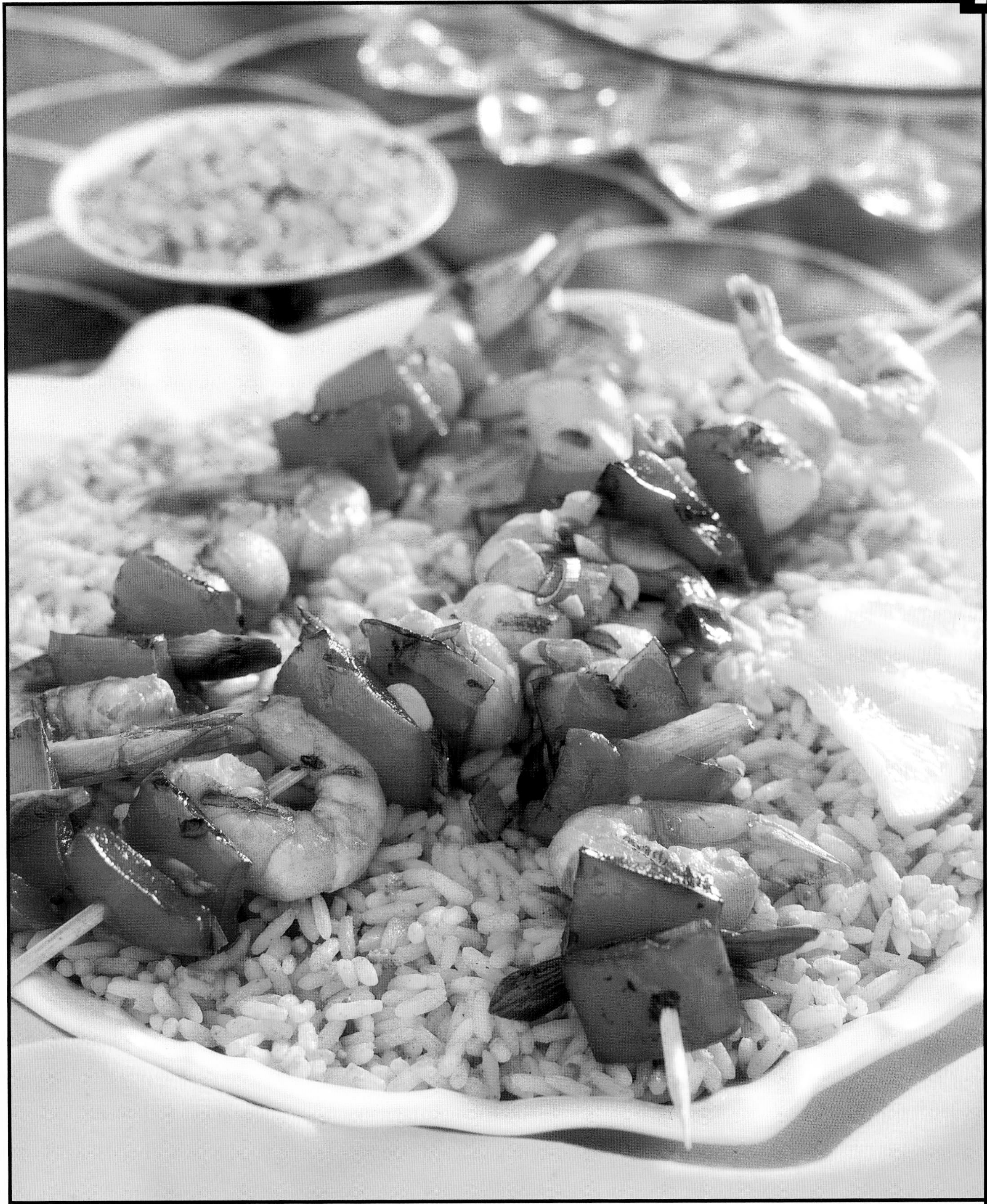

# Tuna Tacos with Grilled Pineapple Salsa

**Tuna Vera Cruz (recipe follows)**
½ **large pineapple, peeled, cored and cut into ½-inch-thick slices**
8 **corn tortillas**
½ **medium red onion, cut into thin slivers**
¼ **cup cilantro leaves, chopped**
1 **tablespoon lime juice**
1 **to 3 teaspoons minced, seeded jalapeño pepper**
1 **garlic clove, minced**
¼ **teaspoon salt**
¼ **teaspoon freshly ground black pepper**

Prepare Tuna Vera Cruz; keep warm. Grill pineapple over medium-hot KINGSFORD® Briquets about 2 minutes per side until lightly browned. Grill tortillas until hot but not crisp; keep warm. Cut grilled pineapple into ½-inch cubes. Combine pineapple, onion, cilantro, lime juice, jalapeño pepper, garlic, salt and black pepper in medium bowl. Break tuna into bite-size chunks. Spoon pineapple salsa down center of each tortilla; top with tuna. Roll to enclose. Serve immediately.     *Makes 4 servings*

## Tuna Vera Cruz

3 **tablespoons tequila, rum or vodka**
2 **tablespoons fresh lime juice**
2 **teaspoons grated lime peel**
1 **piece (1-inch cube) fresh ginger, minced**
2 **cloves garlic, minced**
1 **teaspoon salt**
1 **teaspoon sugar**
½ **teaspoon ground cumin**
¼ **teaspoon ground cinnamon**
¼ **teaspoon black pepper**
1 **tablespoon vegetable oil**
1½ **pounds fresh tuna, halibut, swordfish or shark steaks**
   **Lemon and lime wedges**
   **Fresh rosemary sprigs**

Combine tequila, lime juice, lime peel, ginger, garlic, salt, sugar, cumin, cinnamon and pepper in 2-quart glass dish; stir in oil. Add tuna; turn to coat. Cover and refrigerate at least 30 minutes. Remove tuna from marinade; discard marinade. Grill tuna over medium-hot KINGSFORD® Briquets about 4 minutes per side until fish flakes easily when tested with fork. Garnish with lemon wedges, lime wedges and rosemary sprigs.     *Makes 4 servings*

## Grilled Prawns with Salsa Vera Cruz

1 can (14½ ounces)
   DEL MONTE® Diced
   Tomatoes, drained
1 orange, peeled and chopped
¼ cup sliced green onions
¼ cup chopped cilantro or
   parsley
1 small clove garlic, crushed
1 pound medium shrimp,
   peeled and deveined

**1.** Combine tomatoes, orange, green onions, cilantro and garlic in medium bowl.

**2.** Thread shrimp onto skewers; season with salt and pepper, if desired.

**3.** Brush grill with oil. Cook shrimp over hot coals about 3 minutes on each side or until shrimp turn pink. Top with salsa. Serve over rice and garnish, if desired.

*Makes 4 servings*

**Hint:** Thoroughly rinse shrimp in cold water before cooking.

**Prep Time:** 25 minutes
**Cook Time:** 6 minutes

## Vegetable-Topped Fish Pouches

4 firm fish fillets, such as
   flounder, cod or halibut
   (about 1 pound)
1 carrot, cut into very thin
   strips
1 rib celery, cut into very thin
   strips
1 medium red onion, cut into
   thin wedges
1 medium zucchini or yellow
   squash, sliced
8 mushrooms, sliced
½ cup (about 2 ounces)
   shredded Swiss cheese
½ cup WISH-BONE® Italian
   Dressing*

*\*Also terrific with Wish-Bone® Robusto Italian or Just 2 Good Italian Dressing.*

On four 18×9-inch pieces heavy-duty aluminum foil, divide fish equally. Evenly top with vegetables, then cheese. Drizzle with Italian dressing. Wrap foil loosely around fillets and vegetables, sealing edges airtight with double fold. Let stand to marinate 15 minutes. Grill or broil pouches, seam sides up, 15 minutes or until fish flakes easily with fork.

*Makes 4 servings*

# Pacific Rim Honey-Barbecued Fish

¼ **cup honey**
¼ **cup chopped onion**
2 **tablespoons lime juice**
2 **tablespoons soy sauce**
2 **tablespoons hoisin sauce**
2 **cloves garlic, minced**
1 **jalapeño pepper, seeded and minced**
1 **teaspoon minced fresh gingerroot**
4 **swordfish steaks or other firm white fish (4 ounces each)**

Combine all ingredients except swordfish in small bowl; mix well. Place fish in shallow baking dish; pour marinade over fish. Cover and refrigerate 1 hour. Remove fish from marinade. Grill over medium-hot coals or broil fish about 10 minutes per inch of thickness or until fish turns opaque and flakes easily when tested with fork.

*Makes 4 servings*

*Favorite recipe from* **National Honey Board**

# Grilled Fish with Roasted Jalapeño Rub

3 **tablespoons chopped cilantro**
2 **tablespoons lime juice**
1 **tablespoon minced garlic**
1 **tablespoon minced fresh ginger**
1 **tablespoon minced roasted jalapeño peppers***
1½ **pounds firm white fish fillets, such as orange roughy or red snapper**
**Lime wedges**

*\* To roast peppers, place them on uncovered grill over hot coals. Grill until skin is blistered, turning frequently. Remove from grill and place peppers in large resealable plastic food storage bag for 15 minutes. Remove skins. Seed peppers, if desired, and cut them into thin slices.*

Combine cilantro, lime juice, garlic, ginger and peppers in small bowl. Lightly oil grid to prevent sticking. Grill fish on covered grill over hot KINGSFORD® Briquets 5 minutes. Turn; spread cilantro mixture on fish. Grill 3 to 5 minutes longer or until fish flakes easily when tested with fork. Serve with lime wedges.

*Makes 4 servings*

Pacific Rim Honey-Barbecued Fish

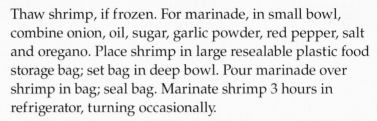

# Bacon-Wrapped Shrimp

1 pound fresh or frozen large raw shrimp, shelled and deveined
1 small onion, finely chopped
½ cup olive oil
½ teaspoon sugar
½ teaspoon garlic powder
½ teaspoon ground red pepper
¼ teaspoon salt
¼ teaspoon dried oregano leaves, crushed
½ pound bacon
   Mexican Fried Rice (recipe follows)

Thaw shrimp, if frozen. For marinade, in small bowl, combine onion, oil, sugar, garlic powder, red pepper, salt and oregano. Place shrimp in large resealable plastic food storage bag; set bag in deep bowl. Pour marinade over shrimp in bag; seal bag. Marinate shrimp 3 hours in refrigerator, turning occasionally.

Halve bacon slices lengthwise and crosswise. In large skillet, partially cook bacon. Drain on paper towels. Drain shrimp; discard marinade. Wrap bacon strips around shrimp; secure with wooden toothpicks. Place wrapped shrimp in wire grill basket or on 12×9-inch piece of heavy-duty aluminum foil. (If using foil, puncture foil in several places.)

Grill shrimp on uncovered grill directly over medium-hot KINGSFORD® Briquets 12 minutes or until bacon is done and shrimp are opaque, turning basket or individual shrimp once. Serve with Mexican Fried Rice.

*Makes 6 servings*

## Mexican Fried Rice

3 tablespoons vegetable oil
1 cup long-grain rice
1 (8-ounce) package frozen raw shrimp, shelled and deveined (optional)
1 cup salsa
½ cup chopped green bell pepper
1 small onion, chopped
1 clove garlic, minced

Heat oil in large skillet over medium heat. Add rice; cook until golden brown, stirring frequently. Stir in shrimp, salsa, bell pepper, onion, garlic and 2 cups water. Bring mixture to a boil; reduce heat to low. Cover; simmer 15 to 20 minutes or until rice is tender. Season to taste; serve with additional salsa, if desired. *Makes 6 servings*

# Tandoori-Style Seafood Kabobs

½ pound each salmon fillet, tuna steak and swordfish steak*
1 teaspoon salt
1 teaspoon ground cumin
¼ teaspoon black pepper
  Dash ground cinnamon
  Dash ground cloves
  Dash ground nutmeg
  Dash ground cardamom (optional)
½ cup plain low-fat yogurt
¼ cup lemon juice
1 piece (1-inch cube) peeled fresh ginger, minced
1 tablespoon olive oil
2 cloves garlic, minced
½ jalapeño pepper, seeded and minced
½ pound large shrimp, shelled with tails intact, deveined
1 each red and green bell pepper, cut into bite-size pieces
  Fresh parsley sprigs
  Fresh chives

*Any firm fish can be substituted for any fish listed above.

Cut fish into 1½-inch cubes; cover and refrigerate. Heat salt and spices in small skillet over medium heat until fragrant (or spices may be added to marinade without heating); place spices in 2-quart glass dish. Add yogurt, lemon juice, ginger, oil, garlic and jalapeño pepper; mix well. Add fish and shrimp; turn to coat. Cover and refrigerate at least 1 hour but no longer than 2 hours. Thread a variety of seafood onto each metal or wooden skewer, alternating with bell peppers. (Soak wooden skewers in hot water 30 minutes to prevent burning.) Grill kabobs over medium-hot KINGSFORD® Briquets about 2 minutes per side until fish flakes easily when tested with fork and shrimp are pink and opaque. Remove seafood and peppers from skewers. Garnish with parsley and chives. *Makes 4 servings*

## GRILLING TIP

*When purchasing fish for grilling, purchase steaks or fillets that are at least 1/2-inch thick; anything thinner will quickly overcook and easily fall apart on the grid.*

# Grilled Paella

1½ to 2 pounds chicken wings or thighs

2 tablespoons plus ¼ cup extra-virgin olive oil, divided

Salt and black pepper

1 pound garlicky sausage links, such as linguisa, chorizo or Italian

1 large onion, chopped

2 large red bell peppers, seeded and cut into thin strips

4 cloves garlic, minced

1 can (14 ounces) diced tomatoes, undrained

4 cups uncooked rice

16 tightly closed live mussels or clams,* scrubbed

½ pound large shrimp,* peeled and deveined with tails intact

1½ cups frozen peas

1 can (about 14 ounces) chicken broth

2 lemons, cut into wedges

1 oval disposable foil pan (about 17×13×3 inches)

*Seafood can be omitted; add an additional 1¼ to 1½ pounds chicken.

Brush chicken with 2 tablespoons oil; season with salt and black pepper. Grill chicken and sausage on covered grill over medium KINGSFORD® Briquets 15 to 20 minutes or until chicken juices run clear and sausage is no longer pink, turning every 5 minutes. Cut sausage into 2-inch pieces.

Heat remaining ¼ cup oil in large skillet over medium-high heat. Add onion, bell peppers and garlic; cook and stir 5 minutes or until vegetables are tender. Add tomatoes, 1½ teaspoons salt and ½ teaspoon black pepper; cook about 8 minutes until thick, stirring frequently. Combine onion mixture and rice in foil pan; spread evenly. Arrange chicken, sausage, seafood and peas over rice. Bring broth and 6 cups water to a boil in 3 quart saucepan. Place foil pan on grid over medium KINGSFORD® briquets; immediately pour boiling broth mixture over rice. Grill on covered grill about 20 minutes until liquid is absorbed. *Do not stir.* Cover with foil; let stand 10 minutes. Garnish with lemon wedges.

*Makes 8 to 10 servings*

## Snapper with Pesto Butter

½ cup butter or margarine, softened
1 cup packed fresh basil leaves, coarsely chopped *or* ½ cup chopped fresh parsley plus 2 tablespoons dried basil leaves, crushed
3 tablespoons finely grated fresh Parmesan cheese
1 clove garlic, minced
Olive oil
2 to 3 teaspoons lemon juice
4 to 6 red snapper, rock cod, salmon or other medium-firm fish fillets (at least ½ inch thick)
Salt and black pepper
Lemon wedges
Fresh basil or parsley sprigs and lemon strips for garnish

To make Pesto Butter, place butter, basil, cheese, garlic and 1 tablespoon oil in blender or food processor; process until blended. Stir in lemon juice to taste. Rinse fish; pat dry with paper towels. Brush one side of fish lightly with oil; season with salt and pepper.

Oil hot grid to help prevent sticking. Grill fillets, oil sides down, on a covered grill over medium KINGSFORD® Briquets, 5 to 9 minutes. Halfway through cooking time, brush tops with oil; season with salt and pepper. Turn and continue grilling until fish turns opaque throughout. (Allow 3 to 5 minutes for each ½ inch of thickness.) Serve each fillet with a spoonful of Pesto Butter and a wedge of lemon. Garnish with basil sprigs and lemon strips.

*Makes 4 to 6 servings*

## Grilled Fresh Fish

3 to 3½ pounds fresh tuna or catfish
¾ cup prepared HIDDEN VALLEY® The Original Ranch® Dressing
Chopped fresh dill
Lemon wedges (optional)

Place fish on heavy-duty foil. Cover with salad dressing. Grill over medium-hot coals until fish turns opaque and flakes easily when tested with fork, 20 to 30 minutes. Or, broil fish 15 to 20 minutes. Sprinkle with dill; garnish with lemon wedges, if desired. *Makes 6 servings*

**Snapper with Pesto Butter**

# Tuna Kabobs with Red Pepper Relish

1 pound tuna steak, cut into
    1-inch squares
6 tablespoons red pepper
    jelly*
⅓ cup *French's*® Bold n' Spicy
    Brown Mustard
2 tablespoons balsamic or red
    wine vinegar
½ teaspoon cracked black
    pepper
¼ teaspoon salt
1 red bell pepper, minced
1 green onion, minced
1 orange, unpeeled, cut into
    1-inch pieces
1 green bell pepper, cut into
    1-inch pieces

*If red pepper jelly is unavailable, combine
6 tablespoons melted apple jelly with
1 tablespoon Frank's® RedHot® Cayenne Pepper
Sauce. Mix well.*

**1.** Place tuna in large resealable plastic food storage bag. Combine jelly, mustard, vinegar, black pepper and salt in 1-cup measure. Pour ½ cup jelly marinade over tuna. Seal bag; marinate in refrigerator 15 minutes.

**2.** Combine remaining jelly marinade, red bell pepper and onion in small serving bowl. Reserve for relish.

**3.** Alternately thread tuna, orange and green bell pepper onto 4 (12-inch) metal skewers. Place skewers on oiled grid. Grill over medium-low heat 8 to 10 minutes or until fish is opaque, but slightly soft in center, turning and basting halfway with marinade.** Serve with red pepper relish.    *Makes 4 servings*

*\*\*Tuna becomes dry and tough if overcooked. Watch carefully while grilling.*

**Prep Time:** 25 minutes
**Marinate Time:** 15 minutes
**Cook Time:** 8 minutes

## GRILLING TIP

*To test for doneness separate the fish with a fork or tip of a knife. The flesh will be just slightly translucent in the center and it will look very moist. As you remove it from the grill the fish will turn from translucent to opaque throughout.*

# Teriyaki Salmon Steaks

½ cup LAWRY'S® Teriyaki
   Marinade with Pineapple
   Juice
¼ cup sherry
2 tablespoons orange juice
1 tablespoon Dijon-style
   mustard
4 salmon steaks (about
   2 pounds)
1 large tomato, chopped
½ cup thinly sliced green
   onion

In large resealable plastic food storage bag, combine Teriyaki Marinade with Pineapple Juice, sherry, orange juice and mustard; mix well. Remove ¼ cup marinade for basting. Add salmon; seal bag. Marinate in refrigerator at least 40 minutes, turning occasionally. In small bowl, combine tomato and green onion; set aside. Remove salmon; discard used marinade. Broil or grill, 4 inches from heat source, 3 to 5 minutes, brushing once with additional ¼ cup marinade; turning salmon once. Spoon vegetables over salmon; broil or grill 3 to 5 minutes longer or until thickest part of salmon flakes easily with fork. *Do not baste during last 5 minutes of cooking.* Discard any remaining marinade. Garnish as desired.

*Makes 4 servings*

# Asian Honey-Tea Grilled Prawns

1½ pounds medium shrimp,
   peeled and deveined
   Salt
2 green onions, thinly sliced

Marinade
   1 cup brewed double-strength
      orange-spice tea, cooled
   ¼ cup honey
   ¼ cup rice vinegar
   ¼ cup soy sauce
   1 tablespoon fresh ginger,
      peeled and finely chopped
   ½ teaspoon ground black
      pepper

In plastic food storage bag, combine marinade ingredients. Remove ½ cup marinade; set aside for dipping sauce. Add shrimp to marinade in bag, turning to coat. Close bag securely and marinate in refrigerator 30 minutes or up to 12 hours.

Remove shrimp from marinade; discard marinade. Thread shrimp onto 8 skewers, dividing evenly. Grill over medium coals 4 to 6 minutes or until shrimp turn pink and are just firm to the touch, turning once. Season with salt, as desired.

Meanwhile prepare dipping sauce by placing reserved ½ cup marinade in small saucepan. Bring to a boil over medium-high heat. Boil 3 to 5 minutes or until slightly reduced. Stir in green onions. *Makes 4 servings*

*Favorite recipe from* **National Honey Board**

Teriyaki Salmon Steak

# BBQ
## SIDEKICKS

## Goat Cheese & Corn Chiles Rellenos

4 large plum tomatoes,
  seeded and diced
1 small red onion, diced and
  divided
3 tablespoons extra-virgin
  olive oil, divided
2 cloves garlic, minced and
  divided
1 teaspoon balsamic vinegar
¼ teaspoon salt
¼ teaspoon black pepper
6 poblano *or* 8 Anaheim
  peppers
2 ears corn, husked*
¾ cup crumbled goat or feta
  cheese
½ cup (2 ounces) shredded
  hot pepper Jack,
  Monterey Jack or sharp
  Cheddar cheese
½ cup minced fresh cilantro
  Fresh cilantro sprigs

*Substitute 1 can (17 ounces) corn, drained, or
1½ cups frozen corn, thawed, for fresh corn, if
desired. Add to filling as directed above.*

Combine tomatoes, ½ onion, 2 tablespoons oil, 1 clove
garlic, vinegar, salt and black pepper in medium bowl;
let salsa stand 15 minutes. Remove stems from poblano
peppers by cutting each pepper about ½ inch from
stem; remove seeds. Grill peppers over medium-hot
KINGSFORD® Briquets until skins are charred on all
sides. Place peppers in large resealable plastic food
storage bag; seal. Let stand 5 minutes; remove skin. Grill
corn over medium-hot briquets 6 to 10 minutes or until
tender, turning every minute; cut kernels from cob.
Combine corn, cheeses, minced cilantro, remaining
½ onion and 1 clove garlic in medium bowl; mix well.
Carefully fill each pepper with cheese mixture, making
cut in side of pepper, if necessary. Secure opening
with wooden pick. (Soak wooden picks in hot water
15 minutes to prevent burning.) Brush peppers with
remaining 1 tablespoon oil; grill over medium briquets
1 minute per side until cheese melts. Serve with salsa.
Garnish with cilantro sprigs.          *Makes 6 servings*

**Goat Cheese & Corn Chiles Rellenos**

# Grilled Vegetables with Balsamic Vinaigrette

1 medium eggplant (about
   1¼ pounds)
2 medium zucchini
2 to 3 medium yellow squash
2 medium red bell peppers
¾ cup olive oil
¼ cup balsamic vinegar
1 teaspoon salt
¼ teaspoon black pepper
1 clove garlic, minced
2 to 3 tablespoons finely
   chopped mixed fresh
   herbs

Trim, then slice eggplant, zucchini and yellow squash lengthwise into ¼- to ½-inch-thick slices. Core, seed and cut red peppers into 1-inch-wide strips. Place vegetables in deep serving platter or wide shallow casserole. Combine oil, vinegar, salt, pepper, garlic and herbs in small bowl. Pour vinaigrette over vegetables; turn to coat. Let stand 30 minutes or longer. Lift vegetables from vinaigrette, leaving vinaigrette that doesn't cling to the vegetables in the platter.

Oil hot grid to help prevent sticking. Grill vegetables on covered grill over medium KINGSFORD® Briquets, 8 to 16 minutes until fork-tender, turning once or twice. (Time will depend on the vegetable; eggplant takes the longest.) As vegetables are done, return them to the platter, then turn to coat with vinaigrette. (Or, cut eggplant, zucchini and yellow squash into cubes, then toss with red peppers and vinaigrette.) Serve warm or at room temperature.

*Makes 6 servings*

## GRILLING TIP

*Dried or fresh herbs impart a distinctive flavor to grilled foods. Add herbs to marinades for extra flavor. Also soak and drain herbs such as rosemary, sage or thyme and sprinkle on hot coals immediately before cooking for another easy and unique way to give flavor.*

**Grilled Vegetables
with Balsamic Vinaigrette**

# Grilled Banana Squash with Rum & Brown Sugar

2 pounds banana squash or
  butternut squash
2 tablespoons dark rum or
  apple juice
2 tablespoons melted butter
2 tablespoons brown sugar

Cut squash into 4 pieces; discard seeds. Place squash in microwavable baking dish. Cover with vented plastic wrap. Microwave at HIGH 5 to 7 minutes, turning once. Discard plastic wrap; pierce flesh of squash with fork at 1-inch intervals. Place squash in foil pan. Combine rum and butter; brush over squash. Sprinkle with sugar. Grill squash on covered grill over medium KINGSFORD® Briquets 20 to 30 minutes until squash is tender.

*Makes 4 servings*

# Mesquite Baked Beans

4 strips 50% less salt bacon
1 large red onion, minced
1 (28-ounce) can low sodium
  baked beans in tomato
  sauce
2 tablespoons MRS. DASH®
  Mesquite Grilling Blend
1 teaspoon dry mustard
½ cup maple syrup

Preheat oven to 350°F. Fry bacon in large skillet over medium-high heat. Cook until lightly browned and crisp. Remove from skillet and set aside. Add onion to skillet and cook until soft. Dice bacon. Place beans, bacon and onion in 2-quart casserole. Combine Mrs. Dash® Mesquite Grilling Blend, dry mustard and maple syrup in bowl and mix well; add to beans and stir. Cover and bake for 25 minutes or until beans are bubbling and heated through.

*Makes 6 servings*

**Note:** This casserole can be made ahead and heated when ready to serve.

**Serving Suggestion:** This is a natural side dish for any barbecue. Serve it with ribs or chicken.

**Prep Time:** 10 minutes
**Cook Time:** 25 minutes

# Risotto with Grilled Vegetables

1 medium yellow onion, cut into ½-inch slices
1 zucchini, cut lengthwise into halves
   Olive oil
1 *each* small red and yellow bell peppers
1 tablespoon butter
1 cup arborio rice
3 to 3½ cups canned chicken broth, divided
½ cup dry sherry
⅔ cup freshly grated Parmesan cheese
   Black pepper
¼ cup toasted pine nuts
   Chopped parsley

Insert wooden picks into onion slices from edges to prevent separating into rings. (Soak wooden picks in hot water 15 minutes to prevent burning.) Brush onion and zucchini lightly with oil. Grill onion, zucchini and bell peppers on covered grill over medium KINGSFORD® Briquets 5 to 10 minutes for zucchini and 20 to 30 minutes for peppers and onion or until crisp-tender. Cut vegetables into chunks. Heat butter and 1 tablespoon oil in 3-quart saucepan over medium heat. Add rice; cook and stir 3 to 4 minutes or until opaque. Add ¼ cup broth and sherry; cook 3 to 5 minutes over medium-low heat until almost all liquid is absorbed, stirring constantly. Continue adding broth in about ¾-cup increments, cooking and stirring after each addition until broth is absorbed and rice is tender and creamy. Stir in Parmesan cheese with last addition of broth. Season to taste with black pepper; stir in pine nuts and grilled vegetables, reserving a few for garnish. Spoon risotto into serving dish; top with reserved vegetables and parsley.

*Makes 6 to 8 servings*

## FOOD FACT

*Impress your family and guests with Risotto, a delicious creamy rice dish originating in Italy. For successful results use arborio rice and add liquid a small amount at a time stirring frequently until rice is firm but creamy.*

# Savory Herb-Stuffed Onions

1 zucchini, cut lengthwise into
　　¼-inch-thick slices
　Nonstick cooking spray
3 shiitake mushrooms
4 large sweet onions
1 plum tomato, seeded and
　　chopped
2 tablespoons fresh bread
　　crumbs
1 tablespoon fresh basil *or*
　　1 teaspoon dried basil
1 teaspoon olive oil
¼ teaspoon salt
⅛ teaspoon black pepper
4 teaspoons balsamic vinegar

**1.** To grill zucchini, spray both sides with cooking spray. Grill on uncovered grill over medium coals 4 minutes or until tender, turning once. Cool; cut into bite-size pieces.

**2.** Thread mushrooms onto metal skewers. Grill on covered grill over medium coals 20 to 30 minutes or until tender. Coarsely chop; set aside.

**3.** Remove stem and root ends of onions, leaving peels intact. Spray onions with cooking spray; grill root-end up on covered grill over medium coals 5 minutes or until lightly charred. Remove; cool slightly. Peel and scoop about 1 inch of pulp from stem ends; chop pulp for filling.

**4.** Combine chopped onion, mushrooms, zucchini, tomato, bread crumbs, basil, oil, salt and pepper; mix until well blended. Spoon equal amounts of stuffing mixture into centers of onions.

**5.** Place each onion on sheet of foil; sprinkle each with 1 tablespoon water. Wrap onions and seal foil. Grill onion packets on covered grill over medium coals 45 to 60 minutes or until tender. Spoon 1 teaspoon vinegar over each onion before serving. *Makes 4 servings*

Savory Herb-Stuffed Onions

# Portobello Mushrooms Sesame

4 large portobello
    mushrooms
2 tablespoons sweet rice wine
2 tablespoons reduced-
    sodium soy sauce
2 cloves garlic, minced
1 teaspoon dark sesame oil

**1.** Remove and discard stems from mushrooms; set caps aside. Combine remaining ingredients in small bowl.

**2.** Brush both sides of mushrooms with soy sauce mixture. Grill mushrooms top side up on covered grill over medium coals 3 to 4 minutes. Brush tops with soy sauce mixture and turn over; grill 2 minutes more or until mushrooms are lightly browned. Turn again and grill, basting frequently, 4 to 5 minutes or until tender when pressed with back of spatula. Remove mushrooms and cut diagonally into ½-inch-thick slices.

*Makes 4 servings*

# Grilled Potato Slices

3 large Idaho or russet
    potatoes
¼ cup CRISCO® Oil*
½ teaspoon salt
¼ teaspoon freshly ground
    black pepper

*Use your favorite Crisco Oil product.*

**1.** Prepare charcoal or gas grill.

**2.** Scrub potatoes under cold running water. Cut into ¾-inch slices. Cover with salted cold water. Bring to a boil on high heat. Boil for 6 minutes. Drain.

**3.** Brush potato slices with oil. Sprinkle with salt and pepper. Grill slices for 3 minutes. Turn with tongs. Grill second side for 3 minutes or until brown. Serve immediately.

*Makes 4 servings*

**Tip:** Always brush the cool grill grids with Crisco® Oil or spray with Crisco® No-Stick Spray before turning on the grill so that food will not stick.

**Prep Time:** 5 minutes
**Total Time:** 30 minutes

# Grilled Vegetables with Olive Sauce

2 frozen ears sweet corn, thawed and cut into rounds
2 large yellow pattypan squash, coarsely chopped
1 medium zucchini, thinly sliced
  Vegetable oil
¼ cup butter, melted
6 green olives with pimientos, finely chopped
1 tablespoon fresh lemon juice
¼ teaspoon dried parsley flakes
1 container (16 ounces) cottage cheese

**1.** Prepare grill for direct cooking. Place corn, squash and zucchini on prepared vegetable grilling grid; brush with oil and season with salt and pepper to taste.

**2.** Grill vegetables on covered grill over hot coals 10 minutes or until crisp-tender, turning halfway. Remove; keep warm.

**3.** Combine butter, olives, lemon juice and parsley; stir well.

**4.** Place vegetables on serving platter; drizzle with 2 tablespoons olive sauce. Serve with cottage cheese and remaining olive sauce. *Makes 4 servings*

**Prep and Cook Time:** 20 minutes

# Grilled Asparagus

1 pound fresh asparagus
  CRISCO® No-Stick Cooking Spray
½ teaspoon salt
¼ teaspoon freshly ground black pepper

**1.** Prepare charcoal or gas grill. Trim woody stems off asparagus by breaking stalks. Spray asparagus with Crisco No-Stick Cooking Spray.

**2.** Grill asparagus for 3 minutes. Turn spears with tongs. Grill 3 to 4 minutes. Sprinkle with salt and pepper. Serve immediately. *Makes 4 servings*

Grilled Vegetables with Olive Sauce

# Ratatouille Salsa

1 medium eggplant

1 medium zucchini

1 medium yellow squash

2 tablespoons *French's®* Worcestershire Sauce

2 tablespoons olive oil

4 ripe plum tomatoes, chopped

½ cup oil-cured olives, pitted

**Herbed Dressing**

½ cup olive oil

3 tablespoons *French's®* Worcestershire Sauce

3 tablespoons *French's®* Napa Valley Style Dijon Mustard

3 tablespoons lemon juice

3 tablespoons minced fresh basil leaves

3 tablespoons minced fresh parsley

2 tablespoons capers, drained

2 cloves garlic, minced

½ teaspoon salt

Cut eggplant, zucchini and squash lengthwise into ½-inch-thick slices. Combine 2 tablespoons Worcestershire and 2 tablespoons oil in small bowl; mix well. Brush vegetables with oil mixture. Place vegetables on grid. Grill over hot coals about 5 minutes or until vegetables are tender, turning often.

Cut vegetables into large chunks. Place in large bowl with tomatoes and olives. Combine Herbed Dressing ingredients in small bowl; mix well. Pour Herbed Dressing over vegetables; toss well to coat evenly. Serve warm or refrigerate until chilled.

*Makes 6 side-dish servings*

**Prep Time:** 20 minutes
**Cook Time:** 5 minutes

# Grilled Greek Vegetables

¼ cup olive oil
1 tablespoon lemon juice
2 teaspoons pressed garlic
1 teaspoon dried oregano
   leaves
1 pound assorted fresh
   vegetables, such as
   eggplant, bell peppers,
   summer squash,
   mushrooms and onions

Combine oil, lemon juice, garlic and oregano in large bowl. Slice eggplant into ½-inch-thick rounds.* Cut small squash lengthwise into halves; cut large squash into ½-inch-thick pieces. Cut bell peppers into large chunks. Cut onions into wedges or thick slices. Toss vegetables with oil mixture to coat. Place vegetables in single layer on grid; reserve remaining oil mixture. Grill on covered grill over medium KINGSFORD® Briquets 10 to 20 minutes or until tender, turning once and basting with remaining oil mixture. *Makes 4 servings*

*If desired, eggplant slices can be salted on both sides and placed in single layer on paper towels. Let stand 30 minutes; blot dry with paper towels.*

# Skewered Vegetables

2 medium zucchini, cut
   lengthwise into halves,
   then cut into 1-inch slices
8 pearl onions, cut into halves
½ red bell pepper, cut into
   1-inch pieces
8 fresh medium mushrooms
   (optional)
16 lemon slices
2 tablespoons butter or
   margarine, melted
   Salt and black pepper

Place zucchini, onions and red bell pepper in medium saucepan with enough water to cover. Bring to a boil; cover and continue boiling 1 minute. Remove with slotted spoon and drain. Alternately thread zucchini, onions, red bell pepper, mushrooms, if desired, and lemon slices onto 8 metal or bamboo skewers. (Soak bamboo skewers in water at least 20 minutes to keep them from burning.)

Oil hot grid to help prevent sticking. Grill vegetables on covered grill over medium-hot KINGSFORD® Briquets, 6 minutes or until tender, carefully basting with butter and turning skewers once. Season to taste with salt and pepper. Serve immediately. *Makes 8 servings*

# Barbecued Corn with Three Savory Butters

**12 ears corn, unhusked**
**Three Savory Butters**
**(recipes follow)**

Carefully peel back husks; remove corn silk. Bring husks up and tie securely with kitchen string. Soak corn in cold water to cover 30 minutes.

Place corn on grid. Grill over medium-high coals 25 minutes or until corn is tender, turning often. Remove string and husks. Serve with your choice of savory butter.

*Makes 12 side-dish servings*

**Prep Time:** 40 minutes
**Cook Time:** 25 minutes

## Three Savory Butters

**Horseradish Butter**
  ½ **cup (1 stick) butter or margarine, softened**
  3 **tablespoons** *French's®* **Bold n' Spicy Brown Mustard**
  1 **tablespoon horseradish**

**Redhot® Chili Butter**
  ½ **cup (1 stick) butter or margarine, softened**
  2 **tablespoons** *Frank's® RedHot®* **Cayenne Pepper Sauce**
  1 **teaspoon chili powder**
  1 **clove garlic, minced**

**Herb Butter**
  ½ **cup (1 stick) butter or margarine, softened**
  2 **tablespoons snipped fresh chives**
  1 **tablespoon** *French's®* **Worcestershire Sauce**
  1 **tablespoon minced fresh parsley**
  ½ **teaspoon dried thyme leaves**
  ½ **teaspoon salt (optional)**

Place ingredients for each flavored butter in separate small bowls; beat until smooth. Serve at room temperature.

*Makes about ½ cup each*

Barbecued Corn
with Three Savory Butters

# Zesty Grilled Potatoes with Lemon Aioli Sauce

4 medium russet potatoes
½ teaspoon salt
⅓ cup melted butter or margarine
3 tablespoons *French's®* Napa Valley Style Dijon Mustard
3 tablespoons *French's®* Worcestershire Sauce
Lemon Aioli Sauce (recipe follows)

**1.** Cut potatoes lengthwise into ½-inch-thick slices. Place potatoes, 1 cup water and salt in shallow microwavable baking dish. Cover and microwave on HIGH (100%) 10 minutes or until potatoes are crisp-tender, stirring halfway through cooking. (If necessary, cook potatoes in two batches.) Drain.

**2.** Combine butter, mustard and Worcestershire in small bowl. Brush on potato slices. Place potatoes on oiled grid. Grill over medium-high heat 8 to 10 minutes or until potatoes are fork-tender, turning and basting often with butter mixture. Serve with Lemon Aioli Sauce.

*Makes 4 servings*

**Prep Time:** 10 minutes
**Cook Time:** 20 minutes

### Lemon Aioli Sauce

½ cup regular or reduced-fat mayonnaise
3 tablespoons *French's®* Napa Valley Style Dijon Mustard
1 tablespoon lemon juice
½ teaspoon grated lemon peel
1 clove garlic, minced

Combine mayonnaise, mustard, lemon juice, lemon peel and garlic in medium bowl. Cover and chill in refrigerator 1 hour.

*Makes about ¾ cup sauce*

**Chill Time:** 1 hour

# Grilled Mesquite Vegetables

2 to 3 tablespoons
    MRS. DASH® Mesquite
    Grilling Blend
4 tablespoons olive oil,
    divided
1 eggplant, trimmed and cut
    into ½-inch chunks
1 zucchini, quartered
    lengthwise
1 red onion, peeled and
    halved
2 red bell peppers, cut into
    large slices
2 green bell peppers, cut into
    large slices
1½ tablespoons balsamic
    vinegar

Preheat barbecue grill to medium. In large bowl, combine Mrs. Dash® Mesquite Grilling Blend and 2 tablespoons olive oil. Add vegetables and toss until well coated with olive oil mixture. Place vegetables on grill. Cover and cook, turning vegetables once during cooking. Cook until tender and vegetables develop grill marks, about 3 to 4 minutes on each side. Remove vegetables from grill as soon as they are cooked. Coarsely chop vegetables into ½-inch pieces. Mix remaining 2 tablespoons olive oil and balsamic vinegar in large bowl. Add cut vegetables and toss to coat. Serve at room temperature.

*Makes 6 servings*

**Note:** Grilling vegetables dehydrates them slightly and intensifies flavors while Mrs. Dash® Mesquite adds a third dimension of flavor. This dish makes a colorful accompaniment to any grilled meat.

**Prep Time:** 10 minutes
**Cooking Time:** 10 minutes

## FOOD FACT

*Vegetable kabobs made with small new potatoes, potato wedges, sweet potatoes, carrots and onions make colorful accompaniments. Parcook these vegetables in the microwave, toss with a small amount of oil and season with salt and pepper and your favorite seasonings before making kabobs. Then cook on the grill until done. Yum! Yum!*

# Mediterranean Grilled Vegetables

4 medium red or Yukon gold
    potatoes, cooked
3 tablespoons orange juice
2 tablespoons balsamic
    vinegar
1 clove garlic, minced
½ teaspoon salt
¼ teaspoon black pepper
⅓ cup plus 3 tablespoons olive
    oil, divided
8 thin slices (4×2 inches)
    prosciutto or ham
    (optional)
3 ounces soft goat cheese, cut
    into 8 pieces (optional)
8 asparagus spears
2 red or yellow bell peppers,
    cut in half, stemmed and
    seeded
2 zucchini, cut lengthwise into
    ¼-inch slices
2 Japanese eggplants, cut
    lengthwise into ¼-inch
    slices
1 bulb fennel, cut in half
8 large mushrooms
2 poblano or green bell
    peppers, cut in half,
    stemmed and seeded

Cut potatoes into thick slices. Combine juice, vinegar, garlic, salt and black pepper in small bowl; whisk in ⅓ cup oil. Set aside. Wrap each slice prosciutto around 1 piece cheese and 1 asparagus spear. Thread cheese bundles onto wooden skewers, piercing asparagus and securing cheese with wooden picks, if necessary. (Soak wooden skewers and picks in hot water 30 minutes to prevent burning.) Brush bundles with 3 tablespoons remaining oil.

Grill bell peppers, skin sides down, over medium KINGSFORD® Briquets 8 minutes until skins are charred. Place in large resealable plastic food storage bag; seal. Let stand 5 minutes; remove skin. Grill remaining vegetables on covered grill over medium briquets 2 to 5 minutes per side until tender. Grill cheese bundles over medium briquets until lightly browned. Arrange vegetables and cheese bundles in 13×9-inch glass dish; drizzle with dressing, turning to coat. Let stand 15 minutes.

*Makes 6 to 8 servings*

# Grilled Vegetables al Fresco

2 large red bell peppers

2 medium zucchini

1 large eggplant

**Spicy Marinade**

⅔ cup white wine vinegar

½ cup soy sauce

2 tablespoons minced ginger

2 tablespoons olive oil

2 tablespoons sesame oil

2 large cloves garlic, minced

2 teaspoons TABASCO®
brand Pepper Sauce

Seed red bell peppers; cut each pepper into quarters. Cut each zucchini lengthwise into ¼-inch-thick strips. Slice eggplant into ¼-inch-thick rounds.

In 13×9-inch baking dish, combine Spicy Marinade ingredients. Place vegetable pieces in mixture; toss to mix well. Cover and refrigerate vegetables at least 2 hours or up to 24 hours, turning occasionally.

About 30 minutes before serving, preheat grill to medium heat, placing rack 5 to 6 inches above coals. Place red bell peppers, zucchini and eggplant slices on grill rack. Grill vegetables 4 minutes, turning once and brushing with marinade occasionally.

*Makes 4 servings*

**To Broil:** Preheat oven broiler and broil vegetables 5 to 6 inches below broiler flame for 4 minutes on each side.

# Burger Topper

¾ cup HIDDEN VALLEY®
The Original Ranch®
Salad Dressing &
Seasoning Mix

¼ cup thinly sliced green
onions

2 tablespoons
KC MASTERPIECE™
Barbecue Sauce

Stir together dressing, onions and barbecue sauce. Serve 1 to 2 tablespoons mixture on a hamburger or turkey burger.

*Makes 1 cup topper*

# Sweet Adobe Sauce

2 to 3 whole chipotle peppers in adobo sauce, finely chopped
½ teaspoon fresh minced garlic
1 jar (10 ounces) KNOTT'S BERRY FARM® Raspberry Preserves or Apricot & Pineapple Preserves
½ tablespoon cider vinegar

In small saucepan over medium heat, sauté chipotle peppers and garlic until garlic is tender; stir constantly. Add preserves and vinegar. Bring to a boil; reduce heat and simmer 5 minutes. Serve warm over grilled or baked ham, pork chops or chicken. *Makes 1¾ cups sauce*

**Prep Time:** 10 minutes

# Peachy Mustard Glaze

¾ cup peach preserves
¼ cup *French's*® Classic Yellow® Mustard
2 tablespoons orange juice

Microwave preserves in small microwavable bowl on HIGH (100%) 2 minutes or until melted, stirring once. Stir in mustard and juice. *Makes 1 cup glaze*

**Tip:** Brush glaze on chicken, turkey or pork during last 15 minutes of grilling. Serve any extra glaze on the side for dipping.

**Prep Time:** 5 minutes

# Jamaican BBQ Sauce

⅓ cup molasses
⅓ cup prepared mustard
⅓ cup red wine vinegar
3 tablespoons Worcestershire sauce
¾ teaspoon TABASCO® brand Pepper Sauce

Combine ingredients in small bowl until well blended. Use as a baste while grilling beef, chicken, pork or game. *Makes 1 cup*

# Honey Barbecue Sauce

1 can (10¾ ounces)
   condensed tomato soup
½ cup honey
¼ cup fresh lime juice
2 to 3 tablespoons
   vegetable oil
2 tablespoons Worcestershire
   sauce
1 tablespoon lemon juice
1 teaspoon prepared mustard
  Dash ground red pepper or
   bottled hot pepper sauce
   (optional)

Combine ingredients in medium saucepan. Bring to a boil over medium heat. Reduce heat to low and simmer, uncovered, 5 minutes. Use as a baste while grilling beef, ribs or poultry. *Makes about 2 cups*

*Favorite recipe from* **National Honey Board**

# Lemon-Garlic Grilling Sauce

½ cup butter or margarine,
   melted
¼ cup lemon juice
1 tablespoon Worcestershire
   sauce
3 cloves garlic, peeled and
   minced
½ teaspoon TABASCO® brand
   Pepper Sauce
¼ teaspoon black pepper

Combine butter, lemon juice, Worcestershire sauce, garlic, TABASCO® Sauce and black pepper in small bowl; mix well. Brush on fish, seafood, poultry or vegetables during grilling or broiling. *Makes ¾ cup*

**Top to bottom: Honey Barbecue Sauce,
Honey Strawberry Salsa (page 345),
Herbed Honey Lime Sauce  (page 338)**

# Sweet 'n' Smoky BBQ Sauce

½ cup ketchup
⅓ cup *French's®* Bold n' Spicy
    Brown Mustard
⅓ cup light molasses
¼ cup *French's®*
    Worcestershire Sauce
¼ teaspoon liquid smoke or
    hickory salt (optional)

Combine ketchup, mustard, molasses, Worcestershire and liquid smoke, if desired, in medium bowl. Mix until well blended. Brush on chicken or ribs during last 15 minutes of grilling.    *Makes about 1½ cups sauce*

**Prep Time:** 5 minutes

# Herbed Honey Lime Sauce

½ cup minced onion
1 tablespoon olive oil
1 cup dry white wine or
    chicken broth
¼ cup honey
¼ cup lime juice
2 teaspoons dry mustard
1 teaspoon minced fresh
    rosemary
½ teaspoon salt
  Dash pepper
1 teaspoon cornstarch
1 teaspoon water

Cook and stir onion in olive oil in medium saucepan over medium heat until onion is softened. Stir in wine, honey, lime juice, mustard, rosemary, salt and pepper; mix well and bring to a boil. Combine cornstarch and water in small bowl or cup, mixing well. Add to sauce. Cook over low heat, stirring until sauce comes to a boil and thickens. Serve over cooked turkey, chicken, fish or pork.    *Makes about ¾ cup*

*Favorite recipe from **National Honey Board***

# Moroccan Charmoula Marinade

½ cup fresh cilantro

½ to 1 jalapeño pepper,*
    stemmed and seeded *or*
    ⅛ to ¼ teaspoon ground
    red pepper

2 tablespoons white wine
    vinegar or rice vinegar

1 tablespoon minced fresh
    ginger

3 cloves garlic, minced

2 teaspoons grated fresh
    lemon peel

1 teaspoon cumin seeds

1 teaspoon paprika

¼ cup fresh lemon juice

*Jalapeño peppers can sting and irritate the skin; wear rubber gloves when handling peppers and do not touch eyes. Wash hands after handling.*

Place cilantro, jalapeño, vinegar, ginger, garlic, lemon peel, cumin and paprika in food processor or blender and process until finely chopped. Add lemon juice* and process until blended.  *Makes 8 servings*

*If using a blender, add only as much lemon juice to mixture as needed to finely chop ingredients, then add remaining juice. Alternatively, mince fresh ingredients by hand, then stir in vinegar and lemon juice; use ground cumin in place of cumin seeds.*

**Tip:** The natural acids contained in lemon juice and vinegar actually precook protein-containing foods, turning them opaque and firm. Marinate fish fillets, scallops or shrimp in this spicy sauce up to 30 minutes and chicken or pork up to 1 day before grilling.

# Korean-Style Honey Marinade

½ cup dry white wine

½ cup honey

½ cup soy sauce

2 green onions, chopped

2 tablespoons Oriental
    sesame oil

1 tablespoon grated fresh
    gingerroot

1 clove garlic, minced

Combine all ingredients in small bowl; mix thoroughly. Use to marinate steak or chicken.

*Makes about 1½ cups*

*Favorite recipe from **National Honey Board***

Moroccan Charmoula Marinade

## Zippy Tartar Sauce for Grilled Fish

1 cup mayonnaise
3 tablespoons *Frank's®*
  *RedHot®* Cayenne Pepper
  Sauce
2 tablespoons *French's®*
  Bold n' Spicy Brown
  Mustard
2 tablespoons sweet pickle
  relish
1 tablespoon minced capers

Combine mayonnaise, *Frank's RedHot* Sauce, mustard, pickle relish and capers in medium bowl. Cover and chill in refrigerator until ready to serve. Serve with grilled salmon, halibut, swordfish or tuna.

*Makes 1½ cups sauce*

**Prep Time:** 5 minutes

## Wyoming Wild Barbecue Sauce

1 cup chili sauce
1 cup ketchup
¼ cup steak sauce
3 tablespoons dry mustard
2 tablespoons horseradish
2 tablespoons TABASCO®
  brand Pepper Sauce
1 tablespoon Worcestershire
  sauce
1 tablespoon garlic, finely
  chopped
1 tablespoon dark molasses
1 tablespoon red wine vinegar

Combine ingredients in medium bowl. Whisk until sauce is well blended. Store in 1-quart covered jar in refrigerator up to 7 days. Use as a baste while grilling beef, chicken, pork or game.

*Makes 3 cups*

**Zippy Tartar Sauce for Grilled Fish**

# Mike's Sensational Salsa

2 cans (14.5 ounces each) HUNT'S® Diced Tomatoes in Juice, one can drained
¼ cup sliced green onion (including white and green portions)
3 tablespoons chopped onion
2 tablespoons chopped fresh cilantro
1 tablespoon diced green chiles
2 teaspoons diced jalapeños (canned or fresh), seeds included
1½ teaspoons sugar
1 teaspoon minced fresh garlic
¼ teaspoon salt
¼ teaspoon cumin
¼ teaspoon hot pepper sauce
Baked tortilla chips *or* fresh cut vegetables

**1.** In medium bowl, combine Hunt's Tomatoes and *remaining* ingredients *except* chips or vegetables.

**2.** Cover and refrigerate at least 2 hours or overnight.

**3.** Remove 30 minutes before serving.

**4.** Stir once before serving. Serve with chips or vegetables. *Makes 12 (¼-cup) servings*

# Pineapple-Mango Salsa

1½ cups DOLE® Fresh Pineapple Chunks
1 ripe DOLE® Mango, peeled and chopped
½ cup chopped red cabbage
⅓ cup finely chopped DOLE® Red Onion
¼ cup chopped fresh cilantro
2 tablespoons lime juice
1 to 2 serrano or jalapeño chiles, seeded and minced

• Stir together pineapple chunks, mango, cabbage, red onion, cilantro, lime juice and chiles in medium bowl. Cover and chill for at least 30 minutes to blend flavors. Serve salsa over grilled chicken with grilled vegetables. Garnish with lime wedges, if desired.

• Salsa can also be served as a dip with tortilla chips or spooned over quesadillas or tacos. *Makes 3½ cups*

**Prep Time:** 15 minutes
**Chill Time:** 30 minutes

# Chunky Salsa

2 tablespoons olive oil
1 cup coarsely chopped onion
1 cup coarsely diced green
bell pepper
1 can (35 ounces) tomatoes,
drained and coarsely
chopped (reserve ½ cup
juice)
1 tablespoon freshly squeezed
lime juice
2 teaspoons TABASCO®
brand Pepper Sauce
½ teaspoon salt
2 tablespoons chopped fresh
cilantro or Italian parsley

Heat oil in large heavy saucepan over high heat. Add onion and bell pepper; cook and stir 5 to 6 minutes, stirring frequently, until tender. Add tomatoes and juice; bring to a boil over high heat. Reduce heat to low and simmer 6 to 8 minutes, stirring occasionally, until salsa is slightly thickened. Remove from heat. Stir in lime juice, TABASCO® Sauce to taste and salt. Cool to lukewarm; stir in cilantro. Spoon salsa into clean jars. Keep refrigerated for up to 5 days. *Makes 3½ cups*

# Honey Strawberry Salsa

1½ cups diced red bell pepper
1 cup sliced fresh strawberries
1 cup diced green bell pepper
1 cup diced fresh tomato
¼ cup chopped Anaheim
pepper
2 tablespoons finely chopped
fresh cilantro
⅓ cup honey
¼ cup lemon juice
1 tablespoon tequila
(optional)
½ teaspoon crushed dried red
chili pepper
½ teaspoon salt
¼ teaspoon pepper

Combine ingredients in glass container; mix well. Cover tightly and refrigerate overnight to allow flavors to blend. Serve on grilled fish or chicken. *Makes 3 to 4 cups*

*Favorite recipe from **National Honey Board***

# Red Pepper and Papaya Salsa

1 large red bell pepper, halved
1 large ripe papaya, peeled,
    seeded and finely diced
2 green onions, thinly sliced
3 tablespoons chopped fresh
    cilantro
2 to 3 tablespoons fresh lime
    juice
1 jalapeño pepper,* finely
    chopped

*Jalapeño peppers can sting and irritate the skin; wear rubber gloves when handling peppers and do not touch eyes. Wash hands after handling peppers.*

**1.** Grill bell pepper halves skin-side down on covered or uncovered grill over medium to hot coals 15 to 25 minutes or until skin is charred, without turning. Remove from grill and place in plastic bag until cool enough to handle, about 10 minutes.

**2.** Place papaya in medium bowl. Stir in onions, cilantro, 2 tablespoons lime juice and jalapeño. Remove bell pepper skins with paring knife and discard. Dice bell pepper and stir into papaya mixture. Add remaining 1 tablespoon lime juice, if desired. Serve chilled or at room temperature over grilled chicken.

*Makes 6 servings*

**Variation:** Vary this intriguing salsa by using a ripe mango or nectarines instead of a papaya. Basil and mint infuse the salsa with an even more tropical flavor. Great with grilled fish, chicken, clams, oysters or fajitas.

# Italian Pineapple Salsa

3 cups DOLE® Fresh
    Pineapple Chunks
½ cup chopped DOLE® Red
    Bell Pepper
3 tablespoons chopped red
    onion
3 tablespoons chopped fresh
    basil
4 teaspoons white wine
    vinegar
1 tablespoon balsamic vinegar
¼ teaspoon red pepper flakes
⅛ teaspoon salt

• Combine pineapple chunks, bell pepper, onion, basil, vinegars, red pepper flakes and salt in medium serving bowl. Cover; chill at least 1 hour to blend flavors.

• Serve over grilled turkey or beef hamburgers, with chips. Salsa can also be served as a dip with tortilla chips or spooned over quesadillas or tacos.

*Makes 10 servings*

**Prep Time:** 20 minutes
**Chill Time:** 1 hour

**Red Pepper and Papaya Salsa**

# Grilled Tomatillo Salsa

1 pound tomatillos, husks
   removed
1 cup diced plum tomatoes
¼ cup finely chopped cilantro,
   plus more for garnish
   (optional)
¼ cup finely chopped onion
1½ tablespoons red wine
   vinegar
1 tablespoon olive oil
1 packet NatraTaste® Brand
   Sugar Substitute
¼ teaspoon salt
   Freshly ground black
   pepper to taste

**1.** Grill tomatillos over medium heat for 3 to 5 minutes, turning until all sides are lightly charred but vegetable is still firm. Remove from heat and cut into pieces. Combine with tomatoes, cilantro and onion in bowl.

**2.** Combine remaining ingredients in a small jar with a lid. Shake; pour over salsa and toss. Garnish with fresh cilantro, if desired, and serve immediately, or cover and refrigerate. Bring to room temperature before serving.

*Makes 4 servings*

**Serving Suggestion:** Serve with flour tortillas as a snack, as a side salad, or with scrambled eggs.

# Pineapple Salsa

1 can (20 ounces) DOLE®
   Crushed Pineapple,
   drained
½ cup finely chopped DOLE®
   Red Bell Pepper
¼ cup finely chopped DOLE®
   Green Bell Pepper
1 tablespoon chopped green
   onion
2 teaspoons chopped fresh
   cilantro or parsley
2 teaspoons finely chopped
   jalapeño peppers
1 teaspoon grated lime peel

• Combine ingredients in small bowl.

• Serve salsa at room temperature or slightly chilled over grilled chicken or fish. *Makes 8 servings*

**Prep Time:** 20 minutes

Grilled Tomatillo Salsa

# SWEET
## TREATS

## Calypso Grilled Pineapple

½ cup *French's®*
   **Worcestershire Sauce**
½ cup honey
½ cup (1 stick) butter or
   margarine
½ cup packed light brown
   sugar
½ cup dark rum
1 pineapple, cut into
   8 wedges and cored*
Vanilla ice cream

*You may substitute other fruits, such as halved peaches, nectarines or thick slices of mangoes, for the pineapple.*

To prepare sauce, combine Worcestershire, honey, butter, sugar and rum in 3-quart saucepan. Bring to a full boil over medium-high heat, stirring often. Reduce heat to medium-low. Simmer 12 minutes or until sauce is slightly thickened, stirring often. Remove from heat; cool completely.

Brush pineapple wedges with some of the sauce. Place pineapple on oiled grid. Grill over hot coals 5 minutes or until glazed, turning and basting often with sauce. Serve pineapple with ice cream and remaining sauce. Garnish as desired. Refrigerate any leftover sauce.**

*Makes 8 servings (1½ cups sauce)*

**Leftover sauce may be reheated in microwave. Microwave and stir for 30 seconds at a time.*

**Prep Time:** 15 minutes
**Cook Time:** 15 minutes

**Calypso Grilled Pineapple**

# Kahlúa® Ice Cream Pie

1 (9-ounce) package chocolate wafer cookies
½ cup unsalted butter, melted
10 tablespoons KAHLÚA® Liqueur, divided
1 teaspoon espresso powder
3 ounces semisweet chocolate, chopped
1 tablespoon unsalted butter
1 pint vanilla, coffee or chocolate chip ice cream
1 pint chocolate ice cream
¾ cup whipping cream, whipped
Chocolate-covered coffee beans (optional)

Preheat oven to 325°F. Place ½ of cookies in food processor, breaking cookies into pieces. Process to make fine crumbs. Repeat with remaining cookies. Add ½ cup melted butter and process with on-off pulses, just to blend. Press crumb mixture evenly onto bottom and up side to rim of 9-inch pie plate. Bake 10 minutes. Cool completely.

In small saucepan, heat 6 tablespoons Kahlúa® and espresso powder over low heat until warm and espresso powder dissolves. Stir in chocolate and 1 tablespoon butter until melted and smooth. Cool completely.

Transfer vanilla ice cream to electric mixer bowl and allow to soften slightly. Add 2 tablespoons Kahlúa® and beat at low speed until blended. Spread over bottom of cooled crust and freeze until firm.

Spread cooled chocolate mixture over ice cream mixture. Freeze until firm.

Transfer chocolate ice cream to mixer bowl and allow to soften slightly. Add remaining 2 tablespoons Kahlúa® and beat at low speed until blended. Spread over frozen chocolate mixture. Freeze until firm.

To serve, pipe decorative border of whipped cream on pie around inside edge. Garnish with chocolate-covered coffee beans, if desired. *Makes one 9-inch pie*

# Grilled Pineapple

1 pineapple
Dark rum
Brown sugar
Ice cream, frozen yogurt or sorbet
Toasted shredded coconut

Peel, core and cut pineapple into ¾-inch-thick rings or thin wedges. Brush generously with dark rum; sprinkle with brown sugar. Lightly oil grid to prevent sticking. Grill 8 to 10 minutes over medium-hot KINGSFORD® Briquets until warm and golden brown, turning once. Top each ring with 1 scoop of ice cream, frozen yogurt or sorbet and a sprinkling of toasted coconut.

# Chocolate Macaroon Heath® Pie

½ cup (1 stick) butter or
   margarine, melted
3 cups MOUNDS® Sweetened
   Coconut Flakes
2 tablespoons all-purpose
   flour
1⅓ cups (8-ounce package)
   HEATH® BITS
½ gallon chocolate ice cream,
   softened

**1.** Heat oven to 375°F.

**2.** Combine butter, coconut and flour in medium bowl. Press into 9-inch pie pan. Bake 10 minutes or until edge is light golden brown. Cool completely.

**3.** Set aside ⅓ cup Heath® Bits. Combine ice cream and remaining Heath® Bits. Spread into cooled crust. Sprinkle with ⅓ cup reserved bits. Freeze at least 5 hours. Remove from freezer about 10 minutes before serving.

*Makes 6 to 8 servings*

# Fresh Fruit Skewers with Zesty Lime Yogurt Dip

1 cup nonfat yogurt
2 tablespoons fresh lime juice
1 tablespoon TABASCO®
   brand Green Pepper
   Sauce
1 teaspoon sugar
   Fresh fruit, such as
      strawberries, cantaloupe,
      apples and pineapple

Combine yogurt, lime juice, TABASCO® Green Pepper Sauce and sugar in small bowl. Cover and refrigerate 1 hour to blend flavors.

Slice fruit into bite-sized pieces and thread 4 to 5 pieces on wooden skewers. Arrange on platter with chilled bowl of Zesty Lime Yogurt Dip.     *Makes about 1 cup dip*

**Tip:** Add a fresh mint leaf to each skewer.

# Barbecue Banana Split

1 banana
   Butter, melted
   Brown sugar
   Ice cream
   Chocolate sauce
   Whipped cream, nuts,
      maraschino cherry

Cut firm, ripe banana lengthwise to, but not through, bottom peel. Brush cut sides with melted butter; sprinkle with a little brown sugar. Grill 6 to 8 minutes on covered grill over medium-hot KINGSFORD® Briquets until banana is heated through but still firm (peel will turn dark). Place unpeeled banana in serving dish; top with small scoops of ice cream. Drizzle with chocolate sauce. Top with whipped cream, nuts and a cherry.

*Makes 1 serving*

# Hershey's White Chip Chocolate Cookies

1 cup (2 sticks) butter or margarine, softened
2 cups sugar
2 eggs
2 teaspoons vanilla extract
2 cups all-purpose flour
¾ cup HERSHEY'S Cocoa
1 teaspoon baking soda
½ teaspoon salt
1⅔ cups (10-ounce package) HERSHEY'S Premier White Chips

**1.** Heat oven to 350°F.

**2.** Beat butter and sugar in large bowl until creamy. Add eggs and vanilla extract; beat until fluffy. Stir together flour, cocoa, baking soda and salt; gradually blend into butter mixture. Stir in white chips. Drop by rounded teaspoons onto ungreased cookie sheet.

**3.** Bake 8 to 9 minutes. (Do not overbake; cookies will be soft. They will puff while baking and flatten upon cooling.) Cool slightly; remove from cookie sheet to wire racks. Cool completely.    *Makes about 4½ dozen cookies*

# Banana Smoothies & Pops

1 (14-ounce) can EAGLE® BRAND Sweetened Condensed Milk (NOT evaporated milk)
1 (8-ounce) container vanilla yogurt
2 ripe bananas
½ cup orange juice

**1.** In blender container, combine all ingredients; blend until smooth. Stop occasionally to scrape down sides.

**2.** Serve immediately. Store covered in refrigerator.
*Makes 4 cups*

**Banana Smoothie Pops:** Spoon banana mixture into 8 (5-ounce) paper cups. Freeze 30 minutes. Insert wooden craft sticks into the center of each cup; freeze until firm. Makes 8 pops.

**Fruit Smoothies:** Substitute 1 cup of your favorite fruit and ½ cup any fruit juice for banana and orange juice.

**Prep Time:** 5 minutes

Hershey's White Chip Chocolate Cookies

# Lemony Cheesecake Bars

1½ cups graham cracker
  crumbs
⅓ cup sugar
⅓ cup finely chopped pecans
⅓ cup butter or margarine,
  melted
2 (8-ounce) packages cream
  cheese, softened
1 (14-ounce) can EAGLE®
  BRAND Sweetened
  Condensed Milk (NOT
  evaporated milk)
2 eggs
½ cup lemon juice from
  concentrate

**1.** Preheat oven to 325°F. In medium mixing bowl, combine crumbs, sugar, pecans and melted butter. Reserve ⅓ cup crumb mixture; press remaining mixture firmly on bottom of ungreased 13×9-inch baking pan. Bake 5 minutes. Remove from oven and cool on wire rack.

**2.** In large mixing bowl, beat cream cheese until fluffy. Gradually beat in Eagle Brand until smooth. Add eggs; beat until just combined. Stir in lemon juice. Carefully spoon mixture onto crust in pan. Spoon reserved crumb mixture to make diagonal stripes on top of cheese mixture or sprinkle to cover.

**3.** Bake about 30 minutes or until knife inserted near center comes out clean. Cool on wire rack 1 hour. Cut into bars to serve. Store covered in refrigerator.

*Makes 3 dozen bars*

**Prep Time:** 25 minutes
**Bake Time:** 35 minutes

# Chocolate-Amaretto Ice

¾ cup sugar
½ cup HERSHEY₂S Cocoa
2 cups (1 pint) light cream or
  half-and-half
2 tablespoons Amaretto
  (almond flavored liqueur)
Sliced almonds (optional)

**1.** Stir together sugar and cocoa in small saucepan; gradually stir in light cream. Cook over low heat, stirring constantly, until sugar dissolves and mixture is smooth and hot. Do not boil.

**2.** Remove from heat; stir in liqueur. Pour into 8-inch square pan. Cover; freeze until firm, stirring several times before mixture freezes. Scoop into dessert dishes. Serve frozen. Garnish with sliced almonds, if desired.

*Makes 4 servings*

**Lemony Cheesecake Bars**

# Triple Chocolate Brownie Sundae

1 brownie
1 scoop chocolate ice cream
  HERSHEY'S Chocolate Shell
    Topping
  REDDI-WIP® Whipped
    Topping

- Place brownie on bottom of sundae dish.

- Place ice cream on top of brownie.

- Shake HERSHEY'S Chocolate Shell Topping according to instructions. Squeeze generous amount over ice cream. Allow to harden for 30 seconds.

- Top with REDDI-WIP Whipped Topping.

*Makes 1 sundae*

# Fresh Fruit with Citrus Glaze

2 cups DOLE® Pineapple,
    Pineapple Orange or
    Pine-Orange-Banana
    Juice
3 tablespoons sugar
1 tablespoon cornstarch
1 tablespoon lemon juice
½ teaspoon grated lemon peel
8 cups cut-up fresh fruit such
    as DOLE® Fresh
    Pineapple, Bananas,
    Strawberries, Red or
    Green Seedless Grapes,
    Cantaloupe, Oranges,
    Peaches, Nectarines
    or Kiwi
Fresh mint leaves (optional)

- Combine pineapple juice, sugar, cornstarch, lemon juice and lemon peel in medium saucepan.

- Cook and stir over medium-high heat 5 minutes or until mixture comes to boil. Reduce heat to low; cook 2 minutes or until slightly thickened. Cool slightly. Sauce can be served warm or chilled.

- Arrange fruit in dessert dishes. Spoon glaze over fruit. Refrigerate any leftovers in air-tight container.

*Makes 8 servings*

**Prep Time:** 5 minutes
**Cook Time:** 5 minutes

Triple Chocolate Brownie Sundae

# Chocolate Chip Applesauce Snacking Cake

1⅓ cups all-purpose flour
1 cup granulated sugar
¾ teaspoon baking soda
¾ teaspoon salt
½ teaspoon ground cinnamon
¼ teaspoon baking powder
¼ teaspoon ground allspice
1 cup chunky applesauce
½ cup shortening
2 eggs
1 teaspoon vanilla extract
½ cup chopped pecans
½ cup HERSHEY'S Semi-
  Sweet Chocolate Chips
Powdered sugar (optional)
Vanilla Frosting (optional,
  recipe follows)
Chocolate Drizzle (optional,
  recipe follows)

**1.** Heat oven to 350°F. Grease and flour 9-inch square baking pan. Combine flour, granulated sugar, baking soda, salt, cinnamon, baking powder and allspice in large bowl. Add applesauce, shortening, eggs and vanilla. Beat on low speed of mixer to combine; beat on medium speed 1 minute or until ingredients are well blended. Stir in pecans and chocolate chips; pour into prepared pan.

**2.** Bake 40 to 45 minutes or until wooden pick inserted into center comes out clean. Cool in pan on wire rack. Sprinkle with powdered sugar or spread Vanilla Frosting on cake. Prepare Chocolate Drizzle, if desired; drizzle over top of Vanilla Frosting.       *Makes 16 servings*

**Vanilla Frosting:** Beat 3 tablespoons softened butter or margarine in small bowl until fluffy. Add 1½ cups powdered sugar and ½ teaspoon vanilla extract alternately with 1 to 2 tablespoons milk, beating to spreading consistency. Makes about 1 cup frosting.

**Chocolate Drizzle:** Place ½ cup HERSHEY'S Semi-Sweet Chocolate Chips and 1 tablespoon shortening (do not use butter, margarine, spread or oil) in small microwave-safe bowl. Microwave at HIGH (100%) 30 seconds; stir. If necessary, microwave an additional 15 seconds or just until chips are melted and mixture is smooth when stirred.

# Kaleidoscope Honey Pops

2¼ cups water
¾ cup honey
3 cups assorted fruit, cut into
  small pieces
12 (3-ounce) paper cups or
  popsicle molds
12 popsicle sticks

Whisk together water and honey in pitcher until well blended. Place ¼ cup fruit in each mold. Divide honey mixture between cups. Freeze about 1 hour or until partially frozen. Insert popsicle sticks; freeze until firm and ready to serve.       *Makes 12 servings*

*Favorite recipe from* **National Honey Board**

# Glazed Fruit Kabobs

2 fresh California nectarines, halved, pitted and cut into 6 wedges

3 fresh California plums, halved, pitted and quartered

½ fresh pineapple, peeled and cut into 2-inch cubes

¼ cup packed brown sugar

2 tablespoons water

1½ teaspoons cornstarch

¾ teaspoon rum extract

Alternately thread fruit onto skewers. Combine sugar, water, cornstarch and rum extract in small saucepan. Bring to a boil, stirring constantly, until thickened and clear. Place fruit kabobs in shallow pan. Brush with glaze mixture. (This may be done ahead.) Grill kabobs about 4 to 5 inches from heat 6 to 8 minutes or until hot, turning once, brushing occasionally with glaze.

*Makes 4 servings*

*Favorite recipe from* **California Tree Fruit Agreement**

# Spiced Grilled Bananas

3 large ripe firm bananas

¼ cup golden raisins

3 tablespoons packed brown sugar

½ teaspoon ground cinnamon

¼ teaspoon ground nutmeg

¼ teaspoon ground cardamom or coriander

2 tablespoons margarine, cut into 8 pieces

1 tablespoon fresh lime juice

Vanilla low-fat frozen yogurt (optional)

Additional fresh lime juice (optional)

**1.** Spray grillproof 9-inch pie plate with nonstick cooking spray. Cut bananas diagonally into ½-inch-thick slices. Arrange, overlapping, in prepared pie plate. Sprinkle with raisins.

**2.** Combine sugar, cinnamon, nutmeg and cardamom in small bowl; sprinkle over bananas and raisins and dot with margarine pieces. Cover pie plate tightly with foil. Place on grid and grill, covered, over low coals 10 to 15 minutes or until bananas are hot and tender.

**3.** Carefully remove foil and sprinkle with 1 tablespoon lime juice. Serve over low-fat frozen yogurt and sprinkle with additional lime juice, if desired. Garnish as desired.

*Makes 4 servings*

# Banana-Coconut Crunch Cake

**Cake**

- 1 package DUNCAN HINES®
  Moist Deluxe® Banana
  Supreme Cake Mix
- 1 package (4-serving size)
  banana-flavor instant
  pudding and pie
  filling mix
- 1 can (16 ounces) fruit
  cocktail, in juices,
  undrained
- 4 eggs
- ¼ cup vegetable oil
- 1 cup flaked coconut
- ½ cup chopped pecans
- ½ cup firmly packed brown
  sugar

**Glaze**

- ¾ cup granulated sugar
- ½ cup butter or margarine
- ½ cup evaporated milk
- 1⅓ cups flaked coconut

**1.** Preheat oven to 350°F. Grease and flour 13×9×2-inch pan.

**2.** For cake, combine cake mix, pudding mix, fruit cocktail with juice, eggs and oil in large bowl. Beat at medium speed with electric mixer for 4 minutes. Stir in 1 cup coconut. Pour into prepared pan. Combine pecans and brown sugar in small bowl. Stir until well mixed. Sprinkle over batter. Bake at 350°F for 45 to 50 minutes or until toothpick inserted in center comes out clean.

**3.** For glaze, combine granulated sugar, butter and evaporated milk in medium saucepan. Bring to a boil. Cook for 2 minutes, stirring occasionally. Remove from heat. Stir in 1⅓ cups coconut. Pour over warm cake. Serve warm or at room temperature.     *Makes 12 to 16 servings*

**Tip:** Assemble all ingredients and utensils together before beginning the recipe.

# Backyard S'Mores

- 2 milk chocolate bars
  (1.55 ounces each), cut
  in half
- 8 large marshmallows
- 4 whole graham crackers
  (8 squares)

Place each chocolate bar half and 2 marshmallows between 2 graham cracker squares. Wrap in lightly greased foil. Place on grill over medium-low KINGSFORD® Briquets about 3 to 5 minutes or until chocolate and marshmallows are melted. (Time will vary depending upon how hot coals are and whether grill is open or covered.)     *Makes 4 servings*

**Banana-Coconut Crunch Cake**

# Creamy Strawberry-Orange Pops

1 (8-ounce) container sugar-
   free strawberry yogurt
¾ cup orange juice
2 teaspoons vanilla
2 cups frozen whole
   strawberries
1 packet sugar substitute or
   equivalent of 2 teaspoons
   sugar
6 (7-ounce) paper cups
6 wooden sticks

**1.** Combine yogurt, orange juice and vanilla in food processor or blender. Cover and blend until smooth.

**2.** Add frozen strawberries and sugar substitute. Blend until smooth. Pour into 6 paper cups, filling each about ¾ full. Place in freezer for 1 hour. Insert wooden stick into center of each. Freeze completely. Peel cup off each pop to serve.                          *Makes 6 servings*

# Chocolate Velvet Pie

1¾ cups (11.5-ounce package)
   NESTLÉ® TOLL HOUSE®
   Milk Chocolate Morsels
1 package (8 ounces) cream
   cheese, softened
1 teaspoon vanilla extract
1 cup heavy whipping cream,
   whipped
1 *prepared* 8-inch (6-ounce)
   chocolate crumb crust
   Sweetened whipped cream
   (optional)
   Chocolate curls (optional)
   Chopped nuts (optional)

**MICROWAVE** morsels in medium, microwave-safe bowl on MEDIUM-HIGH (70%) power for 1 minute; stir. Microwave at additional 10- to 20-second intervals, stirring until smooth. Cool to room temperature.

**BEAT** melted chocolate, cream cheese and vanilla extract in large mixer bowl until light in color. Fold in whipped cream. Spoon into crust. Refrigerate until firm. Top with sweetened whipped cream, chocolate curls and nuts.

*Makes 8 servings*

# Brownie Ice Cream Pie

1 (21-ounce) package
    DUNCAN HINES® Chewy
    Fudge Brownie Mix
2 eggs
½ cup vegetable oil
¼ cup water
¾ cup semisweet chocolate
    chips
1 (9-inch) unbaked pastry
    crust
1 (10-ounce) package frozen
    sweetened sliced
    strawberries
  Vanilla ice cream

**1.** Preheat oven to 350°F.

**2.** Combine brownie mix, eggs, oil and water in large bowl. Stir with spoon until well blended, about 50 strokes. Stir in chocolate chips. Spoon into crust. Bake at 350°F for 40 to 45 minutes or until set. Cool completely. Purée strawberries in food processor or blender. Cut pie into wedges. Serve with ice cream and puréed strawberries. *Makes 8 servings*

# Creamy Chocolate Dipped Strawberries

1 cup HERSHEY'S Semi-
    Sweet Chocolate Chips
½ cup HERSHEY'S Premier
    White Chips
1 tablespoon shortening (do
    *not* use butter, margarine,
    spread or oil)
  Fresh strawberries, rinsed
    and patted dry (about
    2 pints)

**1.** Line tray with wax paper.

**2.** Place chocolate chips, white chips and shortening in medium microwave-safe bowl. Microwave at HIGH (100%) 1 minute; stir. If necessary, microwave at HIGH an additional 15 seconds at a time, stirring after each heating, just until chips are melted when stirred. Holding top, dip bottom two-thirds of each strawberry into melted mixture; shake gently to remove excess. Place on prepared tray.

**3.** Refrigerate about 1 hour or until coating is firm. Cover; refrigerate leftover dipped berries. For best results, use within 24 hours.

*Makes about 3 dozen dipped berries*

Brownie Ice Cream Pie

# Carrot Cake

## Cake
1¼ pounds carrots, scraped and cut lengthwise into 2-inch pieces (about 8 to 10 medium carrots)*
2 cups granulated sugar
1½ CRISCO® Sticks or 1½ cups CRISCO® all-vegetable shortening plus additional for greasing
4 eggs
½ cup water
2 cups all-purpose flour
1 tablespoon ground cinnamon
2 teaspoons baking soda
1 teaspoon salt

## Frosting
1 package (8 ounces) cream cheese, softened
½ Butter Flavor CRISCO® Stick or ½ cup Butter Flavor CRISCO® all-vegetable shortening
1 box (1 pound) confectioners' sugar (3½ to 4 cups)
1 teaspoon vanilla
¼ teaspoon salt

## Garnish (optional)
Chopped nuts
Carrot curls

*Grate carrots very finely if food processor is unavailable.

**1.** Heat oven to 350°F. Grease 13×9×2-inch insulated pan. Flour lightly.

**2.** For cake, place carrots in food processor. Process until very fine and moist. Measure 3 cups carrots.

**3.** Combine granulated sugar and 1½ cups shortening in large bowl. Beat at medium speed of electric mixer until creamy. Beat in eggs until blended. Beat in water at low speed until blended.

**4.** Combine flour, cinnamon, baking soda and 1 teaspoon salt in medium bowl. Add to creamed mixture. Beat at low speed until blended. Beat 2 minutes at medium speed. Add carrots. Beat until well blended. Pour into pan.**

**5.** Bake at 350°F for 40 to 55 minutes or until toothpick inserted into center comes out clean. *Do not overbake.* Cool 10 minutes before removing from pan. Invert cake on wire rack. Cool completely. Place cake on serving tray.

**6.** For frosting, combine cream cheese and ½ cup shortening in large bowl. Beat at medium speed until blended. Reduce speed to low. Add confectioners' sugar, vanilla and ¼ teaspoon salt. Beat until blended. Beat at medium speed until frosting is of desired spreading consistency. Frost top and sides of cake.

**7.** For optional garnish, place nuts and carrot curls on each serving. *Makes 12 to 16 servings*

**If cake is baked in non-insulated pan, baking time will be shorter. Test for doneness at minimum baking time.*

# Banana Boat Sundae

HERSHEY'S Special Dark® Syrup
3 scoops vanilla ice cream
1 banana, peeled and sliced in half lengthwise
REESE'S® Shell Topping®
HERSHEY'S Classic Caramel™ Sundae Syrup
HERSHEY'S Chocolate Shoppe™ Milk Chocolate Sprinkles
HERSHEY'S Double Chocolate Sundae Syrup
REDDI-WIP® Whipped Topping

• Pour layer of HERSHEY'S Special Dark Syrup into banana split sundae dish.

• Place 3 scoops of ice cream next to each other on top of syrup. Place banana half on both sides of ice cream scoops.

• Top first ice cream scoop with REESE'S Shell Topping. Top second scoop with HERSHEY'S Classic Caramel Sundae Syrup and HERSHEY'S Chocolate Shoppe Milk Chocolate Sprinkles. Top third scoop with HERSHEY'S Double Chocolate Sundae Syrup. Top with REDDI-WIP Whipped Topping.
*Makes 1 sundae*

# Peanut Butter Chip Oatmeal Cookies

1 cup (2 sticks) butter or margarine, softened
¼ cup shortening
2 cups packed light brown sugar
1 tablespoon milk
2 teaspoons vanilla extract
1 egg
2 cups all-purpose flour
1⅔ cups (10-ounce package) REESE'S® Peanut Butter Chips
1½ cups quick-cooking or regular rolled oats
½ cup chopped walnuts
½ teaspoon baking soda
½ teaspoon salt

**1.** Heat oven to 375°F.

**2.** Beat butter, shortening, brown sugar, milk, vanilla and egg in large bowl until fluffy. Add remaining ingredients; mix until well blended. Drop dough by rounded teaspoonfuls about 2 inches apart onto ungreased cookie sheet.

**3.** Bake until light brown, 10 to 12 minutes for soft cookies or 12 to 14 minutes for crisp cookies. Remove from cookie sheet to wire rack. Cool completely.
*Makes about 6 dozen cookies*

# Magic Cookie Bars

½ cup (1 stick) butter or
   margarine
1½ cups graham cracker
   crumbs
1 (14-ounce) can EAGLE®
   BRAND Sweetened
   Condensed Milk (NOT
   evaporated milk)
2 cups (12 ounces) semi-
   sweet chocolate chips
1⅓ cups flaked coconut
1 cup chopped nuts

**1.** Preheat oven to 350°F (325°F for glass dish). In 13×9-inch baking pan, melt butter in oven.

**2.** Sprinkle crumbs over butter; pour Eagle Brand evenly over crumbs. Layer evenly with remaining ingredients; press down firmly.

**3.** Bake 25 minutes or until lightly browned. Cool. Chill, if desired. Cut into bars. Store loosely covered at room temperature. *Makes 2 to 3 dozen bars*

**7-Layer Magic Cookie Bars:** Substitute 1 cup (6 ounces) butterscotch-flavored chips for 1 cup semi-sweet chocolate chips. Peanut butter-flavored chips or white chocolate chips can be substituted for butterscotch-flavored chips.

**Magic Peanut Cookie Bars:** Substitute 2 cups (about ¾ pound) chocolate-covered peanuts for semi-sweet chocolate chips and chopped nuts.

**Magic Rainbow Cookie Bars:** Substitute 2 cups plain candy-coated chocolate pieces for semi-sweet chocolate chips.

**Prep Time:** 10 minutes
**Bake Time:** 25 minutes

# Pineberry Smoothie

1 ripe DOLE® Banana,
   quartered
1 cup DOLE® Pineapple Juice
½ cup nonfat vanilla or plain
   yogurt
½ cup fresh or frozen
   strawberries, raspberries
   or blueberries

• Combine all ingredients in blender or food processor container. Blend until thick and smooth. Serve immediately. *Makes 2 servings*

**Prep Time:** 5 minutes

# Chocolate-Caramel S'Mores

12 chocolate wafer cookies or chocolate graham cracker squares
2 tablespoons fat-free caramel topping
6 large marshmallows

**1.** Prepare coals for grilling. Place 6 wafer cookies top-down on plate. Spread 1 teaspoon caramel topping in center of each wafer to within about ¼ inch of edge.

**2.** Spear 1 to 2 marshmallows onto long wood-handled skewer.* Hold several inches above coals 3 to 5 minutes or until marshmallows are golden and very soft, turning slowly. Push 1 marshmallow off into center of caramel. Top with plain wafer. Repeat with remaining marshmallows and wafers.                 *Makes 6 servings*

*\*If wood-handled skewers are unavailable, use oven mitt to protect hand from heat.*

**Notes:** S'mores, a favorite campfire treat, got their name because everyone who tasted them wanted "some more." In the unlikely event of leftover S'mores, they can be reheated in the microwave at HIGH 15 to 30 seconds.

# Oatmeal Cookies

1 cup all-purpose flour
1 teaspoon baking powder
½ teaspoon baking soda
½ teaspoon salt
¼ cup MOTT'S® Cinnamon Apple Sauce
2 tablespoons margarine
½ cup granulated sugar
½ cup firmly packed light brown sugar
1 egg or ¼ cup egg substitute
1 teaspoon vanilla extract
1⅓ cups uncooked rolled oats
½ cup raisins (optional)

**1.** Heat oven to 375°F. Lightly spray cookie sheet with cooking spray.

**2.** In large bowl, mix flour, baking powder, baking soda and salt. In separate bowl, beat together apple sauce, margarine, granulated and brown sugars, egg and vanilla until margarine forms pea-sized pieces. Add flour mixture to apple sauce mixture. Mix well. Fold in oats and raisins.

**3.** Drop rounded teaspoonfuls onto cookie sheet; bake 5 to 7 minutes. Remove cookies from cookie sheet and cool completely on wire rack.                 *Makes 36 cookies*

Chocolate-Caramel S'Mores

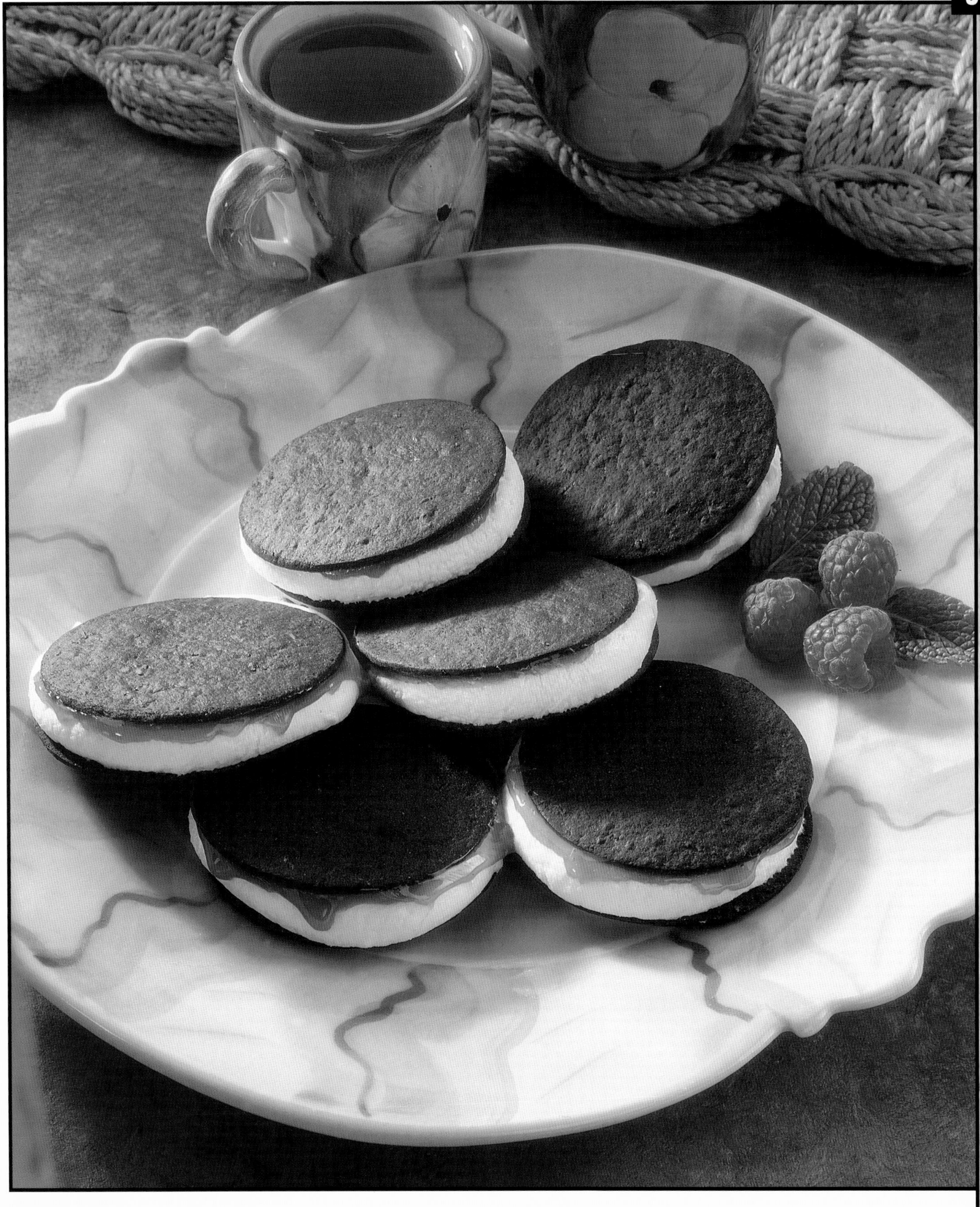

# Acknowledgments

**The publisher would like to thank the companies and organizations listed below for the use of their recipes and photographs in this publication.**

American Lamb Council

BelGioioso® Cheese, Inc.

Birds Eye®

Bob Evans®

Butterball® Turkey Company

California Tree Fruit Agreement

Canada's Canola Industry

Colorado Potato Administrative Committee

ConAgra Foods®

Del Monte Corporation

Dole Food Company, Inc.

Duncan Hines® and Moist Deluxe® are registered trademarks of Aurora Foods Inc.

Eagle® Brand

Filippo Berio® Olive Oil

Grandma's® is a registered trademark of Mott's, Inc.

Hershey Foods Corporation

The Hidden Valley® Food Products Company

Holland House® is a registered trademark of Mott's, Inc.

Kahlúa® Liqueur

The Kingsford Products Company

Lawry's® Foods

McIlhenny Company (TABASCO® brand Pepper Sauce)

Mott's® is a registered trademark of Mott's, Inc.

Mrs. Dash®

National Fisheries Institute

National Honey Board

National Pork Board

National Turkey Federation

NatraTaste® is a registered trademark of Stadt Corporation

Nestlé USA

Newman's Own, Inc.®

Norseland, Inc. / Lucini Italia Co.

North Dakota Wheat Commission

Perdue Farms Incorporated

Reckitt Benckiser Inc.

Reddi-wip® is a registered trademark of ConAgra Brands, Inc.

Sargento® Foods Inc.

The J.M. Smucker Company

StarKist® Seafood Company

Tyson Foods, Inc.

Uncle Ben's Inc.

Unilever Bestfoods North America

USA Rice Federation

Wisconsin Milk Marketing Board

# Index

# METRIC CONVERSION CHART

## VOLUME MEASUREMENTS (dry)

$1/8$ teaspoon = 0.5 mL
$1/4$ teaspoon = 1 mL
$1/2$ teaspoon = 2 mL
$3/4$ teaspoon = 4 mL
1 teaspoon = 5 mL
1 tablespoon = 15 mL
2 tablespoons = 30 mL
$1/4$ cup = 60 mL
$1/3$ cup = 75 mL
$1/2$ cup = 125 mL
$2/3$ cup = 150 mL
$3/4$ cup = 175 mL
1 cup = 250 mL
2 cups = 1 pint = 500 mL
3 cups = 750 mL
4 cups = 1 quart = 1 L

## VOLUME MEASUREMENTS (fluid)

1 fluid ounce (2 tablespoons) = 30 mL
4 fluid ounces ($1/2$ cup) = 125 mL
8 fluid ounces (1 cup) = 250 mL
12 fluid ounces ($1 1/2$ cups) = 375 mL
16 fluid ounces (2 cups) = 500 mL

## WEIGHTS (mass)

$1/2$ ounce = 15 g
1 ounce = 30 g
3 ounces = 90 g
4 ounces = 120 g
8 ounces = 225 g
10 ounces = 285 g
12 ounces = 360 g
16 ounces = 1 pound = 450 g

## DIMENSIONS

$1/16$ inch = 2 mm
$1/8$ inch = 3 mm
$1/4$ inch = 6 mm
$1/2$ inch = 1.5 cm
$3/4$ inch = 2 cm
1 inch = 2.5 cm

## OVEN TEMPERATURES

250°F = 120°C
275°F = 140°C
300°F = 150°C
325°F = 160°C
350°F = 180°C
375°F = 190°C
400°F = 200°C
425°F = 220°C
450°F = 230°C

## BAKING PAN SIZES

| Utensil | Size in Inches/Quarts | Metric Volume | Size in Centimeters |
|---|---|---|---|
| Baking or Cake Pan (square or rectangular) | $8 \times 8 \times 2$ | 2 L | $20 \times 20 \times 5$ |
| | $9 \times 9 \times 2$ | 2.5 L | $23 \times 23 \times 5$ |
| | $12 \times 8 \times 2$ | 3 L | $30 \times 20 \times 5$ |
| | $13 \times 9 \times 2$ | 3.5 L | $33 \times 23 \times 5$ |
| Loaf Pan | $8 \times 4 \times 3$ | 1.5 L | $20 \times 10 \times 7$ |
| | $9 \times 5 \times 3$ | 2 L | $23 \times 13 \times 7$ |
| Round Layer Cake Pan | $8 \times 1 1/2$ | 1.2 L | $20 \times 4$ |
| | $9 \times 1 1/2$ | 1.5 L | $23 \times 4$ |
| Pie Plate | $8 \times 1 1/4$ | 750 mL | $20 \times 3$ |
| | $9 \times 1 1/4$ | 1 L | $23 \times 3$ |
| Baking Dish or Casserole | 1 quart | 1 L | — |
| | $1 1/2$ quart | 1.5 L | — |
| | 2 quart | 2 L | — |